Toward a Native American Critical Theory

Toward a Native American Critical Theory

ELVIRA PULITANO

University of Nebraska Press, Lincoln and London

∞ Library of Congress
Cataloging-in-Publication
Data
Pulitano, Elvira, 1970–
Toward a Native American
critical theory / Elvira
Pulitano. p.   cm.
Includes bibliographical refer-
ences and index.
ISBN 0-8032-3737-5 (cl: alk.
paper)
1. American literature—
Indian authors—History
and criticism—Theory, etc.
2. Indians of North America
—Intellectual life.
3. Criticism—United States.
4. Indians in literature.
I. Title.
PS153.I52P85 2003
810.9′897—dc21
2003042695

For my parents, Luigi and Venera

Contents

Acknowledgments

I would like to thank Paula Gunn Allen, Robert Warrior, Craig Womack, Greg Sarris, Louis Owens, and Gerald Vizenor, whose works allowed me to shape ideas for this book. I have gained enormously from Louis Owens's scholarship on Native American literature, and I particularly wish to acknowledge his constant support over the past several years and his willingness to consider this book's potential from very early drafts. Gary Harrison provided me with excellent suggestions during extensive writing and rewriting, and I wish to thank him for his thoughtful and stimulating critique. Thanks also to Deborah Jenson, who offered valuable recommendations pertaining to the theoretical aspects of this study, and to Gerald Vizenor, for his generous encouragement and valued friendship.

I extend sincere gratitude to Elaine Jahner, for allowing me to cite from her unpublished work and for her kindness over a few telephone conversations, and offer many thanks to Daniel Simon, who read through this manuscript with care and patience. I must also thank Jacquelyn Kilpatrick and A. Robert Lee, for their careful and thoughtful reading and guidance. I am grateful as well for the genuine support that I have received over the past few years from Jim Thorson and for much insight from Pat Smith. Almost a decade after the Fulbright Fellowship that first brought me to the University of New Mexico, I offer bouquets of thanks to Mario Corona, at the University of Bergamo, and to Giuseppe Lombardo, at the University of Messina, for being such an inspiration and for encouraging me to pursue what I thought was an impossible task.

Finally, my greatest debt is to my family and close friends, whose unconditional love and support have guided me through these years. *Grazie a tutti.*

Toward a Native American Critical Theory

Introduction

One of the assumptions most frequently made about critical theory is that it is the elite language of the socially and culturally privileged. Attacks against such a monolithic, hegemonic form of discourse – whether it is called *pure theory*, or *academic jargon*, or simply *incomprehensible language* – have characterized most critical and cultural debates in the past few decades. It is said that *to do theory* means to be working in an Olympian realm, a realm safely located within the confines of an imperialistic West, and thus to ignore the historical realities that invest the rest of humanity. Yet it is undeniable that something called *critical theory* has had a tremendous impact in shaping literary and cultural studies over the past twenty years – to the extent that the foundations of theory itself (in its monolithic, Eurocentric mode) are now being tested.

To begin a discussion about something called *Native American critical theory* means to run into seemingly innumerable problems, the first of which concerns the argument itself. Is there such a thing as a Native American critical theory? If so, how should we define it? As a non-Native critic, am I entitled to define it? Does my "speaking about" necessarily mean "speaking for"? Would my attempt be a further heavy-handed appropriation of the Other since, for more than two millennia, theory has been, as many would argue, the product of Western thinking? These are some of the questions that I intend to pose in the present study, with the hope of beginning a discussion that, far from being definitive or conclusive, might in the end generate further arguments for debate.

In *The Voice in the Margin*, Arnold Krupat claims that "what chiefly marks the Americanist critic from the Native Americanist critic today is the relation of each to that thing called theory" (5). Drawing from Paul de Man's argument concerning the suspicious attitude toward poststructuralist, Derridean, and deconstructivist theories in the past few decades, Krupat laments that, in Native American studies, there has been and continues to be a "resistance to theory tout court" (6). According to Krupat, this resistance results from the general assumption that theory is aligned with the first terms of those binary sets (abstract/concrete, West/East, theory/praxis, etc.) so common within poststructuralist practice and, ironically, so often discredited by poststructuralist and Derridean theories themselves. In *For Those Who Come After*, Krupat posits that "those who do study Native American literatures have thus far tended to avoid critical theory as if it were indeed the French disease, a foreign corruption hostile or irrelevant to their local efforts" (xxviii–ix). Such "resistance to theory" (*Voice in the Margin* 6), Krupat argues, inevitably continues to perpetuate an us/them universe, keeping apart two worlds and two worldviews that could and should talk to one another. As a non-Native critic working in the specific field of Native American studies, Krupat's ongoing project is to eliminate this separatist attitude, by approaching Native American literature, not as an "other" literature, but as a corpus of works that parallel (in their difference) the literary production of Euramerican culture. Krupat's significant lamentation, however, merits consideration.

Despite the fact that many contemporary authors – Native as well as non-Native – have theorized about issues related to Native American culture and literature in particular, to date no monograph-length theoretical account exists that might indicate the development of a Native American critical theory, nor can we talk about a school or circle that has grown up around such a critical endeavor. Even Krupat's own attempt to forge an "ethnocritical" discourse, one originating from "a frontier condition of liminality" and embracing a dialogic approach toward Native American literature, remains substantially a tentative project. As Krupat puts it, "What might be called an 'indigenous' criticism for Indian literature remains to be worked out" (*Ethnocriticism* 44).

Although Krupat's reasoning bears some truth, I will argue, nevertheless, that, in the past few years, rather than simply relying on literary theories borrowed entirely from the West, a number of Native American writers have developed discursive strategies concerning Native American culture and literature, strategies that suggest a theory of reading generated largely, although by no means exclusively, from Native American cultural and intellectual traditions. Paula Gunn Allen, Craig Womack, Robert Warrior, Greg Sarris, Louis Owens, and Gerald Vizenor have produced, from rather different critical positionings and cultural backgrounds, a corpus of works that could represent the beginning of a Native American critical theory, a complex, hybridized project that, while deeply embedded within the narratives of Native American oral tradition and Native epistemology, inevitably conducts dialogues with the larger critical discourse of contemporary theory and significantly disputes the scholarly assumptions of a resistance to theory within Native American studies. Aware that the accepted modes of academic discourse cannot sufficiently explicate the arguments of Native American literature written in English, a literature in which a traditional oral rhetoric is still very much apparent, the above-mentioned authors argue for a literary criticism that brings to light Native ways of articulating the world and that uses indigenous rhetorics along with the instruments of Western literary analysis. A close analysis of their work will give me the opportunity to discuss the different approaches taken toward this complex enterprise and to illustrate how persuasive these different authors' theories are relative both to one another and to the larger field of critical and cultural studies. Since no substantial study has been done on any of the works that I have selected, I want to engage them as closely as possible in my analysis in order both to establish their major premises, arguments, and interrelations and – equally important – to subject them to as rigorous a scrutiny as I can.

As with any discourse involving Native American problematics, the present one cannot escape the overarching question of Indian identity, an identity that is, as Louis Owens points out in *Other Destinies*, a "treasured invention." "The Indian," he writes, "in today's world consciousness is a product of literature, history, and art, and a product that, as an invention, often bears little resemblance to actual, living Native American people" (4). Indeed, the question of how to define a Native American critical theory, as well as how the authors under analysis in this study define it, is primarily determined by such a conception of identity, an identity that, as I will argue, has a rather different meaning for some of these critics than it has for others.[1] Within the specific field of Native American literature itself, discussions and arguments have been produced from so many disparate sites and for so many disparate purposes that to conceive of a single consistent theoretical methodology characterizing such literature is often counterproductive. Similarly, to envision a monolithic discourse that authenticates an ideal form of Native American theory is quite reductive since the needs and contexts that such a discourse would conflate are far too different. While my project does not intend to be prescriptive, it does, however, acknowledge some basic premises, premises heavily determined by the nature of the texts under analysis.

First of all, in using the term *Native American theory* – as opposed, for instance, to *Native American criticism* – I incorporate in my study the recognition that there is no nontheoretical criticism. Theoretical assumptions and implications lurk behind the most practical forms of criticism, even the most text-oriented interpretations and evaluations. As Terry Eagleton points out, "Any body of theory concerned with human meaning, value, language, feeling, and experience will inevitably engage with broader, deeper beliefs about the nature of human individuals and societies, problems of power and sexuality, interpretations of past history, versions of the present, and hopes for the future" (170). Despite the resurgence of anti-intellectualism within leftist thinking in the past few years, the same orientation that has incited the most vigorous attacks against poststructuralist, deconstructivist, and postcolonial critical discourses, I argue that there is a point at which theory and praxis meet and that the intellectual armchair remains a crucial sphere of influence, a place from which it possible to agitate thought and to propose, as Michel Foucault does, "an insurrection of knowledges that are opposed . . . to the effects of the centralizing powers that are linked to the institution" (*Power/ Knowledge* 84).

A second and most important recognition is that no critical theory produced from the so-called margin escapes the question of functioning within a "dominant" discourse, not even a Native American theory. Writing about the relation between Native American literature and Western literary theory, Owens claims that

> we do not have the luxury of simply opting out, because whether or not we are heard by Said, Sollors, or others, we already function within the dominant discourse. To think otherwise is naïve at best, for the choice was made for us generations ago. Half a millennium of European attempts to both eliminate and reimagine the Indian has resulted in a hybridized, multicultural reality clearly recognized in fiction as long ago as the 1920s and '30s by such Native American writers as Mourning Dove, McNickle, and Mathews. . . . The very act of appropriating the colonizer's discourse and making it one's own is obviously collaborative and conjunctural. (*Mixedblood Messages* 52)

Along with Owens, Krupat points out the "conjunction of cultural practices" characterizing the Euramerican and the Native American production. He writes that, "from 1492 on, neither Euramerican intellectuals nor Native American intellectuals could operate autonomously or uniquely, in a manner fully independent of one another, for all the differences in power relations" (*The Turn to the Native* 18).

Within the contemporary scenario of the various "post" isms (postmodernism, poststructuralism, and postcolonialism) where and how would a Native American critical theory fit? Would it just be a new form of colonial enterprise with these authors picking up the master's tools in order to demonstrate that they can function at the same level of the dominant center and, as Owens puts it, "to prove that we [i.e., Native Americans] are tool-using creatures just like him and therefore worthy of intellectual recognition" (*Mixedblood Messages* 53)? Or would it rather be a separatist form of discourse, one that argues for a "Nativist" approach but that inevitably runs the risk of remaining trapped in essentialist positions by merely reversing Western binary structures? Or might it rather be an attempt to mediate between differing discourses and epistemologies? Writing in *Black Literature and Literary Theory* about the validity of applying Western methodologies to black literature, Henry Louis Gates Jr. anticipates the dilemma now facing contemporary Native American authors. "Do we have to 'invent' validly 'black' critical theory and methodologies" in order to explicate the "signifying black differences?" Gates asks. "How 'original' is the use of contemporary theory to read black texts?" (3, 9). By claiming that, in this critical methodology, originality relies more on the process by which the methodology is applied, Gates posits that "the challenge of [this] endeavor is to bring together, in a new fused form, the concepts of critical theory and the idiom of the Afro-American and African literary traditions" (9–10). To those who fear a risk of parroting the paradigms of the academic center Gates replies by saying that "one 'repeats,' as it were, in order to produce *difference*" (10).

In the specific case of Native American studies, where and how is a "signifying" Native difference produced? Does the development of a Native American critical theory necessitate the creation of new critical languages, or does it rather imply a problematic but unavoidable participation in a Western discourse? In *Manifest Manners*, Gerald Vizenor writes: "'The English language has been the linear tongue of colonial discoveries, racial cruelties, invented names, the simulation of tribal cultures, manifest manners, and the unheard literature of dominance in tribal communities; at the same time, this mother tongue of paracolonialism has been a language of invincible imagination and liberation for many tribal people in the postindian world" (105). According to Vizenor, the "same coercive language of federal boarding schools" has now become a language of creative "resistance" and "survivance" among distinguished Native American authors in the cities (106). By challenging the logic of English in its basic structure and subverting the acceptable literary forms, Vizenor, as well as the other theorists discussed in this study, finds a place on the written page by attempting to incorporate patterns and strategies from the oral tradition, what he calls, with a twist on Derrida, "the traces of oral stories" (*Fugitive Poses* 62). If the connection between critical theory and oral tradition might at first appear to be untenable, in the context of my study I argue that it becomes the most subversive and creative way in which to forge a Native voice within the major critical discourse or, to put it in Gates's terms, to produce a "signifying [Native] difference" by repeating. Notwithstanding ideological and methodological differences as far as defining the parameters of a Native American critical theory, and notwithstanding the heterogeneity of discourses produced by the authors under analysis in this study, crucial to all of them is the idea of incorporating the vitality of the oral into the written text while bringing Native epistemology to the attention of First World ideology. Such a basic assumption is what makes them part of a dialogue on Native American critical theory to begin with and, more significantly, perhaps, what makes their work worthy of being explored.

Within such a specific common view, Allen, Warrior, Womack, Sarris, Owens, and Vizenor articulate a unique discursive mode that adequately addresses the complexity of Native American literary texts, including the richly textured and layered worlds of the oral tradition out of which these texts originate, while significantly reflecting their borderland position as mixed-blood authors working at the juncture of different discourses and worldviews. While heavily and inevitably drawing from Western hermeneutical discourse (even when their main intent is to promote a rigidly tribal-centered approach), the above-mentioned authors emphasize a reading of theory that reveals unique characteristics by allowing the Native oral tradition to speak for itself about its nature and various functions, providing the tools, concepts, and languages necessary to a discussion of Native American literature, and adding to the rhetorical systems of Western critical theory. By bringing the liberating and extraordinary vitality of the spoken word onto the written page, these authors suggest in their own ways how the oral tradition can inscribe its own theories of its nature, function within the elaborate hermeneutical systems of the Western tradition, and, ultimately, demystify the curious notion that theory is the exclusive province of Western thought. Instead of taking a resisting stance toward theory, as many scholars have argued should be done, the above-mentioned authors are now "resisting theory" from

within, forging identity out of rupture and inevitably remapping the boundaries of theory itself.

My decision to select Allen, Womack, Warrior, Sarris, Owens, and Vizenor from among the many Native American authors who have written critical works about Native issues – as well as to exclude non-Native critics (e.g.,
Krupat, Alan Velie, Elaine Jahner, and James Ruppert) who have consistently
applied Western methodologies to interpret Native American literary texts –
reflects the primary goal of this study: an attempt to define a Native American critical theory in which the discursive modes are largely generated from
within a Native epistemology while, of course, also subsuming the forms and
methods of Western discourse.[2]

Specifically, the authors selected rely heavily on Native American cultural
and intellectual traditions in the attempt to create discursive strategies that
might explicate the richly layered texts of Native American literary works.
Acknowledging the vitality of the oral narratives, Allen, Womack, Sarris,
Owens, and Vizenor in particular incorporate into their written texts strategies and patterns from the oral tradition, in an attempt to re-create/reimagine
the dialogic quality of the oral exchange.[3] Both in form and in content their
works have, within such a specific point of commonality, begun to define
the characteristics that make Native American theory different, to a certain
extent, from Eurocentric discourse. At the same time, by demonstrating the
crucial ways in which this theory is, of course, in dialogue with, relies on,
and subsumes Western discursive modes, they produce substantially multigeneric, dialogic, and richly hybridized works, texts that shuttle back and
forth between worlds and worldviews and "mediate" strategies that challenge Western ways of doing theory.

Although a dialogic or a crosscultural approach appears as the most natural and effective way to discuss the highly hybridized nature of Native American theory – an approach that, it should be pointed out, not even all the authors selected in the present study seem to agree on – I am also aware of the
significant objections that such a position might raise. Within the current debates over cultural identity and political positioning in postcolonial studies,
an emphasis on hybridity and plural identity has generated significant criticism by scholars such as Robert Young and Benita Parry, who see in such a
tendency a perpetuation of the old notion of humanism.[4] Within the specific
context of cultures, they argue, the term *hybridity* is, much like its opposite
reality, *authenticity*, unintelligible without a notion of cultural purity. Such
a hybridized perspective, they posit, tends to homogenize the center more
or less implicitly and make it monolithic in ways that simply does not do jus-

tice to the variegated (peripheral) realities. On the other hand, in the so-called border zones of cultures, such as Africa, the Caribbean, and the Indian Ocean, the term *hybridity* is conceived as a site of powerful creative resistance to the dominant conceptual paradigms. According to Françoise Lionnet, the message proclaimed by contemporary art and literature from Africa and the Caribbean involves a "move [that] forces individuals to stand in relation to the past and the present at the same time, to look for creative means of incorporating useful 'Western' tools, techniques, or strategies into their own cosmology or weltanschauung" ("Logiques Métisses" 325). By appropriating the term *transculturation* as it was earlier used by the Cuban poet Nancy Morejon, with the prefix *trans-* suggesting the "act of traversing, of going through existing cultural territories" (326), Lionnet insists on a "métissage of forms" and identities that is the result of crosscultural encounters.[5] In such a case, she argues, *transculturation* becomes, unlike *acculturation* and *assimilation*, the terms usually associated with hybridity, "a process whereby all elements involved in the interaction would be changed by that encounter" (323). On a more radical level Chris Bongie envisions, in his historical and theoretical study of the "Creolization" process, the Creole identity as something incessantly produced out of the global crossings of cultures as well as out of identitarian ways (63).[6] Careful to avoid the essentializing trap of opposing the notion of Creolization to the colonial legacy, something that Lionnet herself, according to Bongie, does not do, he insists on the double identity of the Creolization process, a shifting middle ground between a rooted and a relational identity (65).[7] On a discursive level, these advocates of Creolization celebrate the mutual contamination of styles while pointing out how the former colonized culture has, by borrowing from the metropolitan culture, succeeded in the process to subvert and indigenize it.

In the context of my study, I see the hybridized or crosscultural perspective of the Native American discursive modes paralleling more closely the ideological intentions of the Caribbean critics' notion of identity rather than engulfing the assimilationist and pluralist tendencies of its opponents. Those familiar with something called *Native American literature* are fully aware that such literature is, in the end, the product of conjunctural cultural practices, the Euramerican and Native American, and that, whatever our geographic, cultural, or ideological position, we cannot dismiss such a crucial premise in our interpretative acts. Written primarily in English by authors possessing a consistently high level of education, these works are already heteroglot by nature – even as they rely heavily on elements from Native epistemologies, specifically the reality of myth and ceremony as embodied in traditional oral literatures. Novels such as Silko's *Ceremony*, Momaday's *House Made of Dawn*, Welch's *Winter in the Blood*, Carr's *Eye Killers*, Owens's *The Sharpest Sight*, and Vizenor's *Bearheart*, to mention but a few, brilliantly convey this richly hybridized dialogue – or "mediational" strategy – connecting two different worlds and worldviews. The same could be said for the poetry of Luci Tapahonso, Simon Ortiz, and Joy Harjo – and, in fact, for all the literary genres that have contributed in the past few years to the development of Native American literature. Within this context, charges of assimilationism against a theory that relies on the same hybridized strategies and discursive modes utilized by the texts that it sets out to interpret seem, in the long run, an ironic contradiction. How could a Native American theory aim at a "pure" form of (Native) discourse, untouched by the strategies of Western tradition, when Native American literature itself is a product of a crosscultural encounter, what Thomas King labels "interfusional literature, blending the oral and the written" (xii)? How could Native American theorists aim at developing a separatist form of discourse when they are heavily and inevitably implicated in the discourse of the metropolitan center? As I will point out in my discussion, while such separatist sentiments appear legitimate to fervent representatives of nationalistic approaches, they become all the more dangerous as they continue to ossify Native American literary production, as well as Native identity, into a sort of museum culture.

Equally important for my study is the relation that a Native American critical theory bears to current postcolonial discursive modes. Krupat argues, for example, that, in the current climate of literary studies, "it is tempting to think of contemporary Native American literatures as the postcolonial literatures of the world" (*The Turn to the Native* 30). Certainly, he suggests, as the product of the "contact zones," a product originating in response to or in dialogue with the metropolitan representation, the ideological perspective of the literature produced by Native American authors bears interesting parallels with the ideological perspectives of other postcolonial literatures and postcolonial theory. On the other hand, recognizing that there are many forms of postcolonialism and that there is nothing at all "post" about some of these forms, some critics (even within the postcolonial field itself) argue that we must draw distinctions; such critics accuse postcolonialism of being another totalizing method that fails to account for differences, in this case the culturally and historically variegated forms of both colonization and anticolonial struggle. Leela Gandhi, for example, writes, "There is a fundamental incommensurability between the predominantly cultural 'subordination' of settler culture in Australia, and the predominantly administrative and militaristic subordination of colonized cultures in Africa and Asia. A theory of postcolonialism which suppresses differences like these is ultimately flawed as an ethical and political intervention into conditions of power and inequality" (170). Similarly, Anna Johnston and Alan Lawson argue that "not all postcolonial cultures are postcolonial in the same way" and acknowledge that to read "the moment of imperialism in such a unilinear fashion is simply to reconquer the colonial subject" (368).[8] These observations also apply to the situation of Native American cultures.

As critics have pointed out, America never became postcolonial, and what is usually considered Native American literature still operates in an ongoing process of colonialism. To further illustrate this point, we should mention the forceful critique of postcolonial theory conducted by the historian Amy Kaplan, who argues, "The history of American imperialism strains the definition of the postcolonial, which implies a temporal development . . . that relies heavily on the spatial coordinates of European empires, in their formal acquisition of territories and the subsequent history of decolonization and national independence" (17). Obviously, Kaplan suggests, such a "Eurocentric notion of postcoloniality" (17) does not apply to the history of American imperialism, both at home and abroad, where the United States predominates in a power relation often called *neocolonial*. Even Krupat claims, after a first, enthusiastic impulse to align Native American literature among the "postcolonial literatures of the world," that "there is not yet a 'post' to the colonial status of the Native Americans" (*The Turn to the Native* 30). However, while admitting that Native American literature is produced in an ongoing condition of colonialism and that cultural, historical, and ideological differences are crucial in a postcolonial approach to Native American literary production, Krupat convincingly argues that both Native American and postcolonial writers (and theorists) are involved in an intensely subversive ideological project. Drawing from Talal Asad, Krupat uses the term *antiimperial translation* to conceptualize the tension and differences between Native American fiction and the imperial center (*The Turn to the Native* 32).

Such ideological parallels might explain why more and more critics, including Native scholars, have in the past few years turned to the rhetorical strategies of postcolonial theory to elucidate Native American literary narratives. Carlton Smith, for example, explores the cultural and literary borderlands between Native American, postcolonial, and postmodern theories of cultural representation in order to explicate Frederick Jackson Turner's famous frontier thesis in terms of the repressed Other. More specifically, Smith adopts Bhabha's notion of a "third space" as an interpretive lens through which to read Louise Erdrich's Turtle Mountain series of novels. In *Mixed-blood Messages* (whose content will be analyzed in the third chapter of the present study), Owens finds Mary Louise Pratt's terms *contact zone* and *auto-ethnographic text* particularly useful in the context of Native American literature. More extensively, in his "As If an Indian Were Really an Indian," Owens compares the situation of the "migrant, diasporic Native American writer" to the liminal condition of the postcolonial critic (people such as Gayatri Spivak, Homi Bhabha, Trinh T. Minh-ha, and Edward Said, among others) while pointing out how, even within this increasingly anticolonial theoretical site of resistance, the erasure of Native American voices constitutes the norm (209–10). Owens posits that a reader must turn, almost with surprise, from Said's extraordinary denigration of Native Americans in *Culture and Imperialism* and Bhabha's silencing of the indigenous inhabitants of the Americas in his panoply of minority voices in *The Location of Culture* to Trinh's critical narratives in order to find mention of Leslie Marmon Silko's storytelling and Vizenor's trickster, as if the works produced by Native Americans are less marginal and less anticolonial than those produced by African American, Asian American, or Chicano writers.[9]

Elaborating on Owens's and Krupat's formulations, the present discussion will indicate ways in which Native American theory and postcolonial strategies speak to one another despite ideological, historical, and geopolitical differences. Against those who insist on cultural specificity, arguing that the colonization of India, Cuba, or Algeria is not the same as the colonization of the Indians, Cubans, and Algerians, I argue that cultural specificity does not exclude some very real cultural commonalities and that, by overemphasizing (cultural) difference for its own sake, we run the risk of exoticizing the cultures in question. Using Spivak's notion of "catachresis," I will illustrate how Native American theorists both use and go beyond the discursive strategies of postcolonialism by testing its ideas primarily against Native American problematics and predicaments.[10] While the works of Spivak, Bhabha, Trinh, Said, and Fanon, among others, will provide me with a critical vocabulary with which to interrogate the texts of Native American theorists, at the same time, and perhaps more significantly, these same texts will provide me with examples of discursive modes that in most cases challenge the parameters of Eurocentric theory itself. The trickster trope of Vizenor's hermeneutics, as well as the overall patterns from the oral tradition to which almost all the authors I set out to discuss subscribe, provides discursive strategies that speak, actually "perform," the same (anticolonial) lexicon of postcolonialism. In addition, more subversively and provocatively than the often overtly cerebral, Eurocentric grid of postcolonial texts, such strategies succeed in bringing together differing epistemologies and discursive modes. In the words of Homi Bhabha, Native American theorists are, indeed, accomplishing acts of "(cross)cultural translation" (*The Location of Culture* 228), bringing to the attention of the dominant culture other discursive tropes while destabilizing the margin-center opposition so dear to traditional Western hermeneutics.

My first chapter analyzes the critical works of Paula Gunn Allen in an attempt to establish the critic's approach to a Native American critical discourse. In both *The Sacred Hoop* and *Off the Reservation*, Allen explores gender issues from an American Indian perspective. Coming from a gynocratic society, that of the Laguna Pueblo, she places women and ritual at the center of the tribal universe as the nourishing source through which American Indian cultures have survived the genocide perpetrated by Euramerica. Addressing the commodification of women within the larger system of patriarchy, Allen suggests that the colonial models have brought a particular pressure to bear on American Indian women and that these models must be resisted. Allen's discourse, epistemologically rooted in the female-centered universe of Laguna Pueblo traditions, is conceived of as differential to both a patriarchal masculine and a hegemonic feminist perspective. By combining autobiography with historical narrative, poetry, literary analysis, and myth, Allen transgresses preestablished generic boundaries and, along with the other theorists discussed in this study, blurs conventional forms of discourse. From this "threshold theorizing," however, Allen argues for an essentially tribal view as opposed to Western thinking. Even in *Off the Reservation*, notwithstanding her celebration of mixed identity and hybridity, deeply modeled on Gloria Anzaldúa's notion of *mestizaje*, and notwithstanding interesting paths of convergence between her gynocentric theory and some of the critical assumptions of ecofeminist discourse, Allen argues for a critical apparatus through which the texts of *las disappearadas* are explored from a rigidly (gynocentric) Indian perspective. Having never lived in the master's house, Allen argues that she intends to build a more suitable dwelling of her own, a separatist solution that, ironically, does not account for her very interesting hybrid speaking position.

Similar to Allen's position are the critical perspectives of Robert Allen Warrior and Craig S. Womack, the topic of the second chapter. While not dealing specifically with gender issues, both Warrior and Womack argue that, in order to promote an authentic tradition of "Indian intellectualism," scholars should turn to the historical and contemporary voices of American Indian life and experience. In *Tribal Secrets*, Warrior looks at Vine Deloria Jr. and John Joseph Mathews as the "internal historical voices" from which to theorize what he conceives of as a form of "intellectual sovereignty" (xxiii), that is, a process-centered activity through which American Indian intellectuals faithfully devote themselves to their communities and to the building of communities. According to Warrior, Mathews's and Deloria's ideas on land, community, and culture can provide Native American intellectuals with a perfect model for a pragmatic criticism, a criticism that confronts the chaos of contemporary life and that "engages in explicit analyses of economic realities, gender differences, and a host of other areas" (114). Similarly, in *Red on Red*, Womack takes a "Red" approach and turns to Creek history, oral tradition, and literature in order to construct a literary criticism presented as an alternative to that practiced by the Western literary establishment. Like Warrior, Womack envisions a Native American criticism rooted in land and culture, sensitive to the needs of the community, and creating resistance movements against colonialism. Whereas Warrior seems, within his separatist approach, to be at times more open, envisioning the possibility of non-Native critical discourse entering into dialogue with his "intellectual tribalism," Womack categorically dismisses any kind of crosscultural communication with the Western academy. By comparing and contrasting what I term Warrior's and Womack's *tribalcentric* approaches to a Native theory, in this chapter I will illustrate the internal contradictions and linguistic inconsistencies of such methodological strategies. As I discussed earlier, any attempt to recover a "pure" or "authentic" Native form of discourse, one rigidly based on a Native perspective, is simply not possible since Native American narratives are by their very nature heavily heteroglot and hybridized. More significantly, I argue, such separatist sentiments run the danger of embracing another form of colonial invention, perpetuating a sort of "Nativist" nostalgia, to use the words of Kwame Anthony Appiah, the heritage of that Western sentimentalism so familiar after Rousseau. While acknowledging the important role that both Warrior and Womack play in defining a Native American critical theory in which attention is given primarily to the Native/indigenous cultural contexts of the texts themselves, their cultural-separatist ethos remains, I argue, ultimately problematic in a discourse on Native American literature and theory that intends to challenge the parameters of Western hermeneutics.

The idea of crossreading and crosscultural communication as ways of opening up ideas while exploring differing epistemologies becomes the topic of chapter 3. In *Keeping Slug Woman Alive* and *Mixedblood Messages*, Greg Sarris and Louis Owens, respectively, argue for a hybridized, multidirectional, and multigeneric discursive mode, one that reflects the crosscultural nature of Native texts and ultimately and subversively reinvents the monologic utterance of Euramerica. Unlike Allen, Womack, and Warrior, who take separatist approaches to a Native discourse, Sarris and Owens insist on the necessity of displacing the margin-center opposition, not by remaining outside in the margin and pointing an accusing finger at the center, but by implicating themselves in that center and sensing the politics that makes it marginal. As critics already implicated in the discourse of the metropolitan center, Sarris and Owens conceive of writing within and out of the dominant discourse as a powerful, subversive tool through which to redefine a new sense of identity for Native people, one that significantly challenges the stasis and entrapments created by the stereotypes and clichés of the Euramerican imagination. At the same time, their critical methodology – in its polyvocality and heteroglot nature deeply modeled on the richly layered world of oral tradition – intends to challenge the authoritative stance of Eurocentric theory. In *Keeping Slug Woman Alive*, Sarris presents an overlapping of storytelling and theorizing, thus creating criticism that presents itself as a kind of story. Embracing the discourses of contemporary social scientists and reader-response critics, and subsuming them within an oral rhetoric, he intends to convey a Native epistemology not traditionally articulated in conventional academic discourse. Similarly, in *Mixedblood Messages*, Owens blends autobiography, critical theory, film commentary, and environmental reflections in order to come to terms with his mixed heritage while bringing to the reader's attention how, within a Native epistemology, words are inextricably interrelated with the natural world that we inhabit. Particularly useful to the context of my study is Owens's engagement with postcolonialism both in *Mixedblood Messages* and in "As If an Indian." By identifying the transcultural condition of mixedblood authors as a diasporic, migrant location, Owens initiates the debate on how valid the tools of postcolonial theory are for a Native American discourse while reiterating his message of the crucial importance of reading across lines of cultural identity.

Finally, in chapter 4, I look at Gerald Vizenor's critical narratives as the most provocative and definitely the most subversive way in which Native American authors are significantly challenging the parameters of Western, Eurocentric theory. Both *Manifest Manners* and *Fugitive Poses* dissolve any fixed line between essay and story, each more borderland than boundary, and forcefully employ trickster discourse in order to dismantle academic representations of Indianness. In *Gerald Vizenor*, Kimberley Blaeser argues that Vizenor's writing begins in the traditional Chippewa/Anishinaabe tales of his ancestors, in which words have life, vibrancy, force, vitality, and the power to create. Recognizing the vitality of the oral, Vizenor's effort is to "write in the oral tradition" (Blaeser's term; see her *Gerald Vizenor*), to require the same imaginative response that he finds in the oral exchange, and to bring the reader beyond the confining strictures of the written page. If writing tends to close and constrain, Vizenor intends to cross the boundaries of the printed word, subverting these strategies of containment. To accomplish these goals Vizenor relies both on Native American traditions and on contemporary critical theory since the two, for him, ultimately converge in important ways. Vizenor underscores this convergence by incorporating stylistic features of orality – repetition, metaphor, and parataxis as well as the use of allusive titles and names, what he calls "shadow words" (*Manifest Manners* 68) – within quotations and paraphrasing from an extraordinary number of poststructuralist and postmodern theorists. Exploring the manifestations of the tension between the oral and the written, Vizenor discovers in the poststructuralists' use of metaphor, play, utterance, language games, and *différance* attitudes and intentions similar to Anishinaabe ideas on language.

Crucial in Vizenor's work is the presence of the Native American trickster figure conceived, as it is, in absolutely linguistic terms. Like Naanabozho, the mythic figure of the Anishinaabe tales, the woodland tribal trickster, the shape-shifter who mediates between worlds, Vizenor's trickster discourse mediates between traditionally based ideas and Western hermeneutics, with his ultimate goal being that of challenging our cultural beliefs and worldviews. Both in *Manifest Manners* and in *Fugitive Poses*, Vizenor engages in a passionate deconstruction of vexed, age-old representations of Indians. For five hundred years, Vizenor argues, the reality of tribal people has been simulated under this artifact known as "*indian*," a misnomer that testifies more to the absence than to the presence of Native people. Elaborating on Derrida's terminology, Vizenor applies the concepts *absence* and *presence* to a discourse on Native American experience, conducting a penetrating critique of European colonialism in its construction of the "*indian*" as the absent Other. In *Fugitive Poses*, more specifically, Derrida's influence is more evident as the book itself reflects stylist features of *Of Grammatology*.

Recapitulating the overall ideological project of this study, my conclusion will suggest ways in which a Native American critical theory can represent a valid contribution to the field of Native American studies. In contrast to numerous articles and essay collections that rely on Western critical discourse in interpreting Native American texts, I argue that Native American authors themselves have produced (and keep producing) discursive strategies that might and should be taken into consideration in a discussion of Native American literature and culture. If Umberto Eco's reader-response theory applies perfectly well to D'Arcy McNickle's *The Surrounded*, students and readers of Native American literature should also be aware of a similar dialogic approach from within the field, such as Sarris's or Owens's. If poststructuralist and postmodern theories seem the most viable framework within which to read Louise Erdrich's novels, Vizenor's trickster hermeneutics might provide an additional and enriching perspective. Similarly, any feminist approach to Native American writing cannot ignore Allen's gynosophical perspective, even though such a perspective often takes, as I have suggested, an overtly separatist stance. Regardless of the authors' positions regarding defining the parameters of a Native theory, their theoretical principles can, I argue, provide excellent tools with which to explicate the nature of Native American narratives. Why not, for instance, a discussion of Harjo's poetry in the light of Womack's Creekcentric approach? How viable would his perspective be when explicating the permeability of boundaries in Harjo's thought? How does Harjo's poetry validate Womack's argument?

More significantly, a Native American theoretical approach would explicate the complex question of how viable postcolonialism is in a discourse on Native literature. As I argue, while paralleling the critical and ideological work of postcolonial theorists, Native American theory ironically operates in a condition of ongoing colonialism, and, from such a condition, it points out the failure of postcolonial theory itself properly to acknowledge the existence of Native American voices. By appropriating the language of postcolonialism and translating it into a Native epistemology, Native American theorists move beyond the often-Eurocentric grid of postcolonial discourse, revealing a radical ability to shuttle between frontiers while subverting European hegemonic systems.

As I posited earlier, a study of such a complex project cannot hope to be exhaustive, nor can it hope to trace all the various nuances of a Native American critical theory. My purpose here is to establish the parameters that might define this theory as it has been emerging in the past few decades while disputing the popular assumption of a resistance to theory among Native American scholars. Not only do Native American scholars seem to be capable of doing theory, but they have also begun to redefine – more creatively and more subversively than their European counterparts – the boundaries of Western, Eurocentric theory itself, shifting their attention from a monologic, authoritative form to a dialogic, crosscultural perspective. Weaving Native American forms of discourse into the rhetorical patterns of the classical critical tradition, Native American theorists and writers invite all of us to open ourselves to new ways of being in the world, ways that are very different from the models that we have been given by the Western hermeneutical tradition. They invite all of us to listen to other voices and epistemological orientations, those "shadow words" that, as Vizenor puts it, are "the hermeneutics of survivance" (*Manifest Manners* 68).

1

What is considered theory in the dominant academic
community is not necessarily what counts as theory for
women-of-color. Theory produces effects that change people
and the way they perceive the world. Thus we need *teorías*
that will enable us to interpret what happens in the world. . . .
Necesitamos teorías that will rewrite history using race, class,
gender and ethnicity as categories of analysis, theories that
cross borders, that blur boundaries – new kinds of theories
with new theorizing methods.

Gloria Anzaldúa

Back to a Woman-Centered Universe

The Gynosophical Perspective of Paula Gunn Allen's Critical Narratives

In the past few decades, writings by many women of color have been marked
by a desire to resist and resignify dominant modes of theorizing, arguing for
the necessity of creating *teorías* relevant to the lives of women of color rather
than passively accepting the theories given to them by Anglo-American liberal feminists.[1] In fact, because of this resistance, some women scholars of
color have often been regarded as antitheory. Barbara Christian, for example,
voices a suspicion of theory, especially if it is aligned with the hypertheoreti-
cism of postmodernism. Similarly, Tey Diana Rebolledo claims that "by
appropriating mainstream theoreticians and critics we have become so involved in intellectualizing that we lose our sense of our literature and therefore our vitality" (348). Along with Christian's contention that narrative is
also a powerful form of theorizing, Kimberly Blaeser investigates how effective the tools of a U.S. or Continental literary theory are for reading the "hi-
eroglyphs of a Native American system" ("Like 'Reeds through the Ribs of a
Basket'" 266). According to Blaeser, critics should consider more carefully
the Native aesthetics of literature and culture rather than merely imposing
the tools of Western literary analysis on Native literatures. In most cases, she
argues, a culturally accurate critical context develops out of the Native texts
themselves so that "any discussion of tribal literary forms must inevitably engage Native beliefs" (268). Looking at the production of contemporary Native American women, Blaeser finds a creative interweaving of story and theory and concludes that Native storytelling itself can teach critics new ways of

seeing how the literary and the academic are intertwined with the sacred and the daily while redefining the boundaries of Eurocentric theory itself.

Such suspicious attitudes toward Eurocentric theory depend, of course, on how theory itself is defined. In stark contrast to Christian's position, bell hooks claims that it is important that "we do not resist this hierarchical tendency by devaluating theory in general," suggesting that "theorizing, in its most fundamental form, is simply making sense of what is happening" and can also be a "healing place" (*Teaching to Transgress* 61). For Trinh Minh-ha theory is a powerful "tool of survival" (*Woman, Native, Other* 43), and for Gloria Anzaldúa the possibility of doing theory in "other modes of consciousness" – what she calls *mestizaje* theory – "produces effects that change people and the way they perceive the world" (*Making Face* xxv).

As a critic deeply engaged in a project of "doing theory in other modes of consciousness," Paula Gunn Allen seems to fit quite nicely the scenario that I have briefly sketched. A self-identified lesbian of color, Allen aligns herself with the generation of U.S. feminists of color who came of age in the 1960s and 1970s, separated by race, class, or gender identification, but united through similar responses to the experience of racial oppression. In *Off the Reservation*, she claims:

> We are *las disappearadas* (and *desperadas*). We are for the most part invisible, labeled "marginal," the "poor," the "victims," or we are seen as exotica. . . . Right, left, and center see us as their shadows, the part they disown, reject, repress, or romanticize. Our capacities as creative, self-directing, self-comprehending human beings are lost in the shuffle of ideology and taxonomy; the contributions of our peoples to the literatures, philosophies, sciences, and religions of the world are ignored. Our proper place in the view of defining others is that of servant; they have consigned us to the margins, and there we must stay. (164)

Surprisingly, however, despite a significant increase in interest generally in projects involving women of color in coalition, Allen's feminist writing has received little critical attention. Despite Chandra Mohanty's claim that Native people in the United States often refer to themselves as *Third World people*, there is no reference to Allen's critical work in *Third World Women and the Politics of Feminism*. More significantly, it is not mentioned even in Gloria Anzaldúa's collection *Making Face, Making Soul*, which gathers critical essays by Barbara Christian, Alice Walker, Trinh Minh-ha, Norma Alarcón, and Anzaldúa herself, among others.[2] The list could be extended to include other important critical anthologies by women of color published in the last few years, and we would still find that Allen's critical voice is consistently ignored, a fact suggesting how there is still a tendency even among women critics of color to identify themselves in terms of race or ethnicity, creating barriers among the various groups despite political alliances and collaboration across boundaries.

In Allen's case, however, other factors might account for the silencing of her critical narratives within the field of literary theory by women of color. AnaLouise Keating argues, for example, that there is an important connection between the limited recognition of Allen's work in academic circles and the extreme nature of some of her positions. Theorists are often puzzled, Keating says, by "what seem to be monolithic, essentializing views of spiritual forces and the 'feminine' in American Indian traditions" and, therefore, avoid commenting on these aspects of Allen's work (97).[3] While Keating's observations might apply in the context of contemporary poststructuralist debates concerning the (in)effectiveness of woman-centered origin myths and their implications for feminists' representational politics,[4] it is still intriguing that women theoreticians of color themselves, such as Anzaldúa and Audre Lorde, who to a certain extent perpetuate the same essentialist views of Allen's claims, tend to ignore her critical position.[5]

From within the category *women of color*, Allen enters the discourse on Native American critical theory by acknowledging the necessity of generating a form of criticism originating primarily from the Native or indigenous cultural context of the literary texts themselves and producing strategies that suggest how such a discourse can be effectively articulated. Yet her position remains ambivalent throughout the entire critical process. As I argued in the introduction, Allen's critical perspective takes a separatist stance grounded, as it were, in a rigidly gynocentric Indian view. By articulating what the literary critic Chela Sandoval calls "a typology of oppositional consciousness" (3), Allen presents a discourse conceived as different from both a patriarchal-masculine and a hegemonic-feminist perspective.[6] While the basics of her epistemological process are rooted in a female-centered universe, I would argue that Allen's mode of "oppositional consciousness" goes beyond feminist problematics. Insisting as she does on a distinctive Indian perspective, Allen ends up – especially in *The Sacred Hoop* – forging what I call an *ethnographic discourse*, construing and constructing Indianness from the seemingly romantic, sentimentalized perspective of Eurocentric thinking, the same thinking that for more than five hundred years has defined the Indian as the Other of Euramerican consciousness.[7] Despite critics' attempt to read

Allen's theory from within her own paradigm, I argue that Allen's (separatist) critical stance appears problematic in the context of a Native American theory through which authors are attempting to generate a discourse that significantly challenges the authoritative Eurocentric mode. Instead of participating in the critical dialogue from within, showing how it is possible to create new ways of theorizing while adopting the discursive tools offered by the metropolitan center, Allen steps outside, into the margin, and opts for a separatist solution. Such a separatist solution, however, ironically ends up legitimating the binary categories of Western/Eurocentric thinking.

At the heart of Allen's critical theory are the images and symbols of ancient Keres traditions as well as her own self-divided sense of what she calls the "breed" experience. According to Elizabeth Hanson, "the 'breed' experience becomes a mediative, revealing means of adding 'breath' to 'breath' and thereby extending the life of Native American literature in a white American literary context" (10). Allen – who refers to herself as a "multicultural event . . . raised in a Chicano village in New Mexico by a half-breed mother and a Lebanese-American father" (Rev. 127) – occupies what Keating refers to as a "threshold position" (2), participating in a number of apparently separate worlds yet refusing to be contained within any single group or location. Drawing from the poststructuralist insight that language does not merely reflect reality but also reshapes it, Allen, along with the other Native American authors discussed in this study, merges this performative power of the written word with Native American oral traditions, in which words have the power to create, alter, and even destroy. As she rewrites and reelaborates Native belief systems, Allen simultaneously, according to Keating, "spiritualizes" and "politicizes" her work (5). Yet, one could argue, the ways in which Allen's reelaboration of the oral tradition takes place must be very carefully considered in order to evaluate the political effectiveness of her critical strategies.

Published in 1986, *The Sacred Hoop* is the first collection of essays in which gender issues are examined from an American Indian perspective; in the author's words, it is the first "feminist Indian book" (Allen qtd. in Coltelli 38). Allen's "threshold position" is here utilized to explore her interaction with feminist, lesbian, academic, Native, and contemporary spiritual communities. By combining autobiography with historical narrative, poetry, literary analysis, and myth, Allen poses a significant challenge to conventional forms of discourse. At the same time, this "threshold theorizing" invites readers to examine ways in which homophobia, sexism, and racism have significantly distorted the perception of Native cultures and expands existing definitions of lesbian, gay, and female identities. In a 1987 interview with John Purdy, Allen declares that the oral tradition is "what we must look to if we are going to do accurate and responsible criticism" (Purdy 8). *The Sacred Hoop* begins in the oral tradition of the Keres Pueblo:

> In the beginning was thought, and her name was Woman. The Mother, the Grandmother, recognized from earliest times into the present among those peoples of the Americas who kept to the eldest traditions, is celebrated in social structures, architecture, law, custom, and the oral tradition. To her we owe our lives, and from her comes our ability to endure, regardless of the concerted assaults on our, on Her, being, for the past five hundred years of colonization. She is the Old Woman who tends the fires of life. She is the Old Woman Spider who weaves us together in a fabric of interconnection. (11)

From the outset, Allen establishes her position as a "revisionist mythmaker," going back to the roots of American Indian cultures in order to challenge patriarchal constructions of cultural identity.[8] She uses the term *gynocratic* or *gynocentric* to characterize forms of woman-centered communities in a Native American past. In a 1990 interview with Annie Eysturoy, Allen explains that, by *gynocratic* or *gynocentric*, she means "that femaleness or femininity is the central cultural value" within these communities, a value that, unlike those that characterize the patriarchal system, rejects any position of authority or control. She elaborates: "I am not talking about matriarchy, and I won't use that word. It tends to mean that women dominate, because patriarchy means that men dominate" (Eysturoy 101). Allen's notion of gynocentrism, then, seems to operate in the context of balance and mutual respect among the genders as well as in the larger context of harmony and interconnectedness characterizing the tribal universe. The tribal universe is, for Allen, a dynamic, living universe, one that she describes as "the creative flux of things," out of which her own writing process originates. The trick, Allen claims, is "to get back to our origins," that is, to a woman-centered universe, remembering or, as she says, "re-membering" the past, "putting it back together, recovering, knowing who we are and who we have been" (Eysturoy 100).

While the act of re-membering in the attempt to recover a centered sense of identity is a process in which Native American authors are constantly involved, as Owens also argues in his discussion of American Indian fiction in *Other Destinies*, Allen's search for "our origins" has provoked severe critiques by scholars, Native and non-Native alike, who accuse her of attempting to recover a "pure," authentic past with a vein of nostalgia. Arnold Krupat, for example, voices his suspicions of generalizations about the Native American metaphysics or mapping of reality, claiming that sacred hoops and medicine wheels are "both potentially dangerous and, as well, essentially helpless before the complex facts of Native American and Western cultural diversity" (*Ethnocriticism* 42). For Krupat, it is not a matter of denying that the image of the circle is the most appropriate choice to figure the reality construction of a Native epistemology; rather, it is a matter of eliminating oppositional ways of thinking (the circle vs. the line) that "doom Native Americans and Euramericans to repeat the past" (42). He writes: "If lines and circles can meet only *tangentially*, a figural or geometrical imperative acting, as it were in the place of fate, then frontier encounters between the peoples submitted to that fate must continue to be marked by misunderstanding and conflict" (42). More critically, Gerald Vizenor mocks Allen's gynocratic pose and overturning of androcentric structuralism, adding that a celebrated renaissance of the gynocratic cultures is but a perpetuation of "ersatz spiritualism" (*Manifest Manners* 86). As he observes in an interview with Robert Lee, Allen's sense of the mythic "plays to objective reason and . . . weaves arcane traditions into a new feminist enlightenment" (Lee, *Postindian Conversations* 163).

Responding to these critics' arguments that the act of recovery has more important implications than mere nostalgia, Allen writes: "Traditionals say we must remember our origins, our cultures, our histories, our mothers and grandmothers, for without that memory, which implies continuance rather than nostalgia, we are doomed to engulfment by a paradigm that is fundamentally inimical to the vitality, autonomy, and self-empowerment essential for satisfying, high quality life" (*The Sacred Hoop* 214). Allen believes that the loss of tradition and memory – in particular the erasure of tribal gynocentric belief systems – represents the root of oppression. Challenging all feminists to be aware of the history of this continent, to search for the vision of the grandmothers' society, and to take action, she writes: "Traditional lifestyles are more often gynocratic than not, and they are never patriarchal. These features make understanding tribal cultures essential to all responsible activists who seek life-affirming social change that can result in a real decrease in human and planetary destruction and in a real increase in quality of life for all inhabitants of planet earth" (*The Sacred Hoop* 2).

According to Keating, the act of re-membering the past is, for Allen, "a political act situated in the material present" (98). It means recovering, or putting together, an identity as well as attempting a cultural recovery in order to transform existing conditions. As Allen borrows from and rewrites mythic and spiritual traditions, Keating suggests, she simultaneously positions herself in the narrative of the past by rewriting old stories and inventing new ones. Even more significant, in the context of the above-mentioned critiques of Allen's theory, are Allen's ideas concerning the nature of the oral tradition: "The oral tradition, from which contemporary poetry and fiction take their significance and authenticity, has, since contact with white people, been a major force in Indian resistance. It has kept the people conscious of their tribal identity, their spiritual traditions, and their connections to the land and her creatures. Contemporary poets and writers take their cue from the oral tradition, to which they return continuously for theme, symbol, structure, and motivating impulse, as well as for the philosophic bias that animate our work" (*The Sacred Hoop* 53). By acknowledging the adaptability of the oral tradition, its evolving into contemporary forms without, however, abandoning its connection to the past, Allen articulates her idea of recovering the "feminine" in American Indian traditions, an idea intended, as Keating suggests, as "an act of resistance with important implications for all contemporary social actors" (23).

As I argued in the introduction, a Native American theory that brings to the attention of Eurocentric discourse the performative dimension of the oral tradition represents the most significant challenge launched by Native American authors to the discursive modes of Western hermeneutics. Given Allen's premises concerning the vitality of the oral tradition, how do we interpret the charges of essentialism advanced against her theory? Do Krupat and Vizenor, as well as other scholars who have voiced significant reservations about her methodologies, make their accusations out of a rigorously male perspective, ignoring the important implications of gender issues in Allen's critical apparatus, or do their observations respond more consistently to Allen's claims and methodologies? How can a theory that acknowledges the vitality and ongoing adaptability of the oral tradition be essentialist? More significantly, how can Allen's transformational writing, a writing that utilizes the performative dimension of verbal art, remain trapped in essentialist positions? The following declaration might assist us in answering these questions: "The methods used in American Indian Studies are various because it is an interdisciplinary field. So while I employ variously the methodologies of anthropology, folklore, psychology, sociology, historiography, philosophy, culture studies, and women's studies in these essays, my method of choice is my own understanding of American Indian life and thought" (Allen,

The Sacred Hoop 6). Interestingly enough, however, it is Allen's "method of choice" that poses the most puzzling questions to her readers, regardless of gender. Despite her claims in *The Sacred Hoop*, on considering her overall critical methodology one sees that her theoretical response is far from consistent, that in fact it does very little to address her critics' challenges.

Criticizing Western ethnocentric conceptions of mythology as fairy tale, lie, and so forth, Allen argues: "Myth is a kind of story that allows a holistic image to pervade and shape consciousness, thus providing a coherent and empowering matrix for action and relationship" (*The Sacred Hoop* 104–05). While not separating myth from the everyday world of human actions and social roles, Allen emphasizes a metaphysics in which the spiritual and material dimensions of life form a dynamic unity and can be translated into concrete action. Even though her purpose is to bring a Native epistemology to the attention of First World ideology, showing, thus, the holistic nature of the tribal universe, she ironically reverts to the language and methodologies of social-scientific discourse and provides "definitions" and "explanations," albeit from an American Indian perspective. Consider the following: "An American Indian myth is a story that relies preeminently on symbol for its articulation. It generally relates a series of events and uses supernatural, heroic figures as the agents of both the events and the symbols. As a story, it demands the immediate, direct participation of the listener" (105). By taking what I define as an "ethnographic approach," Allen's theory is still trapped in the binary thinking of Western metaphysics; the only difference is that the terms are reversed and the Indian, operating as the "authoritative" voice, is now granted a privileged position within the Eurocentric oppositional system.

The essay "The Sacred Hoop" – in the "Word Warriors" section of *The Sacred Hoop* – contains, perhaps, the most extensive articulation of Allen's methodology and, therefore, merits some consideration. In it, Allen presents a thorough "explanation" of the tribal universe, discussing myths, ceremonies, and structural devices such as ceremonial repetition, all the while pitting her explanation against folklorists and "objective" interpretations in general. Consider the following examples:

In English, one can divide the universe into two parts: the natural and the supernatural. Humanity has no real part in either, being neither animal nor spirit – that is, the supernatural is discussed as though it were apart from people, and the natural as though people were apart from it. This necessarily forces English-speaking people into a position of alienation from the world they live in. Such alienation is entirely foreign to American Indian thought. At base, every story, every song, every ceremony tells the Indian that each creature is part of a living whole and that all parts of that whole are related to one another by virtue of their participation in the whole of being. (*The Sacred Hoop* 60)

Repetition has an entrancing effect. Its regular recurrence creates a state of consciousness best described as "oceanic," but without the hypersentimental side effects implied by that term. It is hypnotic, and a hypnotic state of consciousness is the aim of the ceremony. . . . In this way, the participants become literally one with the universe, for they lose consciousness of mere individuality and share the consciousness that characterizes most orders of beings. (63)

Coming from a critic who insists on the vitality and adaptability of the oral tradition, these statements make us wonder to what extent Allen practices what she preaches. On the one hand, she argues against nostalgic attitudes toward American Indian cultural traditions, showing how these traditions have been reimagined in contemporary Native American literature. On the other hand, and more ironically, perhaps, her methods seem to "freeze" those traditions in a romantic past in which the Indian is still defined as essentially the Other. Culminating in the observation that "American Indian thought is essentially mystical and psychic in nature" (*The Sacred Hoop* 68), Allen's declarations in "The Sacred Hoop," taken in universally accepted terms, inevitably consign to her readers a tribal universe tidily packaged into familiar formulas of exoticism. Despite Hanson's declaration that Allen's critical methodology is designed to stimulate "clarity" and "insight" by demonstrating "how teachers can present this literature" in ways that will allow students to access the universe in which the material belongs (13), as a non-Native teacher and student of Native American literature I find Allen's approach problematic. On carefully reading Allen's explanatory statements, I find myself enticed into a world of mysticism and spirituality, happy to embark on what Owens refers to as a form of "literary tourism" (*Mixedblood Messages* 46), the same thing that we often see in contemporary Native American literature classrooms.[9]

Although my critique of Allen's ethnographic stance aims at showing the limitations of such a methodology in the context of a Native American theoretical discourse whose main goal is to challenge the analytic tools of Eurocentric theory while dismantling romantic definitions of Indianness, other critics have taken a different approach. Renae Moore Bredin, for example, argues that Allen's ethnographic approach can be understood in terms of "guerrilla theory," in which the Laguna author becomes the ethnographer writing about constructions of whiteness. Bredin writes: "Guerrilla ethnography, as I construct it, overturns prototypical ethnography by operating behind the 'enemy' lines of ethnographic discourses, writing an informant, nonhierarchical representation of culture, instigating a reversal of ideology. So we need a Western represented and a non-Western representer to commit guerrilla ethnography . . . a written account of the lives of 'white' people, a picture of what it means to be culturally white by one who is not" (229). Drawing from Homi Bhabha's notion of "mimicry," Bredin claims that Allen's repetition/rearticulation of colonial ethnographic discourse constitutes a "metonymy of presence," an ambivalence suggesting how the "'fetishized colonial culture'" is, in Bhabha's terms, "'potentially and strategically an insurgent counter-appeal'" (240). Limiting her discussion to *Grandmothers of the Light*, Bredin argues that, in using current ethnographic practice, Allen "revises previous images of Indigenous peoples through 'thousands of stories collected from hundred of tribes [that] have been published in the United States'" (238). Through her ethnographic form Allen becomes the shadow "mimicking the colonizer" while "threatening the stability of white identity" (240).

Given what we have seen to be Allen's ambivalent position, I find Bredin's reading strained when applied to the basics of Allen's methodology. Especially in *The Sacred Hoop* it is difficult to see any "reversal of ideology." In order to be effective, mimicry must, according to Bhabha, always produce its slippage/excess/difference. In this "slippage," colonial mimicry ironically produces the disturbing possibility of an Other that can disrupt the authority of colonial discourse itself. This is what Bhabha calls "*the menace* of mimicry" (*The Location of Culture* 91). A careful reading of Allen's ethnographic discourse in *The Sacred Hoop* might show how her construction of *Indianness* plays right into the hands of the romantic, sentimentalized Euramerican notion of the Indian, the same notion that continues to be perpetuated within contemporary American academic discourse. Allen defines Indians as "the Other" of Euramerican consciousness in order to make them different from whites. In her gynocentric cosmology, the Indian is the absent Other, an essentialized and manufactured product, molded after the Euramerican conception of Indianness. Far from being an act of mimicry, Allen's approach is at best emulation, but emulation in opposition. It is like a hand waving in a

mirror to a hand waving in a mirror: both make the same gesture, each thinking that it is waving back when, clearly, it is not.

Bredin concludes her argument by saying: "Guerrilla ethnography is a
strategic response to internal colonialism. In the struggle for land rights and
cultural survivance (in Vizenor's term), those who commit guerrilla ethnography pose more than a theoretical threat to the stability (such as it is) of the
ruling settler classes" (241). By using Vizenor's notion of "socioacupunc-
ture," conceived of as the "the wild reversal of the 'social science monologue
and trope to power'" (241), Bredin further insists on the subversive nature of
Allen's theory, failing to notice, however, that, far from posing a theoretical
threat to the discourse of the establishment, Allen's Eurocentric versions of
Indianness ironically mimic without menacing.

The (in)effectiveness of Allen's ethnographic discourse might be better
understood if we compare it with Trinh's deconstructivist approach. In
Woman, Native, Other, for example, Trinh wittily engages in a conversation
with anthropological discourse, twisting and spinning some of its own "worn
codes" in an attempt to devalue them and question the identity of meaning
and of the speaking/writing subject. Using the language of anthropology,
which is fond of definitions and objective explanations, Trinh reverses these
definitions, reducing this seemingly scientific discipline to a form of far-
fetched storytelling. She wittily defines anthropology as "gossip," a speaking
together about others rather than a conversation: "A conversation of 'us' with
'us' about 'them' is a conversation in which 'them' is silenced. 'Them' always
stands on the other side of the hill, naked, and speechless, barely present in
its absence" (67). In contradistinction to the language of power that she describes in anthropology, Trinh argues for the necessity of a practice of language that remains, through its signifying operations, a process constantly
unsettling the identity of the speaking/writing subject. She writes: "Anthropology as a semiology should itself be treated in semiological terms. It should
situate its position and function in the system of meaning or, in other words,
explicitly assume a critical responsibility towards its own discourse, exposing its status as inheritor of the very system of signs it sets out to question,
disturb and shatter" (71). Far from taking such a poststructuralist stance,
Allen turns to what Trinh defines as the "language of Nativism," constructing in *The Sacred Hoop* definitions of *Indianness* that, unlike any form of
guerrilla theory, ironically leave the Indian "on the other side of the hill,"
silent and significantly Other.

Given the foundations of Allen's theory, it is understandable that critics have overlooked the ironic contradictions of her ethnographic approach, focusing instead primarily on feminist problematics. More specifically, these critics have attempted to see Allen's position from within her own epistemological perspective, reading her gynocentrism as a significant challenge to Western patriarchal structures. As I noted earlier, to date only Keating's study presents an extensive discussion of Allen's critical works as well as a serious attempt to read her recovery of the feminine in a transformational way; it therefore necessitates some attention.

According to Keating, Allen's drawing on Native American worldviews creates a "transformative epistemology" that undermines the binary structure of Western thinking. To describe this process Keating uses the term *embodied mythic thinking*, by which she means "a nondualistic knowledge system in which thoughts, ideas, and beliefs have concrete material effects; and matter itself is a special form of intelligence that human beings can reshape" (27). By replacing the Judeo-Christian worldview (with its binary oppositions) with a Native American mythic tradition, Allen displaces, Keating argues, the boundaries between insider/outsider, subject/object, spirit/matter, and other dichotomous terms and "creates multilayered discourses that replace unified subjects with fluid, shifting speakers" (90). Such embodied mythic thinking generates an epistemological process that challenges Western conventions and could bring about material change. To further support her claims, Keating refers to the preface of *Grandmothers of the Light*, in which Allen explains how the stories collected there reveal " 'the great power women have possessed, and how that power when exercised within the life circumstances common to women everywhere can reshape (terraform) the earth' " (28). Only by fully participating in the prepatriarchal sacred myths, Allen implies, can twentieth-century English-speaking women of any ethnicity or cultural background develop a spiritual mode of perception that would empower them to effect spiritual and material change. With this also comes the much-debated issue of how politically effective prepatriarchal myths are in challenging conventional gender categories, a critique that Keating overcomes by reading Allen's epistemic position beyond the Eurocentric masculinist conventions on which hegemonic feminist theorists often rely.

As I argued earlier, from a poststructuralist feminist perspective, Allen's revisionist mythmaking, grounded as it is in biologically based concepts of womanhood and femininity, inevitably reinscribes phallocentric definitions of the notion *woman*. Consider, for instance, the following assertions in *The Sacred Hoop*:

Pre-contact American Indian women valued their role as vitalizers because they understood that bearing, like bleeding, was a transformative ritual act. Through their own bodies they could bring vital beings into the world – a miraculous power unrivaled by mere shamanistic displays. They were mothers, and that word implied the highest degree of status in ritual cultures. (28)

Among the tribes, the occult power of women, inextricably bound to our hormonal life, is thought to be very great; many hold that we possess innately the blood-given power to kill – with a glance, with a step, or with a judicious mixing of menstrual blood into somebody's soup. (47)

Women are by the nature of feminine "vibration" graced with certain inclinations that make them powerful and capable in certain ways (all who have this temperament, ambience, or "vibration" are designated as women and all who do not are not so designated). (207)

Coupled with many other claims disseminated in the various essays that form the theoretical subject of *The Sacred Hoop*, Allen's position inevitably reinscribes a concept of female identity rooted in a biology that still locates creative power in the (female) body. The "feminine" that Allen attempts to recover is, one might argue, an ahistorical, unchanging essence that supports conventional phallocentric definitions of *woman*. As Keating also points out, viewed from within the academy, Allen's claims are "highly suspect, if not outright laughable" (110). From a poststructuralist Western perspective, feminist celebrations of womanhood can, indeed, be problematic. Judith Butler, for example, claims that, by positing the category *woman* as a "coherent and stable subject," feminism must face the political problem that the signifier *women* refers to a common identity: "If one 'is' a woman, that is surely not all one is; the term fails to be exhaustive . . . because gender is not always constituted coherently or consistently in different historical contexts, and because gender intersects with racial, class, sexual, and regional modalities of discursively constituted identities" (3). More critically, Donna Haraway argues that "there is nothing about being 'female' that naturally binds women." Indeed, "there is not even such a state as 'being' female, itself a highly complex category constructed in contested sexual, scientific discourses and other social practices" (155). Similarly, Teresa de Lauretis posits that there is "no

going back to the innocence of 'biology'" (20), or to biologically based concepts of gender, since gender is inevitably produced by a wide range of social
discursive practices. As Haraway provocatively puts it, for these theorists it
is better to be "cyborgs" than "goddesses" (181).

However, Keating posits, any attempt to define *woman* obviously depend
on one's perspective. Unlike Butler, de Lauretis, and Haraway, Keating suggests that women of color would seem to accept Allen's claims since they
also acknowledge and critique the Eurocentrism of hegemonic feminist theory. Yet, I argue, Keating herself does not comment on the fact that Allen's
theory is simply ignored by theorists of color, which might indicate that rejecting Eurocentric hegemonic feminist theory does not necessarily make
women of color a monolithic, unified group. In the attempt to read Allen
from within her own critical paradigm, Keating posits that Allen's use of
North American feminist creatrix figures "demonstrates the possibility of
writing 'the feminine' in open-ended, non-exclusionary ways" (96). Allen's
writings affirm, for Keating, a form of "feminine mestizaje": "'feminine' in its
re-metaphorized images of Woman; 'mestizaje' in its fluid, transformational,
transcultural forms" (96). Discussing Allen's use of Native American mythic
creatrixes, Keating argues that, in Allen's work, the category *woman* is de-
tached from the "'heterosexual matrix' underlying western images of gender
identities" (104). Keating claims that, in the various essays that form *The Sacred Hoop*, Allen points out the "creative power" of Thought Woman and
presents definitions of creation based on a cosmic intelligence rather than on
a biological one. In a discussion of Keres theology, for instance, Allen claims,
"Creation does not take place through copulation. In the beginning existed
Thought Woman and her dormant sisters, and Thought Woman thinks creation and sings her two sisters into life" (*The Sacred Hoop* 16). Rather than
reducing woman to the maternal function, Allen expands definitions of ma-
ternity, Keating suggests, to incorporate all forms of creativity and change as
well as all aspects of human existence. Allen writes: "A strong attitude inte-
grally connects the power of Original Thinking or Creation Thinking to the
power of mothering. The power is not so much the power to give birth . . .
but the power to make, to create, to transform" (*The Sacred Hoop* 29). By
framing a cosmic feminine intelligence that "thinks" creation, Allen redefines, Keating argues, the notion of femininity and disrupts "the hierarchical
dichotomous worldview that equates 'masculine' with transcendence, culture, and the mind, and 'feminine' with immanence, nature, and the body –
a perpetuation of the Cartesian dualism of body vs. Mind" (107). The result
is a "performative epistemology" aimed at transcultural transformation.

Keating concludes: "Instead of recovering a pre-colonial mythological system erased by patriarchal structures, Allen invents an ethical, *artificial* mythology – ethical, because her new Indianized metaphors of Woman provide imaginary alternatives to contemporary definitions of the 'feminine'; and artificial, because the 'feminine' she affirms does not – yet – exist" (111). Claiming that the "feminine" that Allen is trying to recover cannot be reduced or identified with the lives of actual women, cannot be adequately represented as "the elsewhere to masculine discourse," Keating concludes – in line with such French feminist theorists as Hélène Cixous and Luce Irigaray – by positing this "feminine" as an "imaginative universal," one that exists at the threshold of textual and psychic locations, "where transcultural identifications – mestizaje connections – can be made" (117).[10]

As intriguing as this position might seem, I find Keating's defense of Allen's critical epistemology highly problematic in that, ironically, it perpetuates the same contradictions that I see in Allen's theory itself. If this "artificial feminine" cannot be identified with the life of actual women, how do we account for Allen's call for all women, feminist scholars included, to go back to the gynocosmos of the tribes and learn from the grandmothers? In other words, how politically effective is this transcultural, fluid, *mestizaje* feminine if it can be found neither within nor without the prevailing sociosymbolic structure? How does Allen's criticism effectively challenge mainstream critical positions if it steps outside them into a vague "imaginative universal"? What, if not a retreat into a nostalgic cultural past, is Allen's reliance on spirit guides, supernatural informants, and female gods? Despite Keating's attempt to view Allen's theoretical approach from the position of a Native worldview (one defined by Allen), she does not acknowledge the problems that doing so might entail.

In the first place, the question of how matrifocal/matrilineal/gynocratic Native American tribes really were or are is puzzling to Western and Third World critics alike (including male critics). According to Hanson, "Allen's vision of tribal life as gynocratic in nature, rather than simply mystical or psychic, reveals a remarkable contention, one that Allen herself recognizes as supported by limited verifiable evidence" (16). Notwithstanding Allen's speculations that "the invaders have exerted every effort to remove Indian women from every position of authority," thus ensuring a complete erasure of gynocracy, which, as she puts it, was "the primary social order of Indian America" (*The Sacred Hoop* 3), Hanson points out that there is too little evidence either to confirm or to disprove Allen's hypotheses.[11] Supporters of Allen's theory tend to dismiss such observations, arguing, as Keating does, that Allen's epistemology is "performative" rather than "descriptive" (111) and that, by attempting to validate it, critics are simply asserting positivist methodologies. While it is tempting to agree with Keating's observations, especially in the light of a Native American theory that draws from systems of knowledge other than the Western or the Eurocentric, one might nevertheless wonder to what extent Allen's theoretical assumptions escape the entrapments of the conventional epistemological methods mentioned by Keating.

In the context of my study, Allen's critical position, a species of what Edward Said defines as a "strategic location" or "a way of describing the author's position in a text with regard to the . . . material he writes about" (*Orientalism* 20), is, indeed, one that we must consider very carefully. In the introduction to *The Sacred Hoop*, Allen writes that "the essays in this collection do not particularly reflect a white mind set," being "unfiltered through the minds of western patriarchal colonizers" (6). Vigorously rejecting Western theories (poststructuralism in particular) as well as any form of Eurocentric or masculinist convention, Allen provides her own "factual" evidence for her assertions: "Whatever I read about Indians *I check out with my inner self.* Most of what I have read – and some things I have said based on that reading – is upside down and backward. *But my inner self, the self who knows what is true about American Indians because it is one*, always warns me when something deceptive is going on. . . . Sometimes that confirmation comes about in miraculous ways; that's when I know guidance from the nonphysical and the supernaturals, and that the Grandmothers have taken pity on me in my dilemma" (6–7; emphasis added). How are we to read these statements in the light of Keating's interpretations of Allen's theory? To what extent is Allen's theory a "threshold position," one in which "transcultural identifications" can be made, if it relies exclusively on the author's inner self? How does this inner self know "what is true about American Indians," and, more important, how does this inner self define *Indianness?*

If, as critics have observed, Allen's multicultural experience – what Keating calls a "threshold identity" (2) and Hanson a " 'breed' experience" (10) – is at the foundation of her literary theory, a concept that illustrates the potentially transformational implications of her work, her definition of a unified "inner self" inevitably contradicts the multiplicity contained within her identity as a "confluence." [12] In addition, by conceiving an inner self that often receives guidance from supernatural informants, Allen ends up perpetuating romantic images of a mystic tribal universe to which Euramerica can securely escape in a desire to find an exotic, authentic Native Other. Even more problematic are Allen's supposed knowledge of "what is true about American Indians" and her definition of *Indian* itself. Is Allen's Indianness a guarantee of authentic knowledge, a position that makes her a representative "Native informant," to use Spivak's term, whose claims and observations are evidence of infallible truth? Given her multicultural experience, what makes Allen an authoritative source on Indian material? All these questions inevitably relate to the way in which we define who and what an Indian is.

Arguing for an essentially tribal as opposed to a Western view, Allen seems in defining *Indianness* to be repeating the discursive modes of Euramerica's imagination, the same discourse that has constructed the Indian as the distinctively Other of Euramerican consciousness. In *Manifest Manners*, Vizenor points out that the word *Indian* was "a colonial enactment . . . an occidental invention that became a bankable simulation; the word has no referent in tribal languages or cultures" (11). In his ongoing project of discarding the institutional and academic stereotypes invented for Native Americans by Euramerican culture, Vizenor clearly indicates the suicidal and destructive quality of what he calls "terminal creeds," or beliefs that try to confine and imprison Native Americans in the static, unchanging domain of words, as they have been confined in reservations. By relying on authentic notions of Indianness as opposed to Western discursive paradigms, Allen inevitably perpetuates those "terminal creeds" that prevent the signifier *Indian* from being freed from all the romantic entrapments that Euramerica has created for it for more than five hundred years.

Allen's view of Indianness as a sentimentalized version of Eurocentric discourse is particularly evident in her attempt to come to terms with (cross-cultural) interpretative readings of tribal material. What follows is a discussion of "Kochinnenako in Academe: Three Approaches to Interpreting a Keres Indian Tale," which is one of the essays in the last section of *The Sacred Hoop*, the section entitled "Pushing Up the Sky." By way of comparison, and to further illustrate the pitfalls and inconsistencies in Allen's methodology, I will also briefly consider Gayatri Spivak's discussion of the Bengali story "Stanadayini" (Breast-Giver), by Mahasweta Devi, which Spivak herself translates in *In Other Worlds*.

"Kochinnenako in Academe" is Allen's most extensive discussion of contemporary white readings of English translations of traditional Native American tales as well as an attempt to create a dialogue with Western feminist theory. The story of Sh-ah-cock and Miochin, or "The Battle of the Seasons," is a narrative version of a ritual that Allen relates as recast by her mother's uncle, John M. Gunn, in his book *Scat Chen*. Claiming that Gunn's rendering inevitably reflected European traditions and simultaneously distorted Laguna-Acoma ones, Allen intends her three readings (Keres, modern feminist, and feminist-tribal) to provide students with a "traditionally tribal, nonracist, feminist understanding of traditional and contemporary American Indian life" (*The Sacred Hoop* 223).

From the very beginning, then, Allen assumes the pose of Native informant, suggesting that her position as a "traditional Indian" (whatever that might be) authenticates her reading of the story. Such a position, however, is problematic since, as Spivak argues, "the complicity between subject and object of investigation" is something that the critic cannot escape and something that establishes an inevitable parasitic relationship between the two discursive parties (*In Other Worlds* 221). Spivak writes: "Situated within the current academic theatre of cultural imperialism, with a certain *carte d'entrée* into the elite theoretical *ateliers* in France, I bring news of power-lines within the palace. Nothing can function without us, yet the part is at least historically ironic" (221). In *The Postcolonial Critic*, Spivak talks about the "tokenization" of Third World critics, who are often invited to participate in First World academic debates only to present the "authentic" Third World point of view (61). Similarly, writing about difference and authenticity, Trinh observes that "the Third World representative the modern sophisticated public ideally seeks is the *unspoiled* African, Asian, or Native American, who remains more preoccupied with her/his image of the *real* native – the *truly different* – than with the issues of hegemony, racism, feminism, and social change" (*Woman, Native, Other* 88). By acting as a Native informant, as the insider who possesses the authentic version of the story, Allen inevitably contributes to the tokenization of the Native while failing to acknowledge that, as a critic implicated in the discourse of Western imperialism, she is also part of the construction of her (Native) object of knowledge.

Allen begins her interpretative analysis by arguing that "The Battle of the Seasons" is a female-centered story – one in the tradition of "Yellow Woman." It is a story that reflects the gynocratic cosmology of prepatriarchal communities in which women are central to the harmony, balance, and prosperity of the tribe. In the battle between Sh-ah-cock ("the spirit of winter") and Miochin ("the spirit of summer"), there is no winner; neither is Kochinnenako's love the real motif for the battle. As Allen notices, the story is patterned after the transfer of power from winter to summer, a harmonious transfer – effected by Kochinnenako – that reflects the earth's bilateral division between summer and winter.

When a "traditional Keres" listens to the story, Allen argues, she "is

satisfied with [it] because it reaffirms a Keres sense of rightness, of property"
(*The Sacred Hoop* 234). Such a reader might be puzzled to find the term *rulers* applied to the social stratification of the Keres world.[13] She might also be
puzzled by the tone of epic romance. But, Allen notes, "the primary Keres
values of harmony, balance, and the centrality of woman to maintain them
have been validated" (234). Problems occur, instead, when a non-Keres feminist, one trained in "Western technological-industrialized minds" (243), approaches the story. Allen claims that this reader inevitably reads the traditional version of the story imagining that, like many women, Kochinnenako
has been socialized into "submission" and supposes that "this narrative is
about the importance of men and the use of a passive female figure as a pawn
in their bid for power" (234-35). Here, Allen is obviously speaking of the
problems inherent in contemporary non-Native readings of English translations of traditional Native American tales while indirectly referring to issues
of cultural appropriation.[14] Yet some of her statements are puzzling – particularly those dealing with what she calls a "non-Indian mind" – and, therefore, merit careful consideration. Allen writes: "Reading American Indian
traditional stories and songs is not an easy task. Adequate comprehension requires that the reader be aware that *Indians never think like whites* and that
the typeset version of traditional materials is distorting. In many ways, literary conventions . . . militate against an understanding of traditional tribal materials. Western technological-industrialized minds cannot adequately interpret tribal materials because they are generally trained to perceive their entire
world in ways that are alien to tribal understanding" (242-43; emphasis
added). What, if not further restatements of her ethnographic stance, are
such observations? By writing that "Indians never think like whites," Allen
ironically implies that, in their difference, Indians are the Other of Euramerican consciousness, suddenly deciding, like anthropologists before her, what
is authentic and what is not. Relating her anthropologized version of Indianness to her feminist concerns, she argues that such inadequate interpretation
of traditional material plagues, not Native, tribal writers alone, but all ethnic
writers who write out of a folk or tribal tradition and women as well since
women, after all, "inhabit a separate folk tradition" (243).

 As a critic trained in a Western-technological mentality, I feel uneasy with
Allen's declarations. Given her premises, one must assume that it is possible
to define the essential *Indian*, that only such Indians can adequately interpret tribal material, and that any attempt by "outsiders" to learn about other
cultures is futile. But does reading and learning necessarily mean appropriating or attempting to colonize? Is it possible to reach some kind of cross-

cultural understanding without necessarily stealing or appropriating? What is at stake here?

Satya Mohanty perfectly illustrates the source of my uneasiness when he poses the ironic question: "What better way of ensuring the equality of cultures than to assert that, since all explanations of the other risk repeating the colonizers' judgments, we should simply refuse to judge or explain, forsaking understanding for the sake of respect?" ("Epilogue" 111). Mohanty argues against this refusal claiming that a relativism that refuses to judge or explain for fear of colonizing turns out to cripple our chances of genuine cross-cultural understanding: "If 'we' decide that 'they' are so different from us that we and they have no common 'criteria' (Lyotard's term) by which to evaluate (and, necessarily, even to interpret) each other, we may avoid making ethnocentric errors, but we also, by the same logic, ignore the possibility that they will ever have anything to teach us" (112). Even more ironically, he concludes: "There is simply no need to worry about the other culture's view; they provide no reason to make us question our own views or principles. That culture and ours are equal but irredeemably separate" (112).

A similar concern, albeit in a feminist framework, is expressed by Kathleen M. Donovan when she claims that the "issue of voice" – who is entitled to speak and "what can be said" – is perhaps the most fundamental issue raised by both Native American literature and feminist theories (8). Writing specifically about the objections to the dominant culture advanced in the past few decades by women of color, Donovan wonders whether, in our critical valorization of specificity, we might be in danger of denying the possibility of commonality in cultural and aesthetic expression (12). Are specificity and commonality mutually exclusive? she asks. Can Paula Gunn Allen and Toni Morrison be analyzed for what they have in common more than for what separates them? Can the lyrical theory of the French feminist Hélène Cixous be employed in reading the poetry of the Native American Joy Harjo? These and other, similar questions shore up Donovan's advocacy of cross-cultural dialogue, an advocacy in direct opposition to Allen's separatist position.

In "Kochinnenako in Academe," Allen does attempt to tone down her separatist position by providing a "feminist-tribal" interpretation of the story. Here, however, her perspective as a Native informant appears all the more problematic since, as Greg Sarris points out in *Keeping Slug Woman Alive*, "she closes discussion with those women and the texts she sets out to illuminate" while making broad generalizations about tribal thought and feminist points of view (126). Sarris claims that each point of view appears to be a generalization created by Allen. He states:

[Allen] writes for example: "A Keres is of course aware that balance and harmony are two primary assumptions of Keres society and will not approach the narrative wondering whether the handsome Miochin will win the hand of the unhappy wife and triumph over the enemy, thereby heroically saving the people from disaster." Is this the case for *all* Keres individuals? Another example: "A feminist who is conscious of tribal thought and practice will know that the real story of Sh-ah-cock and Miochin underscores the central role that woman plays in orderly life of the people." And again, I ask: A Feminist who is aware of *which* [*sic*] tribal thought? What tribe? What feminist? In creating and presenting multiple points of views, how might Allen, as a creator/writer of these points of view, have diminished the complexity and power of those points of view? Who is Allen as a mediator and presenter of the different points of view? (126–27) [15]

As my discussion of *Keeping Slug Woman Alive* will show, the issue of insider/outsider is one that Native critics should carefully consider since, as Sarris argues, being Indian or part Indian does not necessarily guarantee authentic insight into the critic's cultural background. To use Spivak's terms, Allen forgets as a critic to consider that her privilege is her loss and that, by theorizing about the Keres story (subaltern material), she is inevitably acting as the investigating subject who constructs her object of investigation/ knowledge.

As a "real Indian" who implicitly participates in the production of colonial discourse and in the construction of the commodified Other of which she is also a part, Spivak positions herself (as a Third World woman, a hyphenated American, a Bengali exile) in ways and assumes critical methodologies (Marxist, feminist, deconstructivist) that are all the more interesting to consider in the light of Allen's speculations. [16] Along with a translation of Devi's story, Spivak also provides in *In Other Worlds* a critical analysis in which elite methodologies (Western Marxist feminism, Western liberal feminism, and French high theory of the female body) are employed to interpret subaltern material. To a certain extent, Spivak is repeating Allen's experiment, approaching a text of counterinsurgency where the subaltern has been represented and assigning to it a new subject position. True, "Stanadayini" is not an oral tale appropriated by a Westernized masculine mind but instead a story written by a (female) teacher of English who, after all, participates in the colonial production that Spivak is trying to critique. Nevertheless, because of the "ravenous hunger for Third world literary texts in English translation"

(Spivak, *In Other Worlds* 253), and because of the "pedagogical and curricular appropriation" of these texts by "feminist teachers and readers who are vaguely aware of the race-bias within mainstream feminism," I argue that Spivak's experiment with and translation of the story resembles Allen's approach in that both critics (with their own interpretations) become investigating subjects inevitably involved in a complicitous relation with the object of their knowledge. Unlike Allen, however, Spivak acknowledges her complicity and attempts to come to terms with it.

"Stanadayini" is a story about a gendered subaltern, Jashoda, used by Mahasweta as the measure of the dominant sexual ideology in India. Jashoda is a professional woman and mother who becomes a wet nurse for the wealthy family whose son crippled her husband. Her repeated gestation and lactation become the "means of production" supporting her family until a consuming breast cancer puts an end to her life and, thus, to her "value." As Spivak sees it, "It is the *loneliness* of the gendered subaltern that is staged in 'Stanadayini'" (*In Other Worlds* 253). Unlike Devi's reading of the story (presented in *In Other Worlds* along with Spivak's own) – that it is about British colonial oppression in India (India being symbolized by the mother for hire, abused and exploited by all classes of people) – Spivak's focuses more on a study of the subaltern, arguing against a continual subalternization of Third World material and aiming at deconstructing the epistemological and ontological confusion that pits elite methodology against subaltern material.[17]

If a story such as "Stanadayini" invokes the singularity of the gendered subaltern, Spivak asks, why should we employ elite methodologies in interpreting the story?

> This is part of a much larger confusion: can men theorize feminism, can whites theorize racism, can the bourgeois theorize revolution and so on. It is when *only* the former groups theorize that the situation is politically intolerable. Therefore it is crucial that members of these groups are kept vigilant about their assigned subject-positions. It is disingenuous, however, to forget that, as the collectivities implied by the second group of nouns start participating in the production of knowledge about themselves, they must have a share in some of the structures of privileges that contaminate the first group. (Otherwise the ontological errors are perpetuated. . . .) (*In Other Worlds* 253)

Claiming that knowledge relies, not on identity, but on irreducible difference, Spivak concludes by saying that "what is known is never adequate to its object" (254). In translating Mahasweta's story for the elite and as an elite critic and including both Mahasweta's reading of the story and her own, Spivak suggests that both participate in the colonial production: "Because we are after all talking about India as a place with a history, where the idea of literature and the reading of literature are also produced through the very mechanism that I am trying to critique. So it is not as if I am over Mahasweta as the authentic voice and me as the U.S. scholarly reader. Mahasweta herself was a teacher of English so that what we're looking at is two different kinds of readerly production" (*The Postcolonial Critic* 158). More important, by using elite methodologies in her reading of the story, Spivak shows how it significantly deconstructs them by pointing out limits and limitations.

A Marxist feminist reading of the story subverts, as Spivak notes, the general Marxist feminist assumption according to which it is the provision of the means of subsistence by men during the childbearing period that forms the basis for women's subordination in a class society. In "Stanadayini," Jashoda's gestation and lactation are, by the logic of the production of value, both means of production, just as Jashoda's husband is (by the logic of sexual reproduction). According to Spivak, "a certain version of the elite versus the subaltern position is perpetuated by non-Marxist antiracist feminism in the Anglo–United States toward Third World women's texts in translation" (254). For example, a Western liberal feminist perspective tends to privilege the indigenous, diasporic elite from the Third World and identifies woman with the reproductive and copulative body. In the story, Spivak posits, having children is also accession to free labor, an act that implies productive rights as well as reproductive ones. However, these acts are denied Jashoda, not only by men, but also by elite women, who tend to undermine this (and other) significant factors (*In Other Worlds* 258).

Ultimately, within the context of French feminist theory of the body, frequently perceived as unrealistic and elitist by Western liberal feminism, Spivak's analysis of the question of *jouissance* as orgasmic pleasure in the story shows limits in that theoretical space as well. Unlike critics who claim that "Stanadayini" remains silent on the issue of orgasmic pleasure since Mahasweta "writes like a man" – a position that reinforces a hegemonic gendering of the subaltern – Spivak argues that Jashoda's body, not her fetishized deliberative consciousness, is the place of knowledge: "The role of Jashoda's body as the place where the sinister knowledge of decolonization as failure of foster-mothering is figured forth produces cancer, an excess very far from the singularity of the clitoral orgasm" (*In Other Worlds* 260). Within this context, Mahasweta's story offers an interesting response to Jacques Lacan's notion that woman's *jouissance* in the narrow sense is "fairly trivial" (Lacan 89). In addition, by turning fostering into a profession, Mahasweta's story presents mothering in its materiality while inevitably critiquing Kristeva's version of the "divine mother." [18]

It is beyond the scope of this chapter to engage in a thorough discussion of Spivak's critical interpretations of Mahasweta's story or in an analysis of the story itself. My intention in addressing Spivak's analysis has been simply to illustrate the danger in Allen's separatist position concerning the politics of interpretation. Whereas Allen forcefully argues that any interpretation of tribal material by a non-Indian mind is ultimately inadequate, insisting on a continual subalternization of Native texts, Spivak (a subaltern herself) convincingly shows how this separation between "us" and "them" is impossible. In the ongoing debate concerning the Native's resistance to theory, Spivak posits, some claim that, whereas First World literature has become little more than language games, Third World literature is still grounded in realism. A critical approach such as Allen's would endorse this position, perpetuating the ontological and epistemological confusion that pits "subaltern being against elite knowing" (268). As a critic and writer from the margin whose work is inevitably produced within the dominant discourse of the metropolitan center, Allen does not have the choice to opt for a separatist approach simply because she already functions within the discourse of the mainstream establishment. Her strategic location of investigating subject puts her in a parasitic relation with the subaltern material that she sets out to analyze and discuss. Avoiding recognition of this paradox simply leads to the position that Sarris points out: the critic closing discussion with the protagonist of the Keres story, Kochinnenako, leaving her once again in the utterly silent position of the Native or subaltern.

In the context of Allen's theory in general, a separatist approach such as the one pursued in *The Sacred Hoop* ironically contradicts Allen's self-positioning at the border of various discourses and theoretical identities. Rather than demonstrating how Native epistemological processes subsume Western discursive modes, producing a *teoría* that, in Anzaldúa's terms, might cross borders and blur boundaries, Allen's theoretical approach perpetuates instead the us/them universe of Western metaphysics, creating a binary opposition in which the Indian is now granted a privileged position.

Published in 1998, collecting essays spanning the thirty years from the late 1960s to the late 1990s, *Off the Reservation* is, in the author's words, "a re/col-

lection of contemporary coyote Pueblo American thought" (5). From the outset, then, Allen adopts the trickster figure as a metaphor for transformation
and border crossing while reflecting Stanley's observation that "women of
color have often taken on the subversive roles of women warriors, tricksters,
wild women, and guerrilla tacticians" in order to critique multiple systems of
domination (1). More consistently and more effectively in this new collection
than in *The Sacred Hoop*, Allen celebrates her multicultural experience both
on a thematic and on a formal level, producing a multigeneric, hybrid text
that blends myth, history, literary studies, philosophy, and personal narrative. Whereas the essays in the previous collection were "unfiltered through
the minds of western patriarchal colonizers" (*The Sacred Hoop* 6), each essay
in the new collection "is equally a product of Western thought, necessarily
so" (*Off the Reservation* 6) – but still suiting a Native turn of mind. Within
this context, the use of the essay as a discursive, open form to convey the primary tenet of Allen's threshold theory – the dialogic quality of the oral tradition – is interesting. Allen writes: "In my mind, critical essays – indeed,
'nonfiction' writing in general – is [*sic*] simply another way of telling a story.
Each has a narrative line, a plot if you will, and that line must unfold in accordance with certain familiar patterns, just as any story must. An essay contains all the elements of a good plot: conflict, crisis, resolution. Concepts take
the role of character, and, of course, the unities of time, place, and action
must be respected" (10).

Allen's views on the nature of the essay seem to be shared by the other Native American theorists whose work I am going to discuss in the subsequent
chapters of this study. As I argued in my introduction, crucial in all these authors is the idea of bringing into the discursive modes of Eurocentric theory
forms and patterns from the oral tradition in order to show the interface between the indigenous American discourse and the contemporary American
discourse. Like Allen, Womack, Sarris, Owens, and Vizenor in particular
adopt storytelling strategies that, while pushing the boundaries of theory itself, teach their audiences significant new ways of reading and listening.

According to Allen, "Stories, whether narrative or argumentative in nature, tell us not who we are, not who we are supposed to be, but instead describe and define the constraints of the possible" (*Off the Reservation* 11). In
her specific case, then, stories tell her about her mixed heritage, about the
crossing of borders of her ancestors, about the boundaries that have become
permeable, and about her identity that cannot be "fenced in," made into a
fixed, stable category (1). By locating herself at the intersections of what oth-

ers assume to be separate entities, Allen assumes a strategic location similar to the one adopted by Gloria Anzaldúa in *Borderlands/La Frontera*. Anzaldúa writes:

> I am a border woman. I grew up between two cultures, the Mexican (with a heavy Indian influence) and the Anglo (as a member of colonized people in our own territory). I have been straddling that *tejas*-Mexican border, and others, all my life. It's not a comfortable territory to live in, this place of contradictions. Hatred, anger, and exploitation are the prominent features of this landscape. However, there have been compensations for this *mestiza*, and certain joys. Living on borders and in margins, keeping intact one's shifting and multiple identity and integrity, is like trying to swim in a new element, an "alien" element. (preface)

Both in form and in content, *Off the Reservation* parallels Anzaldúa's hybrid text with the intent to inscribe the author's threshold identity into her creative and critical writings while challenging the dominant culture's sociopolitical inscriptions, those labels that tend to define each person according to gender, ethnicity, sexuality, class, and other systems of difference. Like Anzaldúa, Allen enacts Keating's notion of "embodied mythic thinking," bringing to our attention the nondualistic knowledge system of Native cultures, a system characterized by reciprocity among the intellectual, the physical, and the spiritual.

Allen's gynosophy, or female-centered perspective, informs the nature and content of *Off the Reservation*. The essays in the first section, entitled "Haggles/Gynosophies," take up many of the issues explored in *The Sacred Hoop* as far as recovering the feminine in American Indian traditions. Again, Allen refers to the gynocentrism of Laguna-Pueblo life, to the matrilineal, matrilocal, and matrifocal structures that, as she puts it, "include multiplicity, nurturing, respect for all that lives, harmony, peacefulness, kinship, integrity, honor, and profound engagement with the world of the supernatural" (*Off the Reservation* 80). Again, Allen emphasizes the spirituality of tribal cultures, arguing that there is not "a clear line between sacred and secular for tribal traditionals" (45). However, whereas in *The Sacred Hoop* the spiritualism and mysticism of tribal cultures is explored to perpetuate nostalgic views of Indianness, in *Off the Reservation* Allen's sense of the sacred expands to embrace ecological and political concerns.

The essay "Radiant Beings" explores the correlation between the uranium mines on Laguna Pueblo land, the atomic bomb – made in New Mexico with

uranium dug from those same mines – and the stories that reveal the transformational nature of the power that nuclear fission unleashed. Referring to
the old stories of Yellow Woman, particularly to the version in which Naotsete (Sun Woman) quarreled with Uretsete (later Iyatiku or Ic'city), her sister, and went away (to the East), Allen links the facts of the past five hundred
years (including the bomb) to Naotsete's return. She writes: "Gossips hint
that her return signals the end of Western colonial domination and the destruction of the patriarchy. The legend suggests that it heralds something
even we can't conceptualize. . . . It is clear that the fission of the atom signals
loud and bright that something sacred is going on in the universe. And it is
equally clear that respect for the Great Mysteriousness . . . is demanded in
such a sacred time. Perhaps it is because of our collective disrespect of Her
awesomeness, rather than radioactive substances per se, that we sicken and
die" (*Off the Reservation* 106). Rejecting Western, scientific thought, which
does not acknowledge the power of the sacred, consigning it to the level of
superstition and myth, Allen insists on the necessity of looking at the devas-
tating effects of imperialist power from within an indigenous perspective in
order to find a cause and then a cure for the current cancer-related diseases
that are killing millions of people as well as for planetary destruction. She
writes: "My point is that it is not the radiation, toxins, electro-magnetic over-
kill, or holes in the ozone that are causing planetary wipe-out. It's not about
immune systems failing. . . . It's what they signify – the adamant inability of
the white world to see the reality of the sacred, to acknowledge its living presence, and to pay homage through properly constituted ceremony" (115).

Native American women writers such as Marilou Awiakta (Cherokee/Ap-
palachian) have written about the relation between the atom and the land specifically in the context of a Native feminine perspective. Considering woman's affinities with the atom, Awiakta argues that women's responsibilities for
its use are more profound than we might have imagined. She writes: "Nuclear energy is the nurturing energy of the universe. Except for stellar explosions, this energy works not by fission (splitting) but by fusion – attraction
and melding. With the relational process, the atom creates and transforms
life. Women are part of this life force. One of our natural and chosen purposes is to create and sustain life – biological, mental, and spiritual. . . . To be
productive and safe, the atom must be restored to its harmonic, natural pattern. It has to be treated with respect. Similarly, to split woman from her
thought, sexuality and spirit is unnatural. Explosions are inevitable unless
wholeness is restored" (*Selu* 69). Embracing Allen's gynocentric vision, Awiakta posits that, in its perpetuation of Cartesian dualities, the same dualities

that relegate women to the role of a passive, all-giving, and all-suffering one, the West will not be able to see the holistic nature of the universe, a world with no division and no separation. Like the child protagonist of her poem "Beneath My Feet," who resists the hard Cartesian world that splits souls ("Concrete . . . won't do / for me" the poetic voice claims [*Abiding Appalachia* 55]), Awiakta constantly reminds us that our soul needs contact with the whole world we inhabit, the cosmos.

According to Patricia Clark Smith and Paula Gunn Allen, in the American Southwest there is an inextricable relation between the land, American Indian women, ritual, and American Indian women's writing (see Smith and Allen 176). The land is Spider Woman's creation, "the whole cosmos" in which everything is woven together in an exquisite, delicate balance. For Smith and Allen, no contemporary Native American text explores the complex interplay between women, land, and ritual better than Silko's *Ceremony*. Writing about the novel in *The Sacred Hoop*, Allen claims: "While *Ceremony* is ostensibly a tale about a man, Tayo, it is as much and more a tale of two forces: the feminine life force of the universe and the mechanistic death force of the witchery. And Ts'eh is the central character of the drama of this ancient battle as it is played out in contemporary times" (119). It is the same witchery that both exploits the earth through the mining of uranium and creates the atomic bomb. The only way for Tayo to heal both himself and the land is to turn away from his own pattern of destruction (the pattern perpetuated by Western metaphysics, with its impulse to separate and divide) and embrace the thinking of Spider Woman, who derives her power from the web of interconnections that runs through the cosmos.

Addressing in *Off the Reservation* the feminine, ritual-centered nature of the tribal universe, with its related ecological and nuclear problematics, Allen seems (to a certain extent) to move beyond the hypersentimentalism and nostalgia that characterize the gynocentric perspective of *The Sacred Hoop*. True, poststructuralist feminist theorists would still be troubled by her biologically based concepts of woman and references to Mother Earth as the "mother of us all." [19] Similarly problematic, in the context of my discussion, are Allen's references to spiritual paths and vision quests to describe her own critical methodology, an approach that, while perpetuating the ethnographic stance of her previous work, inevitably produces a sort of theoretical tourism particularly appealing to a white audience. Having said that, however, we cannot deny the novelty of Allen's position in *Off the Reservation* compared to that in *The Sacred Hoop*, especially in the context of her attempt to mediate different critical discourses and theoretical perspectives.

While deeply grounded in a gynocentric Laguna Pueblo view, Allen's notion of the feminine in *Off the Reservation* bears interesting ideological parallels with the current debates on ecofeminist discourse. As critics have
pointed out, ecofeminism (ecological feminism) is a "philosophy whose primary tenet is that the same patriarchal world view motivating the oppression
of women and minorities motivates human oppression of nonhuman nature
as well" (Schweninger 38). According to Françoise D'Eaubonne, who coined
the term *ecofeminism* in the early 1970s, we have as a species very little chance
of surviving unless we come to terms with our interrelatedness with our environment. For ecofeminist scholars, then, survival depends on a radical approach to the biosphere, on our recognizing that human beings are no longer
the only agents responsible for knowledge, that the whole world is an or-
ganism with all parts inextricably related. As Carolyn Merchant writes, "All
parts are dependent on one another and mutually affect each other and the
whole. . . . Ecology, as a philosophy of nature, has roots in organicism – the
idea that the cosmos is an organic entity, growing and developing from
within, in an integrated unity of structure and function" (99–100). By offering an approach based on a post-Cartesian, postmodern epistemology,
ecofeminism calls for a reexamination of a worldview that sanctions the domination of women and nature as well as the domination of minority groups
and people of lower classes. Such a reexamination will recognize a worldview
that emphasizes interdependent rather than hierarchical structures.

Given the philosophical tenets of ecofeminism, it seems obvious why an
ecofeminist approach would respond to the theoretical foundations of Native
American women writers such as Allen who keep arguing for a subversion of
patriarchal hierarchical systems by recovering the feminine view of traditional cultures. The essay "The Woman I Love Is a Planet, the Planet I Love
Is a Tree" is perhaps the best example of the way in which Allen's gynocentric epistemology merges with ecofeminist concerns. Discussing Western society's debasement of the physical sphere, including the body, Allen claims
that a society grounded on "body-hate destroys itself and causes harm to
all of Grandmother's grandchildren" (*Off the Reservation* 119). She writes:
"The mortal body is a tree; it is holy in whatever condition; it is truth and
myth because it has so many potential conditions; because of its possibility,
it is sacred and profane. . . . Healing the self means honoring and recognizing the body, accepting rather than denying all the turmoil its existence
brings, welcoming the woes and anguish flesh is subject to, cherishing its
multitudinous forms and seasons, its unfailing ability to know and be, to
grow and wither, to live and die, to mutate, to change" (122). Unlike the West-

ern (masculine) historical privileging of the purely conceptual over the cor-
poreal and the subsequent denial of the (feminine) body, Allen's gynocentric
epistemology presents a dynamic, all-inclusive, intellectual, creative, maternal power. Such power she equates with Thought Woman, whose intelligence encompasses human beings as well as the physical world.

In an essay titled "The Body as Bioregion," whose argument is strikingly
similar to Allen's in "The Woman I Love Is a Planet," ecofeminist critic Deborah Slicer merges personal narrative and philosophical cultural criticism in
order to condemn the ways in which social meanings define, control, and de-
limit a woman's experience of the bioregion that is her body. Slicer writes:
"Most Westernized men and women stand in a similar confused and unhealthy relationship to both their bodies and the earth, and what we do to
both, with frequency, is sacrilege" (113). Arguing against the Western worldview that sees the body as an object and something else as the holy, Slicer
contends that the body is "the sacred itself" (113) and that, by continuing to
objectify the body as well as all the creatures that inhabit the earth, we run the
risk of destroying, not just ourselves, but all life on the planet. Envisioning
a web of interconnections between the physical and the spiritual, between
human and nonhuman forms, while questioning patriarchal, homocentric
patterns of beliefs, ecofeminism as a heuristic method thus offers Allen valid
tools with which to initiate a dialogue between Western and non-Western
critical discourses.

More forcefully and more effectively than in *The Sacred Hoop*, Allen's mediative strategies in *Off the Reservation* are conveyed on a formal level as well.
Unlike the essays in the earlier collection, in which the discursive mode is
primarily objective and, as I have argued, often relies on a reverse ethnographic or anthropological paradigm, Allen's writing in *Off the Reservation*
attempts to write "feminine(s)," as she puts it, embracing multiplicity and
conceiving new multiplicitous paradigms that will, she hopes, bring women
"out of the Master's House of monstrosity, monopoly, monotony, and all his
other mono's unities" (78). Paralleling the ideological assumptions of French
feminist critics such as Hélène Cixous, Allen argues for an *écriture féminine*
through which women will challenge the existing knowledge system, going
beyond the Cartesian binary structure that separates the body from the soul.
In the classic manifesto of French feminist theory, "The Laugh of the Medusa," Cixous argues that "women must write through their bodies, they
must invent the impregnable language that will wreck partitions, classes,
and rhetorics, regulations and codes, they must submerge, cut through, get
beyond the ultimate reserve-discourse" (256). Reclaiming the (feminine)

body will, according to Cixous, allow women to develop revolutionary, self-affirming forms of discourse that defy phallocentric meaning systems. Indeed, Allen's fluid writing in *Off the Reservation*, with essays continuously shifting from the analytic to the poetic and to the personal, must to a certain extent remind readers of Cixous's "orgasmic writing." However, given the forceful critique by women of color of hegemonic feminist theory, and given Allen's own mistrust of French critics and Continental theory in general, it might not be correct to trace Allen's influence exclusively to French feminist theory.

Allen's version of writing the feminine(s) in *Off the Reservation* parallels, more than the French critics, Anzaldúa's notion of *mestizaje* writing, what Keating, drawing on Cixous, calls *mestizaje écriture* (122). While acknowledging the influence of French feminist theory on Anzaldúa, Keating argues that she "expands her definition of 'writing the body' to encompass 'writing the soul'" (121), creating thus a writing process that reflects the specific needs of self-identified women of color. Similar to her reading of the feminine in Allen's *The Sacred Hoop*, an open-ended, nonexclusionary, yet culture-specific recovery of the feminist perspective, Keating's reading of Anzaldúa interprets her *mestizaje écriture* as "nonsymmetrical oppositional writing tactics that simultaneously deconstruct, reassemble, and transcend phallocentric categories of thought" (122).[20] Failing to acknowledge the critique advanced against Anzaldúa by those critics who accuse her of fetishizing Mexican identity by relying on earlier constructs of Aztec mythology and *mestizaje*, Keating attempts to read Anzaldúa's text from within Anzaldúa's own indigenous paradigm, rather that from within merely Western conventions. By emphasizing the permeable, constantly shifting boundaries between inner and outer realities, Anzaldúa demonstrates, according to Keating, that "oppositional forms of resistance can subvert culture from within" (122).

It is not within the scope of this discussion to assess the various critical interpretations of Anzaldúa's *Borderlands/La Frontera*, nor is it my intention to embark on my own. Yet, given the close parallels between Allen's and Anzaldúa's ideological positions, I do take Keating's reading as a starting point – noting, of course, my own reservations and questions – in order to establish to what extent *Off the Reservation* embraces Anzaldúa's notion of *mestizaje écriture* and *mestizaje* theory. Despite the convergence of discourses and fluidity of styles, I would argue that Allen's theoretical position in *Off the Reservation* is far from articulating a consistent theoretical methodology. If, as it first appears, Allen seems to have come a long way from the separatist and

nostalgic attitude expressed in *The Sacred Hoop*, taken as a whole her critical apparatus in this latest collection still perpetuates some of the ideological
claims of the previous work.

Both in form and in content *Borderlands/La Frontera* calls for "a massive
uprooting of dualistic thinking" and maintains that "mestiza consciousness"
enables the writer "to break down the subject-object duality that keeps her
prisoner and to show . . . through the images in her work how duality is tran-
scended" (80). Anzaldúa claims that the new mestiza "has a plural personal-
ity," that "she operates in a plural mode": "Nothing is thrust out, the good
and the bad and the ugly – nothing rejected, nothing abandoned. Not only
does she sustain contradictions, she turns the ambivalence into something
else" (79). Like many U.S. women of color who depict themselves as sites
of plural and shifting identities, Anzaldúa's ability to contain and transform
contradictions enables her to resist oppressive social systems from within. As
Keating puts it, "Instead of rejecting dominant U.S. culture, Anzaldúa's *mestiza* deconstructs it; she takes it apart, exposes its underlying tensions, and
builds a new consciousness, *una cultura mestiza*" (131). As I argued earlier,
Allen's fluid writing in *Off the Reservation* embodies quite nicely Keating's
version of *mestizaje écriture* as applied to *Borderlands/La Frontera*. Weaving
in and out of the theoretical, the mythic, and the personal, Allen envisions a
text that, while resembling contemporary poststructuralist expressive modes,
perfectly conveys the web-like complexity of oral narratives. Specifically, the
essays in the second section, "Wyrds/Orthographies," offer the most significant examples of Allen's experimentation with Western rhetorical frameworks as she challenges the linear structure of Eurocentric discourse. In
"Looking Back: Ethnics in the Western Formalist Situation," Allen inserts
excerpts of poems by Native American authors, fragments from Laguna
Pueblo oral songs, personal anecdotes, and bits of conversational language,
provocatively blending the lyrical with the analytic while fully enacting Anzaldúa's notion of *mestizaje* writing.

Discussing the situation of Native Americans as well as other ethnic people
in American academic institutions, Allen characterizes that situation as one
of alienation owing to the fact that the thinking mode, in these institutions,
still remains essentially Eurocentric and oppressive. She writes:

> I am not opposed to structure in academic life. . . . I am seriously con-
> cerned that structure means oppression, ignorance, and perpetuation of
> ideas and attitudes that have historically resulted in the extinction or
> near extinction of countless cultures and civilizations. . . . I don't mind

reading John Locke. I do mind being stuck with the idea that Locke, Marx, et al. came to their ideas totally within a Western framework, when I know better. I resent the idea that non-Western peoples had no influence on Western civilization, when I know differently. I resent the inference that Mankind means Western Man, who somehow found himself (never herself) surrounded by non-Westerners who never had two ideas to rub together. (*Off the Reservation* 140)

According to Allen, in a structure-oriented educational system such as the Euramerican, any attempt to challenge the foundations of its thinking mode – by, for example, presenting alternative epistemological paradigms – is often looked at with skepticism and mistrust. Despite more than five hundred years of contact between the Indian and the white world, the dynamics of communication still fail, and the Indian is still confined to the margin of European discourse. Yet, Allen argues, such marginal status can also become an empowering condition, one sufficient to mount a significant challenge to the boundaries of Western discourse, as the literature produced by Native American authors (as well as by other people of color) in the past few decades clearly suggests. As she critiques Western aesthetics and rational modes of thinking while at the same time recovering and examining nonrational realities, Allen both embraces the creative and critical perspective of women of color and responds to Anzaldúa's call for *teorías* that will rewrite history, using class, gender, and ethnicity as categories of analysis. Anzaldúa writes: "In our *mestizaje* theories we create new categories for those of us left out or pushed out of the existing ones. We recover and examine non-Western aesthetics while critiquing Western aesthetics; recover and examine nonrational modes and 'blanked-out' realities while critiquing rational, consensual reality; recover and examine indigenous languages while critiquing the 'languages' of the dominant culture" (*Making Face, Making Soul* xxvi).

In "Who's Telling This Story, Anyway?" Allen's idea of breaking down the monolithic Western (masculinist) Aristotelian tradition is directed toward the development of critical strategies that are inclusive rather than exclusive. Allen argues that American literature is more than a mere copy of the literature of England and Western Europe, that it is a New World literature and shares many features with African, Indian (from India), Japanese, Arab, and indigenous literature in America. Allen claims: "New World means non-European; it means new; it means big; it means heterogeneous; it means unknown; it means free; it means an end to feudalism, caste, privilege, and the violence of power" (*Off the Reservation* 148). As people of the twenty-first century, she posits, we should consider it imperative that a "theory of relativity" be applied to literature so that cross-cultural communication can be established and so that we realize that "the center cannot hold because there never was one center only but a myriad of centers in constant flux" (150). In Einstein's formulations – which respond perfectly to her idea of merging Western and non-Western forms of consciousness – Allen finds the quintessential translation of a Native epistemology. As she puts it, "Indians have long recognized the principle of relativity, though they did not articulate it in a recognizable Western scientific framework but within the ritual framework that is the ground and sky of their being" (156).

Allen's vivid example of this "theory of relativity" is displayed in her cross-reading of Hemingway's Nick Adams stories and N. Scott Momaday's *House Made of Dawn*. Despite the many discontinuities between the two texts, one written in the early 1920s, the other in the late 1960s, they do, Allen claims, possess a certain sameness in both form and content. Both, for example, are stories of alienation, of antiheroes, stories in which characters are both "particles" and "waves," moving always indeterminately across a "forever moving field among other equally indefinable wavicles, part of the whole in a way that is simultaneously fragmented and complete" (*Off the Reservation* 159). In Allen's "relativity strategy," texts can be perceived as a multiplicity of phenomena interrelating in a dynamic field and moving in endless conversation with each other. Within this context, Allen insists that it is somehow absurd to speak of either margin or center since, by consigning specific texts to the margin, we make them, ironically, the center of attention, "an odd way for margins to act" (162). Unlike her position in *The Sacred Hoop*, in which she excluded any possibility of dialogue between different discourses (as in her interpretation of the Keres tale), Allen's critical stance now ironically parallels Spivak's position. Like Spivak, Allen insists on the necessity of displacing the center (and showing its marginality), not by remaining outside in the margin, but by implicating herself into that center and sensing, as Spivak puts it, "what politics make it marginal" (*In Other Worlds* 107). By analyzing the way in which Momaday's and Hemingway's texts "move in their inner conversation," as she puts it (*Off the Reservation* 161), Allen clearly demonstrates the interconnectedness of Western genres with non-Western consciousness. She demonstrates how "the West joins the rest of humanity in the complex level of consciousness" that its monolithic, totalitarian thinking modes had heretofore denied it (160). In other words, she succeeds in subverting the structure from within, by opening up the space through which the American story can be heard, "illuminated, explored, in its multiple voices, its ceaseless telling" (161).

Allen's position concerning literature and cross-cultural reading in *Off the Reservation* seems definitely to have shifted from the exclusionary, separatist stance of *The Sacred Hoop* to a more inclusive, open-ended one. However, owing perhaps to the fragmented nature of *Off the Reservation* and to the fact that the essays collected there cover a significant span of time, contradictions and ambiguities in the author's strategic location inevitably emerge. The essay "Thus Spake Pocahontas," the most clearly "thea-retical" piece in the collection, as Allen defines it, presents the most articulate discussion of her theory from within the perspective of a woman of color while contradicting the argument of the previous essays. Discussing the creative, literary status of women of color in the mainstream academy, Allen defines it as one of "invisibility" and "speechlessness." Drawing from Emily Dickinson's famous "I am nobody," a poem by another "sister," "albeit white and Calvinist but marginalized, closeted and all but disappeared" (*Off the Reservation* 167), Allen claims that those who are on the borders, who experience non-Western modes of consciousness, are still ignored, not only by mainstream scholars, but also by scholars in the disciplines of minority or ethnic studies, most of whom are still heavily enmeshed in the training that they received in Western-biased institutions. Forcefully rejecting the assumption that "the cultural matrix from which all literature derives its meaning is the one described by French critics and other Continental intellectuals" (169), Allen calls for a critical apparatus that explores the texts of *las disappearadas* by attending to "the actual texts being created, their source, their source texts, the texts to which they stand in relation, and the otherness that they both embody and delineate" (177). Noting that, according to Henry Louis Gates, the meaning of texts by black authors derives from the systems of significance revealed and shaped by Ifa, Allen argues that, within a Native American context, the primary texts "are the myths and ceremonies that compress and convey all the meaning systems a particular consciousness holds" (168). Critiquing mainstream feminist theorists such as Julia Kristeva and Toril Moi, whom she sees as servants of patriarchal structures, "Freud, Marx and Nietzsche – the triumvirate at whose altar [they] pay homage" (173), Allen opts for separatism as the only solution: "To my Indian eyes it is plain that subversion cannot be the purpose or goal for women of color who write. . . . For to subvert, to turn under, is only the first step in the generation of something yet unborn; no, even less; it is the first step in the process of death. . . . Subversion, dissidence, and acceptance of the self as marginal are processes that maim our art and deflect us from our purpose. They are enterprises that support and maintain the master, feeding his household on our energy, our attention, and our strength" (173–74).

To a reader who has just examined Allen's essay on the theory of relativity, where her notion of motion and interconnectedness is applied to an intriguing discussion of Momaday's and Hemingway's works, such comments would appear questionable. To begin with, in her reading of Gates, Allen conveniently avoids the fact that Gates himself draws on contemporary Western theories of reading, as well as on Afro-American mythic discourse, to explicate black literary texts. In addition, within a specific feminist context, Third World theorists such as Spivak and Trinh have aptly demonstrated that, by engaging with the discourse of patriarchal thinking (Marx, Freud, Nietzsche in Spivak's case; Lévi-Strauss in Trinh's), feminist theorists can, indeed, rewrite the canonical texts of the patriarchal system while indicating some of its significant limitations.

Allen's separatist solution raises even more troubling questions as far as a definition of *Indianness* is concerned. With the expression *to my Indian eyes* Allen seems to revert to the essentialist position conveyed in *The Sacred Hoop*, in which she argues that "Indians never think like whites" and goes on to assert: "Whatever I read about Indians I check out with my inner self." In the light of her underlying assumption of border crossing and boundary busting, Allen's wish for all women of color to "build a far more suitable dwelling of [their] own" (*Off the Reservation* 175), rather than merely inhabiting the master's house, inevitably runs contrary to her overall approach. While her intent is to bring attention to the metatext of Native American literary works, to the ritual and ceremonies that inform the nature and content of the narratives, Allen does not, however, consider the fact that cross-reading and cross-writing work both ways. As products of conjunctural cultural practices, Native American literary texts present from the outset a high level of hybridization and heteroglossia, one that reflects the hybridized nature of the oral texts as well. A critical interpretation that argues exclusively for a recovery of the Native cultural matrix is, thus, inevitably reductive, if not all the more inadequate.

The third section of *Off the Reservation*, entitled "*La Frontera*/Na[rra]tivities," poses even more significant questions as to the effectiveness of Allen's strategy. Here, Allen embarks on a personal journey in that portion of the oral tradition that she calls "my life." All the essays in this section are autobiographical narratives, exploring her mixedblood experience, her relation with the land, myth, the oral tradition, and its grounding. In a sense, these essays are cross-category pieces, with a rich layering of voices in which the personal verges into the impersonal. In "Yo Cruzo Siete Mares," for instance, Allen explores her Lebanese heritage through oral reminiscences. By juxtaposing her voice and those of her father and grandfather, she blurs temporal and spatial lines while bringing the narrative into the "immemorial time" of the oral tradition, into the realm of stories that tell people who they are and how to live in the world.

In "The Lay of the Land: Geospiritual Narratives and the American Southwest," Allen presents a "threnody to her land," the confluential Southwest defined by the Native American, the Hispano-Mexican, and the Anglo-American cultural identity. Here Allen's gynosophical perspective finds full development, and the essay as a whole brings "her story" full circle. The "lay of the land" that nurtures the spirit of the Southwest points toward the "feminine," the *gyne*, the nurturing element that gives shape and existence to the universe and to everything alive. The land that, in Annette Kolodny's words, was made woman by the first explorers – who, in the act of civilizing it, "[cast] the stamp of human relations upon what was otherwise unknown and untamed" (Kolodny 9) – has, Allen posits, always been feminine:

> In the beginning was Thought, and she was Grandmother; the people emerged into the fourth world guided and led by our dear mother, Beautiful Corn Woman; under the continued guidance of Thought Grandmother, we migrated from wherever we were to our present homelands. Then there was a reprise of that cycle. . . . The people were created as Pueblo by the coming of others from the east; we migrated in Thought and custom from where we had been situated to where we are situated now, and our thought migrated over the globe, sending Grandmother Thought/Consciousness outward toward the web of life (again). (13)

As a nurturing element, the land is the umbilical cord to the various immemorial stories that function as cultural geographies, far more telling than maps: "Besides food, which may be the single most definite aspect of a sense of place, stories provide a deep sense of continuity within a psychespace. A region is bounded, characterized by geographical features, but these features take on a human and spiritual dimension when articulated in language" (*Off the Reservation* 234). These stories, Allen posits, are as old as the land and reflect the confluential aspect of the Southwest; they are the "*Frontera* na[rra]tivities." The story of the wicked giantess whose body was split from her head, a Laguna story that Allen recounts in the words of her great-grandmother, coexists with that of La Llorona, the origins of which go back to the court of Monteczuma, and with that of Billy the Kid, the most representative of the Southwestern Anglo narratives. As a separate section, "*La Frontera*/Na[rra]tivities" functions well in defining Allen's mixedblood experience and in articulating the overall message of the book. However, when compared to the theoretical position outlined in "Thus Spake Pocahontas," in which Allen presents separatism as the only solution to hegemonic academic discourse, it leaves many questions and contradictions unresolved.

Defenders of Allen's critical theory might, of course, refer to Spivak's notion of "strategic essentialism" to justify Allen's theoretical position in *Off the Reservation*.[21] Such critics would see Allen's employment of strategic ideas as a necessary part of the process by which women of color can achieve a renewed sense of the value of their precolonial cultures while significantly challenging Western discursive modes. Keating's reading of Allen's notion of the feminine in *The Sacred Hoop* – a reading that, Keating argues, occurs from within Allen's own paradigm rather than from Western perspectives – would definitely fit this category. However, as Spivak herself points out:

> The strategic use of essentialism can turn into an alibi for proselytizing academic essentialisms. The emphasis then inevitably falls on being able to speak from one's own ground, rather than matching the trick to the situation, that the word strategy implies. Given the collaboration between techniques of knowledge and structures of enablement, better I think to look for the bigger problem: that strategies are taught as if they were theories, good for all cases. One has to be careful to see that they do not misfire for people who do not resemble us and do not share the situation of prominent U.S. universities and colleges. (*Outside in the Teaching Machine* 4)

As I argued earlier, Allen's own strategic location within the discourse of the mainstream academy inevitably makes her complicit with the (Western) system from which she wants to be separated. From within such a position, a separatist approach such as hers is highly problematic. Moreover, in the context of my study, the question concerning Allen's theory goes beyond a mere question of essentialism, strategic or not. As I noted earlier, on considering Allen's critical narratives, we might want to investigate to what extent her theoretical stance might assist us in constructing a Native American critical theory, a theory that, by relying on both Western and non-Western paradigms, can explicate the richly hybridized texts of Native American literature while significantly challenging the parameters of Eurocentric discourse. While Allen's critical voice brings an interesting contribution to the overall field of Native American critical theory – suggesting how such a theory should originate primarily from a Native or indigenous cultural orientation (in Allen's case specifically from a Laguna Pueblo perspective) and showing how such a discourse can effectively coexist with Western rhetorical strategies – her overtly separatist position ultimately results in an untenable explication of the high level of hybridization substantiating Native American literary texts, including her own. Allen's separatist position, along with her definition of *Indianness*, perpetuates the oppositional or binary thinking of Western metaphysics and, far from "signifying" any difference, as Gates suggests, dangerously essentializes Native identity and Native American studies in the mold of the Euramerican conception of Indianness. While pretending to write back against Euramerican imperialist power, Allen's theoretical position can be seen, when considered as a whole, inevitably to perpetuate the same discursive modes of the hegemonic academic center.

2

A world in which knowledge of each people was owned exclusively by that people itself would be culturally totalitarian. Just as it is indefensible to have an anthropology in which only outsiders know, and insiders are only known, so it is simply to reverse that inequity. None of us is able to stand outside ourselves sufficiently to know ourselves comprehensively.

Dell Hymes

Intellectual Sovereignty and Red Stick Theory
The Nativist Approach of Robert Allen Warrior and Craig S. Womack

At the "Translating Native Cultures" conference, held at Yale University in February 1998, the Santee Sioux writer and critic Elizabeth Cook-Lynn delivered a passionate keynote address significantly drawing a line between those whom she described as being on the right and the wrong sides of American Indian studies. Referring to concepts such as multiculturalism, postmodernism, and postcolonialism, she asked: "What do these terms mean in terms of sovereignty, land, and the revitalization of our languages?" She ended with the rhetorical question (which she answered herself, in the negative): "Are we satisfied to be 'post' – colonial, modern, Indian?" (Cook-Lynn qtd. in Lee, *Loosening the Seams* 280).

Cook-Lynn's position in the field of Native American studies has been long known to writers and critics in the field. As Arnold Krupat points out, her 1993 essay "Cosmopolitanism, Nationalism, the Third World, and Tribal Sovereignty" remains perhaps "the strongest and best account of the 'nationalist,' 'nativist,' and 'anti-cosmopolitan' position" in evaluating Native American literatures today (*The Turn to the Native* 4). In the essay, Cook-Lynn argues that what among Third Word literary decolonization theoreticians (i.e., Bhabha et al.) is usually referred to as *cosmopolitanism* ironically erases the search for sovereignty and tribalism that legitimates First Nation status: "Yet the American Indian writers who have achieved successful readership in mainstream America seem to avoid that struggle in their work and present Indian populations as simply gatherings of exiles, emigrants, and refugees, strangers to themselves and their lands, pawns in the control of white manipulators, mixed-bloods searching for identity, giving support, finally, to the idea of nationalistic/tribal culture as a contradiction in terms" ("Cosmopolitanism" [in Purdy and Ruppert] 29–30). The term *nationalism* itself, Cook-Lynn suggests, takes on a pejorative connotation when it is used by the representatives of cosmopolitanism and the work of traditional Native thinkers usually dismissed as "mere political action for political gain and dangerous authoritarianism" (30). By accepting the notions of hybridity, cosmopolitanism, and cultural translation, American Indian writers legitimate, according to Cook-Lynn, an unhealthy determinism that will, eventually, lead them away from discussions of decolonization in contemporary America.

The critical perspectives of Robert Allen Warrior and Craig S. Womack closely resemble Cook-Lynn's position insofar as both authors are highly suspicious of discursive modes that embrace Western theoretical paradigms or notions of cultural hybridity. Arguing for the necessity of creating a mature Native cultural and literary criticism, Warrior and Womack envision this criticism as being rooted in the land and culture of American Indian communities, focusing on issues of Native sovereignty and nationalism, discussing concepts such as autonomy and self-determination, and, ultimately, emphasizing a Native resistance movement against colonialism. In *Tribal Secrets*, Warrior turns to Vine Deloria Jr. and John Joseph Mathews as the internal historical voices from which to promote what he terms "intellectual sovereignty" (xxiii). In *Red on Red*, Womack takes a "Red Stick" approach and turns to Creek history, oral tradition, and literature in order to construct a literary criticism presented as an alternative to the Western literary establishment.[1] Whereas Warrior at times seems, within his separatist stance, to be more open, envisioning a moment in which a non-Native critical discourse will be engaged in his intellectual tribalism, Womack categorically dismisses any possibility of dialogue with the Western academy and forcefully endorses the necessity of a "Native American literary separatism" (as he subtitles *Red on Red*).

This chapter examines Warrior and Womack's "tribalcentric" approach to a Native American critical theory and interrogates the significance of such an approach in the context of a Native American discourse that intends to challenge the parameters of Western, Eurocentric hermeneutics. Like Allen, Sarris, Owens, and Vizenor, Warrior and Womack acknowledge the necessity of generating discursive modes originating primarily from the Native or indigenous cultural context, as it informs Native American literary texts, and suggest ways in which such discursive strategies can be articulated. While their work makes an interesting contribution to the overall field of Native

American critical theory, their position remains problematic, eliciting severe criticism from those who reject Nativist or nationalist ideologies. In the attempt to isolate and define a kind of Native American intellectualism rigidly based on an Indian perspective, Warrior and Womack produce a critical strategy that ultimately collapses back in on itself because of failed logic, internal contradictions, and linguistic inconsistencies. By envisioning a Native American theory exclusively grounded in indigenous categories, the product of a unitary, a priori given identity, both critics seem to overlook the complex level of hybridization and cultural translation that is already operating in any form of Native discourse (including their own) – the product of more than five hundred years of cultural contact and interaction. As Krupat points out, for all the radically asymmetrical relations of power, prevailing from the outset, in the history of the Americas, "neither Euramerican intellectuals nor Native American intellectuals could operate autonomously or uniquely, in a manner fully independent of one another" (*The Turn to the Native* 18). Similarly, I argue, identities significantly shaped by these intersecting trajectories could never be conceived as monolithic and fixed but, instead, must be recognized in their plural, complex, and socially constructed nature.

In the current debate on nationalism, indigenism, and cosmopolitanism as categories applied to Native American literatures, Krupat appears as the most prominent voice attempting to move Native American studies toward a cosmopolitan perspective.[2] In a 1998 essay, he argues that, although the nationalist and indigenist positions often overlap and both nationalists and indigenists tend to see themselves quite apart from the cosmopolitans, the cosmopolitan critic ultimately stands "in more nearly oxymoronic than oppositional relationship to the nationalists and indigenists" ("Nationalism" 617).[3] In other words, the cosmopolitan critic who acknowledges the long-term process – inevitable and persistent – of cultural hybridization is also inclined to recognize the importance of the issue of sovereignty in the political struggle of colonized people all over the world as well as the significance of traditional, place-specific values and principles. By adopting Kwame Anthony Appiah's definition of *cosmopolitan patriot*, itself an oxymoron, Krupat posits that supporters of a cosmopolitan perspective believe that "the use of the master's tools, as it were, in conjunction with Native tools constitutes the most powerful *hybrid* or mixedblood strategy available against cultural colonialism" (624).[4] Forcefully critiquing rigid nationalist and separatist practices, Krupat consistently emphasizes the profound level of cultural hybridization taking place in what Mary Louise Pratt has called the "contact zones" of cultures and inevitably reflected in the literary works of the cultures themselves. As he convincingly argues in *The Turn to the Native*, "Some contemporary Native American discourses committed to cultural sovereignty, cultural autonomy, or cultural separatism [all products of a nationalist or indigenous approach], in an apparently absolute sense, readily subvert themselves . . . in the very texture of the language they use" (16). Whether we like it or not, Krupat claims, Native American writing, in whatever language, is the product of the conjunction of cultural practices, Euramerican and Native American; any claim to a radical cultural independence or autonomy is, therefore, untenable.

On carefully considering the implications of a strictly nationalist or indigenous position for a Native American discourse, we are immediately faced with the dilemma articulated by Gates in his analysis of black literature and literary theory. A separatist or nationalist perspective, such as the one promoted by Warrior and Womack, runs the risk, I argue, of essentializing Native American discourse, limiting Native studies in a way that does not allow the discipline to evolve, and, in the end, parroting the master's language, but with the terms reversed and without "signifying" any difference. The term *Nativist*, which I use to characterize Warrior and Womack's critical approach, is one that is frequently encountered among colonial discourse theorists, particularly those operating in the postcolonial sites of Africa. As Ashcroft et al. have pointed out, the term suggests that "colonialism needs to be replaced by the recovery and promotion of pre-colonial, indigenous ways" (*Key Concepts in Post-Colonial Studies* 159). Even though objections could be made as to the applicability of such a term to Warrior and Womack's critical perspectives, I will argue that their cultural separatism eventually leads to the hopeless project of recovering a Native essence, a project that, ironically, embraces another sort of colonial invention.

At the heart of *Tribal Secrets*, a comparative study of the works of Vine Deloria Jr. (Standing Rock Sioux) and John Joseph Mathews (Osage), is Warrior's call for the emergence of a mature Native cultural and literary criticism, a criticism not merely preoccupied "with parochial questions of identity and authenticity" (xix) but addressing, instead, issues of economic and social class, gender, and sexual orientation. The book is divided into three major chapters: In the first, Warrior establishes contexts for Deloria and Mathews, contextualizing their work among American Indian intellectuals of the twentieth century. In the second, he provides a critical discussion of Mathews's novel *Sundown* in the light of Deloria's ideas regarding land and community. In the third, he envisions the role of American Indian intellectuals in the future of American Indian communities and, in order fully to describe the experience of Mathews and Deloria, introduces the problematic concept *intellectual sovereignty.*

According to Warrior, even though Deloria and Mathews do not focus on many of these issues in their major works, they do open up possibilities for talking about these contemporary challenges. Indeed, one of the main questions that Warrior's study addresses is how the engagement with American Indian writers of earlier periods can affect contemporary Native American intellectuals in the development of Indian critical studies. Reviewing the relevant academic criticism produced since the mid-1980s, Warrior sees it as divided into two major streams: the idealist and the essentialist.[5] As he points out, "Essentialist categories still reign insofar as more of the focus of scholarship has been to reduce, constrain, and contain American Indian literature and thought and to establish why something or someone is 'Indian' than engage the myriad critical issues crucial to an Indian future" (*Tribal Secrets* xix). Deloria and Mathews, for Warrior, work against the grain of contemporary discourse for at least two reasons: their commitment to the community and its future and their global and international experience, which dismisses any stereotypical formulation of Indianness. According to Warrior, Deloria's and Mathews's ideas concerning the way in which American Indians form their views about land and community are crucial to the preservation of traditional discourses about Native life. American Indian discourse has its own intellectual tradition, and, if Native scholars intend to realize responsible criticism, they must, Warrior warns, start taking into serious consideration their intellectual heritage.

From the outset, Warrior establishes the critical direction of his study while also acknowledging the "countless objections" to his approach. Writing that "the present work is concerned primarily with American Indian creative and critical writers, and a look at the Bibliography reveals that it is dominated by references to American Indian writers," Warrior is fully aware that he is taking an "overly separatist" position (*Tribal Secrets* xx, xxiii). Such a position leads his argument and analysis into problematic contradictions. If, owing to their international and global experience, Deloria and Mathews provide an ideal direction for the development of an American Indian discourse, why would Warrior's study remain confined within an American Indian perspective? How does Deloria's and Mathews's global perspective translate into Warrior's own work? Warrior writes that a study such as his own, grounded in the influences and complexities of contemporary and historical American Indian life, will (eventually) engage non-Native critical discourse, but he does not clearly define when and how this moment of engagement will occur. Throughout *Tribal Secrets*, Warrior insists on the parameters of his critical position and clearly reiterates his primary concerns: "The first priority of developing American Indian criticism is *to step back from current critical strategies* and find within the internal variety of historical and contemporary voices the sources of such a criticism. A critical accounting of the differences between Mathews and Deloria illustrates what such an approach can produce and what sorts of resources are available" (57; emphasis added). Coming from a critic who asserts that the purpose of his study is to remove American Indian critical discourse from what he considers "its essentialist, parochializing strategies" (xxiii), such a statement does, indeed, seem contradictory, particularly in relation to a discourse on a Native theory that, as I argued in the introduction, is already hybridized and heteroglot in its own nature.

Even on only a quick review of the biographical information on Deloria and Mathews scattered throughout the first chapter of *Tribal Secrets*, the reader is immediately confronted with issues of cultural hybridization characterizing their experiences. The son of an English Protestant whose lineage traced back to an Osage woman, Mathews was conscious of not belonging properly to any one group, refusing, therefore, both the fullblood and the mixedblood status. As Warrior states, "[Mathews's] associations with all groups were somewhat tenuous, and he belonged, finally, to none of them" (16). Even more significant, for Warrior, is Mathews's international dimension, beginning with the offer of a Rhodes scholarship, in 1921, to attend Oxford University. (While he refused the Rhodes on the grounds that it was too restrictive, he did attend Oxford a year later, paying his own way.) Warrior claims, "Mathews was born in 1894 in the period before the Osage Reservation was allotted and became a county of the state of Oklahoma. Of the Native intellectuals in his time he went on to become the most cosmopolitan, most philosophical, and most suspicious of Euro-American values" (15). Traveling extensively in Europe, North Africa, and the Middle East, Mathews was able, according to Warrior, to develop a political consciousness that did not fit into any of the typical patterns characterizing Indian intellectuals of his time; such a consciousness accounted for his future political and literary success.

Although less cosmopolitan than Mathews's, Deloria's cultural background also reveals, Warrior suggests, an "open-ended framework" (*Tribal Secrets* 44). Born in 1933, in Martin, South Dakota, a town that bordered the Pine Ridge Reservation, to a Standing Rock Sioux, Episcopalian minister father, Deloria attended a prep school in Connecticut, graduated from Iowa State University, served in the U.S. Marine Corps, attended seminary at Augustana (later the Lutheran School of Theology) in Chicago, and eventually earned a law degree from the University of Colorado (32–33). In college, Warrior notices, "Deloria's consciousness of the centrality of Native tradition to the Indian future grew" (32), a consciousness that would play a crucial role in his future commitment to pragmatic politics. As Warrior remarks, "What comes out of Deloria's writings is a portrait of a search, at once pragmatic and visionary, for answers to the problems of Native communities in the context of the world as a whole" (33–34). Again and again, Warrior emphasizes how Deloria's idea of tradition, as it is developed in his major writings in the early 1970s (e.g., *Custer Died for Your Sins*; *We Talk, You Listen*; *God Is Red*; *Behind the Trail of Broken Treaties*), is never conceived of in a manner that might be considered fetishized. He writes: "First, [Deloria] contended, the affirmation of tradition provides the necessary raising of consciousness among those who have been taught that the ways of their ancestors were barbaric, pagan, and uncivilized. Second, tradition provides the critical constructive material upon which a community rebuilds itself" (*Tribal Secrets* 95). According to Warrior, in all his works Deloria aims at developing political and cultural strategies that maintain Native cultures while adjusting to contemporary challenges and necessities. Deloria argues that "Truth" "is in the ever-changing experiences of the community" (qtd. in Warrior, *Tribal Secrets* 94) and that the traditional Indian who fails to acknowledge this aspect of his or her heritage is destined to fall into the trap of Western religion.

Warrior's reading of Deloria assumes a significant aspect in his overall theory, an aspect aimed at establishing the importance of tradition in the future of American Indian communities. Arguing that "tradition provides the critical constructive material upon which a community re-builds itself" (*Tribal Secrets* 95), Warrior positions himself among those thinkers who, in the postcolonial world, have forcefully critiqued the danger of mythologizing the past for nationalist concerns. Frantz Fanon's ideas on national culture and national consciousness compare neatly with Warrior's observations. In *The Wretched of the Earth*, Fanon argues that the passion with which contemporary postcolonial writers remind their people of the great events of their history is a reply to the lies told by colonialism, "the logical antithesis of that insult the white man flung at humanity" (213). On the other hand, however, such a return to the glorious past proves to be a blind alley; it is an approach in danger of becoming nothing more than sterile exoticism. Fanon writes:

"The desire to attach oneself to tradition or bring abandoned traditions to life again does not only mean going against the current of history but also opposing one's own people. When a people undertakes an armed struggle or even a political struggle against a relentless colonialism, the significance of tradition changes" (224). The intellectual who does not recognize this dangerous possibility behaves, according to Fanon, like a foreigner, attaching himself to the outer "garments of the people," which are, in the end, merely "the reflection of a hidden life, teeming and perpetually in motion" (224). Similarly, Warrior suggests, Deloria and Mathews would seem to insist that people who have never considered the real meaning of cultural change and traditional revitalization end up losing their sense of pragmatism and falling instead into the trap of idealism.

Given the richly hybridized nature of Mathews's and Deloria's cultural backgrounds, and given the privileged discourse within which they inevitably speak, a reader might question what makes them the internal historical voices and major intellectual sources out of which, according to Warrior, an American Indian discourse, a mature Native cultural and literary criticism, should originate. Is it that they conceive of their work as inseparable from political activism (i.e., that the notion of art for art's sake is, essentially, meaningless for them)? Is it, rather, their Indianness? Or is there a logical inconsistency in Warrior's reasoning, an inconsistency suggested by their cosmopolitanism, which, according to Warrior, sets them apart from the other intellectual figures of their time? From Mathews's and Deloria's perspective, the category of an authentic tradition of Indian intellectualism is a priori ambiguous since it implies problematic definitions of Indian identity. In response to Warrior, then, one might argue that Deloria and Mathews might, indeed, function as a valid source for the contemporary Native intellectual developing Indian critical studies – but for reasons that Warrior himself seems to undervalue. Mathews's and Deloria's cosmopolitanism is a vivid example of how any discourse within Native American studies cannot ignore the intricate interrelation between Native and Euramerican cultural practices. Reading Mathews and Deloria only for their ideas concerning tribal sovereignty and self-determination – the same ideas that, in Warrior's view, can promote an authentic discourse of Indian intellectualism – simply means reverting to a separatist or nationalist position that, ironically, perpetuates the categories of Western binary thinking.

One of the major accusations that Warrior launches at contemporary critics is that they still reduce American Indian literature and thought to, and therefore constrain and contain them within, the parochial question of what an "Indian" is (*Tribal Secrets* xix). The fact that only limited attention has been given to American Indian critical writing, as opposed to fictional, poetic, oral, and autobiographical works, is, for Warrior, indicative of the "unfortunate prejudice among scholars" (xv) toward the American Indian intellectual heritage and those works that do not fit into standard notions of Indian writing. It can be argued, however, that Warrior's position itself points toward a definition of *Indianness* that, in the end, anthropologizes and ossifies Native experience. What, if not a "parochial question of identity and authenticity," is Warrior's reliance on such problematic categories as *self-determination, tribal,* and, most important, perhaps, *sovereignty?*

Warrior himself acknowledges the problems that his terminology raises, claiming, "I have tried to recognize that these words are problematic in spite of continuing to carry a certain political, emotional, and critical force. This is perhaps most true for *sovereignty, a term from European theological and political discourse* that finally does little to describe the visions and goals of American Indian communities that seek to retain a discrete identity" (xxi; emphasis added). In his attempt to be "convincingly suggestive, rather than conclusive" (xv), Warrior avoids detailed definitions, thus sidestepping the double bind that these words – whose epistemological roots take us back to Europe and to forms of colonial discourse – inevitably convey. As I argued earlier, nowhere in *Tribal Secrets* does Warrior clearly define the term *sovereignty.* Drawing extensively from Deloria, Warrior spins an intricate web, going back and forth between Deloria's understanding of the term and his own ideas, arriving ultimately at the problematic notion *intellectual sovereignty,* which he conceives of as the main conceptual category characterizing any form of Native American criticism. Interestingly enough, Deloria's objections to the concept of sovereignty clarify Warrior's position significantly, and it will be useful, therefore, to consider some of these objections carefully. Similarly, it will be useful to look at Deloria's reflections on sovereignty in general terms in order to get a better sense of the inconsistencies in Warrior's position.

Deloria has been thinking and writing about sovereignty for several decades, pointing out the adaptability and flexibility of the term in the face of new historical challenges. By the time he wrote *God Is Red,* he believed that the key to an American Indian future was the return to Native ceremonies and traditions within a context that asserted sovereignty. In *We Talk, You Listen,* for example, Deloria had already suggested: "The responsibility which sovereignty creates is oriented primarily toward the existence and continuance of the group. As such, it naturally creates a sense of freedom not possible in any other context" (123). For Deloria, Warrior suggests, "the path of sovereignty is the path to freedom" (*Tribal Secrets* 91). But, as Warrior also points out, "That freedom . . . is not one that can be immediately defined and lived. Rather, the challenge is to articulate what sort of freedom as it 'emerge[s]' through the experience of the group to exercise the sovereignty which they recognize in themselves" (91). In Warrior's interpretation, Deloria's notion of sovereignty becomes a process-centered activity – that of building community – that will define the future. In accordance with Deloria's ideas, Warrior seems to envision sovereignty as a concept primarily ingrained in the life and tradition of American Indian communities, a concept that cannot be defined a priori but, instead, emerges as the community builds itself.

Interestingly enough, however, it is when Warrior extends Deloria's analysis of the rhetoric of sovereignty to American Indian intellectual discourse, envisioning some kind of intellectual sovereignty as the first step to be taken by all those who engage in community, federal, and other American Indian work, that one finds the most ironic contradictions in his argument. Warrior writes: "I contend that it is now critical for American Indian intellectuals committed to sovereignty to realize that we too must struggle for sovereignty, *intellectual sovereignty*, and allow the definition and articulation of what it means to emerge as we critically reflect on that struggle. If, as Deloria argues, tradition cannot and should not be a set of prescribed activities, but rather a set of processes, does it not make sense that our work and our lives as American Indian writers and thinkers should be a part of those processes?" (*Tribal Secrets* 97–98). Taking from Deloria the idea of sovereignty as a process-centered activity, Warrior employs it to characterize the role of American Indian intellectuals as faithfully devoted to the community and to the building of the community, overlooking the complicated issue of the double bind characterizing Native American writers and critics, who are both inside and outside the metropolitan academic center.

In his attempt to further clarify the concept of sovereignty as it applies to intellectual discourse, Warrior turns to Mathews as a figure who did practice intellectual sovereignty, a figure whom American Indian intellectuals should definitely imitate. Mathews's writing and reflection were not, according to Warrior, activities that could be isolated from the material experience on which he was reflecting – his life at the Blackjacks.[6] The concept of the land itself and the processes through which the land passes in adapting to new challenges, the same concept that Deloria emphasizes in all his works, is essential to Mathews's reflection. Warrior quotes a crucial passage from *Talking to the Moon* to reinforce Mathews's idea of moving toward "the maturity of intellectual experience and action" (*Tribal Secrets* 104):

> But one cannot appreciate what it means to step out of the natural background where one has lived alone, with only the voices of the ridges, into the society of one's own kind. One being fresh and alert one's self sees only freshness and beauty in others. How beautiful are women in the soft light of the dinner table and on the dance floor, and how wonderful the music. How heavenly is the scotch-and-soda, the wine, and the taste of a cigarette, and how interesting the conversation . . . no matter on what subject. How clearly one seems to see the social, economic, and political problems through the spectrum of one's own freshness, and how much greater is the magic of the indefinite "They" who have made the wonders of civilization; the magicians who have brought forth the radio, television, chromebright mechanisms, skyscrapers, and electrical gadgets. And how beautiful is romance, filling every cell of one's capacity for emotion, and how delightfully inspiring to ornamental expression. (*Talking to the Moon* 125)

What Warrior wants us to see in Mathews is the example of one person, one intellectual, who could make sense of the material realities faced by American Indian communities and the lands on which they live. Avoiding slipping into a rhetoric that separates American Indians either from the rest of humanity or from their own past, Mathews perfectly embodies, in Warrior's view, Deloria's notions of tradition and sovereignty as open-ended processes and "gives us an example of intellectual sovereignty deeply committed to humanism" (*Tribal Secrets* 103). Mathews's "withdrawal," Warrior concludes, "is experience and leads to experience" (104). Mathews challenges us as critical readers to move always toward mature understandings of "how the localized roots of a tree move and grow toward its cosmopolitan trunk, branches, and leaves" (86).[7]

According to Warrior, as critics deeply committed to achieving intellectual sovereignty, American Indian intellectuals have "to make the connection between what is going on in communities and the various factors of influence we encounter" (*Tribal Secrets* 112). In contrast to an intellectual production reduced to mere aestheticism, Warrior calls for a pragmatic criticism that confronts the economic and political realities of everyday experience. As Warrior points out, Mathews's experience at the Blackjacks should teach American Indian intellectuals that the process of sovereignty is a matter, not of removing themselves and their communities from the influences of the world in which they live, but of learning how to interact with that world. In other words, by *sovereignty* Warrior appears to mean a kind of intellectual activity in which one is completely committed to the life and experiences of one's community in order to build the social structures of the community itself. In addition, following the example of Mathews and Deloria, Warrior's intellectual appeals to the fundamental principles of humanism, recognizing that self-reliance is not necessarily dependent on isolation and that, by withdrawing from the outside world, a group can severely limit its future development. Again and again, Warrior goes back and forth between localism and cosmopolitanism as the major categories characterizing the life of American Indian intellectuals. But how can one reconcile Mathews's and Deloria's humanist principles with Warrior's idea of the intellectual deeply engaged in the process of community building? At what point does Warrior's Native intellectual come out of his Native community to embrace a dialogue with outside communities? These are some of the questions that Warrior's study tends to overlook, causing his overall argument to remain trapped in ironic contradictions.

At its foundation, Warrior's major problem rises out of his attempt to isolate the phenomenon that he calls "Native American intellectualism" and define it as an expression of "intellectual sovereignty." How can Warrior argue for a rigid Native American intellectualism, one based primarily on the work of Deloria and Mathews, when Deloria and Mathews themselves live fully at the crossroads of cultures? At what point do Deloria's and Mathews's intellects cease being Euramerican and become "Uramerican" or tribal?[8] More important, how can the notion of tribal sovereignty define any form of Native intellectualism (whatever that might be) when the term *sovereignty* itself is a Western epistemological concept? As I argued earlier, Deloria and Mathews do, indeed, develop in their work an international or cosmopolitan perspective that contradicts Warrior's interpretation of their position. Similarly contradictory is Warrior's use of *sovereignty* as a category rigidly defining an authentic tradition of Indian intellectualism, a category to which Deloria himself has given some attention in his work.

In *The Nations Within* Deloria and Clifford Lytle make very clear that what is meant today by *Native sovereignty* bears little resemblance to the principles of Native American societies. Their position indirectly provides an answer to our earlier questions concerning the complexity of the term *sovereignty*. They claim: "When we look back at the treaty negotiations between the United States and the respective Indian tribes, there is little mention of the complex ideas that constitute nationhood. Indeed, we find very little awareness in either the Indians or the American treaty commissioners that an important status was being changed by the agreement that people were then making" (7). In almost every treaty, the major concern for the Indians was the preservation of the people, and it is in this concept that we will find the psychological and political keys with which to unlock the puzzling dilemma of Warrior's dubious terminology. Deloria and Lytle write: "The idea of peoplehood, of nationality, has gradually been transformed over the past two centuries into a new idea, one derived primarily from the European heritage, and with a singular focus distinct from the old Indian culture and traditions" 12). In other words, to appeal to terms such as *self-government*, *nation*, *sovereignty*, or *self-determination* as parameters of authenticity is self-defeating, an exercise doomed to failure, because these concepts are of European origin and do not express indigenous realities.

Various critics have noticed the linguistic inconsistencies of the categories employed by Warrior in his attempt to establish a tradition of authentic Indian intellectualism. Krupat, for example, writes: "Native societies, thus, do not conceive of themselves in any manner equivalent to Euramerican states or governments (e.g., with generalized and abstract notions of law, right, and justice). Rather, Native societies conceive of themselves as nations, where the nation is not the modern nation-state but a synonym for the people (who, to repeat, have specific and concrete relations, entailing responsibilities). It is nation-to-nation relations as people-to-people that are thus particularly meaningful to Native Americans" (*The Turn to the Native* 14). Jack Forbes writes that *sovereignty* "denotes a state of being rather than a process of becoming" and suggests that "we can apply traditional Native ideas about individual freedom . . . to refer to individuals as well as to tribes" since, among most Native groups, it is the people who were sovereign, not the nation-state ("Intellectual Self-Determination" 14). According to Forbes, we must redefine *sovereignty* if we are to understand more precisely the complex reality of traditional indigenous societies and if we want to avoid the adoption of new tribal ideologies that, instead of reflecting a Native heritage, simply mirror European ideas. Forbes asks: "Can we not legitimately ask if sovereignty in the sense of supremacy [from Latin *Superanus*, from *super*, meaning "above"] was possessed by everyone, or if the concept of supremacy is not a totally European paradigm that some are seeking to impose upon a much more complex indigenous reality?" (15).

Forbes's question here cuts to the core of Warrior's argument and helps us clarify some of the logical inconsistencies that I have pointed out throughout my discussion. Can we, as critics, appeal to concepts originating in the European or colonial authoritative discourse and still claim to practice an "authentic" Native American criticism? More important, is there in fact such as thing as an authentic Indian discourse? Without dismissing the legal-historical heritage of the term *sovereignty*, we must, eventually, come to terms with the fact that whatever is intended by legal and/or cultural sovereignty is, as Forbes also notes, a "double-edged sword" ("Intellectual Self-Determination" 16), often used against what we might term the *traditional Indian* (whatever that means).

Even more critical is Deloria's position in the essay "Intellectual Self-Determination and Sovereignty," written as a response to Forbes. Deloria writes: "From what I remember of the old days, we began to use these concepts in a context in which they had specific meanings and from which, when the opposition agreed to their meanings, changes and benefits then flowed. I am not sure this is still the case" (25). Today, Deloria claims, terms such as *sovereignty*, *self-determination*, *hegemony*, and *empowerment* are abstract concepts producing no concrete action in the real world. Everything boils down to an empty bundle of ideologies that keep perpetuating Western epistemological concepts: "This generation of Indians now coming to power shows a strange alienation from the community setting. . . . Everyone is proud to claim a tribal heritage, but many times it appears not as a commitment but as a status symbol of 'Indianness.' *Individual self-determination* and *intellectual sovereignty* are scary concepts because they mean that a whole generation of Indians are not going to be responsible to the Indian people, they are simply going to be isolated individuals playing with the symbols of Indians" (28).

Deloria's position would seem to be a valid response to Warrior's notion of intellectual sovereignty. Deloria convincingly suggests that, insofar as such a term is in the intellectuals' minds and not realized in practice, it can be discussed endlessly without, however, conveying any meaning for the tribal communities living their everyday lives. Among all the misinformation concerning the history and culture of indigenous people, and in the midst of constant attempts to turn tribal cultures into cultural artifacts, relics of an irredeemable, nostalgic past, do we, Deloria asks, "have the luxury of . . . whining about our lack of 'intellectual sovereignty'?" ("Intellectual Self-Determination" 29). If Native people want to bring some substance to concepts such as *self-determination*, *empowerment*, and *hegemony*, they need, Deloria suggests, to begin to turn those concepts into action; only then, he argues, will the study of the past bring about effective engagement with the present and with the future. While providing an insightful commentary on Warrior's argument, Deloria's questions also raise the important issue of the role and responsibility of Native intellectuals toward their own communities, an issue with which all the authors under consideration in this study are, to a certain extent, involved and on which I will comment more extensively in the next chapter.

Implicit in Warrior's notion of intellectual sovereignty is, as I argued earlier, the idea of the Native writer or critic deeply engaged with the life of the community. Only such active participation can, Deloria suggests, validate the otherwise abstract concepts of sovereignty and self-determination. While such reasoning might at first seem legitimate, it overlooks the complicated issues of the variety of Native communities as they exist today. Warrior does not seem to consider the reality of the many Native American writers and critics who reside far away from their traditional homeland, operating primarily in an urban context, the product of more than five hundred years of colonialism. Within the parameters suggested by Warrior and significantly reinforced by Deloria, how would their intellectual sovereignty find validity? Would it?

In his essay "Native American Authors and Their Communities," Jace Weaver focuses on some of these issues. According to Weaver, Native writers may not always agree on the terms and conditions of what he calls *communitism*. He writes: "Community is a primary value, but today we exist in many different kinds of community – reservation, rural village, urban, tribal, pan-Indian, traditional, Christian. Many move back and forth between a variety of these communities. Our different locations, physical, mental, and spiritual, will inevitably lead to different conceptions of what survival, liberation, and communitism require" (53–54). Weaver cites the example of the Navajo poet Luci Tapahonso, for whom writing becomes "a vehicle for reversing the diaspora begun after European invasion" (52), as well as that of many other contemporary Native writers, for whom writing "prepares the ground for recovery, and even re-creation, of Indian identity and culture" (53).

Similarly, considering more specifically the ambivalent position of Native American authors, Louis Owens writes:

It is perhaps time to recognize that what we are calling Native American literature is represented largely, if not exclusively, . . . by those migrant or diasporic Natives who live lives of relatively privileged mobility and surplus pleasure. As a group, published Native American authors have an impressively high rate of education, most possessing not merely a university degree but at least some graduate work if not an advanced degree. We may go back to our families and communities periodically or regularly, we may – like N. Scott Momaday – even be initiated into a traditional society within our tribal culture, but we are inescapably both institutionally privileged by access to Euramerican education and distinctly migrant in the sense that we possess a mobility denied to our less privileged relations. ("As If an Indian" 224)

Owens's observations well describe the "strategic location" of Deloria and Mathews and, even better, provide a critical lens through which more closely to scrutinize Warrior's position. Any form of discourse involving notions of tradition, sovereignty, and commitment to communities should at first acknowledge the level of complicity between Native intellectuals (regardless of the kind of community in which they operate) and the dominant academic discourse. In addition, it becomes even more contradictory to argue for an autonomous tradition of Indian intellectualism by ignoring "the conjunction of cultural practices" (to use Krupat's term [*The Turn to the Native* 17]), the Euramerican and the Native American, that have characterized the history of this continent for more than five hundred years.

In *Imperial Eyes*, Mary Louise Pratt defines *contact zones* as "social spaces where disparate cultures meet, clash, and grapple with each other, often in highly asymmetrical relations of domination and subordination – like colonialism, slavery, or their aftermaths as they are lived out across the globe today" (4). In an attempt to understand how modes of representation between borders and the imperial metropolis have influenced each other, Pratt looks at "autoethnographic texts" as expressions of the partial collaboration between the colonized and the colonizer and as examples in which the colonized appropriates and turns to his or her own advantage the idiom of the conqueror (7). To a certain extent, Deloria's and Mathews's texts are examples of such "autoethnographic" expression, texts that, far from being autochthonous forms of self-representation, constitute the authors' point of entry into the metropolitan literate culture. In the light of Mathews's and Deloria's cosmopolitanism, a position that Warrior himself has ironically emphasized, readers of *Tribal Secrets* may find it problematic to consider these authors as ideal subjects for a constructive engagement with an authentic tradition of Indian intellectualism. The same readers might, then, on considering Mathews's and Deloria's autoethnographic writing, also wonder about Warrior's rhetorical strategies and how effectively they produce a response or challenge to the idiom of mainstream discourse.

When compared with the discursive approaches taken by Allen, Womack, Sarris, Owens, and Vizenor, Warrior's methodology appears to be more visibly grounded in the Western rhetorical pattern of the classical critical tradition rather than in a Native epistemological orientation. As I argued in my introduction, crucial to the authors discussed in this study is the idea of bringing forms and patterns from the oral tradition onto the written page, challenging the rhetorical structure of Western discourse while suggesting new, alternative ways of producing theory. Regardless of the differing approaches that they might take in defining the parameters of a Native theory, the above-mentioned authors do attempt to articulate in writing ways in which Native epistemology significantly merges with Western philosophical paradigms. In Allen's case, for example, my discussion has indicated how the fluidity of her texts – in which the narratives shift in and out of different genres – clearly reveals an attempt to break down the monolithic, Western, Aristotelian linear tradition to include the circular pattern of Laguna Pueblo epistemology. The same applies to the storytelling quality of Womack's and Sarris's works, the crosscultural nature of Owens's texts, and the trickster element of Vizenor's textual landscapes. A close reading of Warrior's critical strategy shows that such experimentation with Western techniques is primarily absent from the text; not only do we find a more traditional (Western) rhetorical pattern, but Warrior's own reflections regarding such important issues also raise even more logical inconsistencies in his argument.

As I noted earlier, at the beginning of his study, Warrior argues that fictional, poetic, oral, and autobiographical writings are not the only literary manifestations through which tradition is able to live in new written forms. As his comparative study of Mathews and Deloria intends to suggest, tradition, conceived as an open-ended process, can and should permeate the intellectual production of American Indian critical studies in order effectively to promote some sort of intellectual sovereignty. In the final chapter of *Tribal Secrets*, Warrior resumes this argument, writing: "As many of the poets find their work continuous with, but not circumscribed by, Native traditions of storytelling or ceremonial chanting, we can find the work of criticism continuous with Native traditions of deliberation and decision making" (117–18). Ironically, however, instead of suggesting how works of criticism (including his own) can pragmatically convey the idea of tradition in new written forms, Warrior proceeds to analyze the poetry of Jimmy Durham and Wendy Rose, thus reinforcing the idea that poetry remains the primary choice in promoting the kind of intellectual sovereignty that he has been theorizing throughout his work.

Even more problematic, in the context of my study, are Warrior's reflections in the final section of *Tribal Secrets*, where he again insists on looking at Deloria's and Mathews's experience as something on which Native intellectuals should model their own critical path. He claims: "Through Euro-American style education, we can bring critical knowledge of what has happened in the history of that dominating society that helps explain the situations in which we find ourselves" (123). More significantly, Warrior invites us to reject any form of either/or perspective and embrace a humanistic philosophy in the attempt to bring the Native American experience into a wider context. He writes: "We see first that the struggle for sovereignty is not a struggle to be free from the influence of anything outside ourselves, but a process of asserting the power we possess as communities and individuals to make decisions that affect our lives. . . . We must, as Deloria suggests, withdraw without becoming separatists, being willing to reach out for the contradictions within our experience and open ourselves to the pain and the joy of others" (124).

Warrior is quite right in asserting that education can be a powerful avenue through which to validate the activity of any form of theoretical discourse and give pragmatic context to what would otherwise be mere aestheticism. Through "Euro-American style education" a Native American theoretical discourse can add its own voice and bring its own perspective to the voices already existing in the academy, challenging the parameters of Western theory itself and writing back against cultural versions of Euramerican imperialism. Given these premises, an either/or perspective would not be altogether effective, and Warrior is all the more correct in discouraging it. However, after reading *Tribal Secrets*, a reader might wonder how well Warrior himself has put into practice his theoretical assumptions. While calling for the abolition of binaries, Warrior appears to be constructing one in his definition of a Native American intellectualism based exclusively on indigenous conceptual categories. By appealing to concepts such as *sovereignty*, *self-determination*, and *tribal* as identifiers of his Native intellectualism and overlooking the epistemological root conveyed by such terms, Warrior simply ignores the double bind characterizing his overall theoretical approach.

One might ask how Warrior justifies the fact that, in his ideal erasing of binaries, *Tribal Secrets* does not engage in any significant way with the critical discourse of Western tradition, not even to mount a forceful critique. Perhaps an answer to such a question might be found in a brief discussion of an earlier version of the third chapter of *Tribal Secrets*, "Intellectual Sovereignty and the Struggle for an American Indian Future," published in a 1992 issue of the *Wicazo Ša Review*. In this essay, Warrior looks at the work of Gerald

Vizenor as writing that offers important insights into the framework of intellectual sovereignty that he has developed through his reading of Deloria and Mathews. Along with his criticism of traditionalist and nationalistic activities of the early 1970s, Vizenor's notion of tradition represents, according to Warrior, the culmination of Deloria's and Mathews's thought. Warrior writes: "Rather than relying on an ideology that turns tradition and ritual into 'a kind of standardized liturgy, as if it were scripture,' Vizenor argues that tradition comes alive through allowing those traditions to break open the creativity and imagination of those who practice them. In this, he is similar to Mathews – committed to finding the living power of the oral tradition in circumstances radically different than those in which they were born" (16). Even the concept of sovereignty is, according to Warrior, a primary concern in Vizenor's writing, to the point that some of Vizenor's novels are "about the creations of sovereign Native communities" (16).⁹

If Vizenor's work seems to reflect some of the ideological assumptions of Mathews and Deloria, why is it that Warrior mentions it only marginally in the introduction to *Tribal Secrets*? A closer look at the rest of the *Wicazo Ša* essay might help us come to terms with Warrior's formulations here. In Warrior's view, Vizenor's trickster discourse, heavily influenced by Continental (French) theory, provides a sort of imaginative landscape without a pragmatic basis. More important, Warrior claims,

> Vizenor replicates the conclusions and praxes of French theory. Like Foucault, he is resigned to allowing power and knowledge to play out their own control. Like Baudrillard, he is resigned to there being only more simulation underneath the simulacrum of the world that modernism and capitalism has produced. Like Derrida, difference becomes the only politics that the creative artist or intellectual can offer. While he opens tremendous avenues at the level of creativity and critical reflections, at the level of program, Vizenor offers us little. Deloria and Mathews . . . are just as influenced by European and Euro-American intellectual traditions as Vizenor. The difference between them, though, is the suspicion with which Deloria and Mathews regard that influence. ("Intellectual Sovereignty" 17)

Regardless of whether we agree with Warrior's interpretation of Vizenor's theory here – Vizenor's engagement with French theory is, as my discussion in chapter 4 will indicate, much more complex than it at first appears to be – what is significant in these statements of Warrior's is his suspicious attitude toward any form of Western critical discourse. It would seem that, for Warrior, in order to be effective or pragmatic, Native American literary criticism must dismiss Euramerican intellectual traditions and critics must, in fact, "decolonize" their minds, eliminating from them any form of colonial discourse. But is this act of decolonization possible? How would Warrior justify such a rejection of Eurocentric theory in the light of his discussion of Mathews's and Deloria's cosmopolitanism? At the conclusion of his discussion of Vizenor, Warrior suggests that Vizenor's theory would be especially challenged and strengthened were it to engage other oppositional discourses "outside of Europe and Euro-America" ("Intellectual Sovereignty" 19). Warrior argues that, if Vizenor's criticism is to enter an international dialogue, it must embrace such critics as Said, Spivak, Gates, and Cornel West (19). But could such an international dialogue detach itself from Eurocentric discourse? Can we read Spivak without reading Derrida? Can we read Gates without reading Saussure or any of the other structuralist (and poststructuralist) thinkers? In addition, how does Warrior's own theory dialogue with such international voices? These are the questions that Warrior's argument inevitably raises. While they cannot be completely resolved here, a closer look at *Tribal Secrets* will at least allow us to make a start.

Undoubtedly, Warrior has undertaken a very ambitious project, attempting to construct some kind of American Indian criticism with Mathews and Deloria as the primary material on which to base this discourse. Owing to their international and, I would add, hybridized experience, Mathews and Deloria seem to be the perfect candidates to bring the Native American experience into a wider context and give some pragmatic foundation to a Native American critical theory. However, by failing to translate Mathews's and Deloria's international and hybridized experience into his own study, and by insisting throughout on a cultural criticism rigidly rooted in the American Indian experience, Warrior leaves unsolved the question of how a criticism that aims at eradicating binaries can argue for a tradition of Indian intellectualism or intellectual sovereignty. Despite its premises, Warrior's critical approach remains, in his own words, "[un]convincingly suggestive rather than conclusive" (*Tribal Secrets* xv).

At the heart of *Red on Red* is Craig Womack's attempt to recover a Native intellectual tradition and open a dialogue among Creek people, specifically, and Native people, more generally. Like Warrior, Womack appeals to concepts such as *autonomy, sovereignty,* and *self-determination* in order to theorize a "Native" perspective that allows Indian people to speak for themselves.[10] Against the postmodernist claim that Native and non-Native are constantly deconstructing each other, Womack posits: "Whatever one might argue about postmodern representation, there is the legal reality of tribal sovereignty, recognized by the U.S. Constitution and defined over the last 160 years by the Supreme Court, that affects the everyday lives of individuals and tribal nations and, therefore, has something to do with tribal literature as well" (6).[11] More forcefully than Warrior, Womack insists on a Native consciousness and a Native viewpoint out of which a Native American critical theory should originate. Unlike Warrior, he does not envision any moment of dialogue with Western critical discourse, claiming that "the primary purpose of [his] study is not to argue for canonical inclusion or opening up Native literature to a broader audience" (6) but to develop a theoretical discourse that will allow Native people to decolonize themselves.

Lamenting the paucity of criticism among Native authors (a further example of how, for Womack, Natives have internalized colonization by thinking that only white intellectuals can "do theory"), he takes a Red Stick approach and turns to Creek history, oral tradition, and literature in order to construct a literary criticism presented as a meaningful alternative to the Western literary establishment. Similar to the anticolonial movement of the Red Sticks, Womack's reliance on tradition is more an initiation and innovation on the part of Native people than a victimization. He writes: "I am more interested in what can be innovated and initiated by Native people in analyzing their own cultures rather than deconstructing Native viewpoints and arguing for their European underpinnings or even concentrating on white atrocities and Indian victims" (*Red on Red* 12). Like Deloria and Warrior, Womack looks at tradition as a dynamic entity, something that is perpetually in motion and that adapts to new cultural challenges. Like Deloria and Warrior, Womack envisions Red Stick literary criticism rooted in land and culture, sensitive to the needs of the community, and creating resistance movements against colonialism. As he puts it, "This criticism emphasizes unique Native worldviews and political realities, searches for differences as often as similarities, and attempts to find Native literature's place in Indian country, rather than Native literature's place in the canon" (11). While dismissing postmodernism and poststructuralism *tout court*, considering them merely "literary trends" (6), Womack is even more critical of postcolonial approaches that, in their emphasis on how the settler culture views the Others, largely miss the point of how Indians view Indians.[12] Again and again, Womack appeals to issues of authenticity and nationhood to legitimate space for a Native American critical theory that is defined by internal, or tribal, rather than by external sources. In this section, I discuss Womack's separatist approach, showing how his call for a Native American literary separatism and for a Native perspective ultimately reinscribes colonial definitions of Indianness and simply reverses the Western binary structure of an us/them universe through which Native American studies continues to be the Other of Euramerican discourse.

Crucial in Womack's ideology is the necessity of breaking down the dichotomy that separates orality and literacy, "wherein the oral constitutes authentic culture and the written contaminated culture" (*Red on Red* 15). Against this anthropological, ethnological stance, Womack seeks to politicize the oral tradition, claiming that the ongoing expression of a tribal voice through imagination, language, and literature gives identity to the citizens of a nation and legitimates their sovereign status. Womack's critical enterprise, thus, responds to the challenge of writing in the oral tradition, a concept that, to a certain extent, all the other theorists discussed in this study embrace, in order to subvert Western discursive modes. More effectively than does Warrior, Womack puts the notion of tradition as revitalization into practice, creating a dialogue between essays on Native literature and culture, on one side, and fictional letters from Creek characters commenting on the essays, on the other. As the blurb on the dustjacket of *Red on Red* tells us, the exchange of letters between Hotgun (a character in Alexander Posey's letters, published in the *Eufaula Indian Journal*) and his buddy Jim Chibbo (a fictional character created by Womack) assumes the function of a "Creek chorus," with the characters at the end of each essay exchanging views on the events narrated and launching ironic thrusts against the discipline of literary criticism. In a self-parodying mode, Womack writes: "To avoid the nastiness of a profession that is just pitiful mean, Jim tries to tell funny stories here and again to consider the most serious critical issues in the book without becoming mean himself. Him and Hotgun found that they could get to the heart of the matter quicker by funning each other than by writing literary criticism, and they could use jokes instead of taking up the hickory sticks themselves as a bloody cudgel on everybody who disagrees with them. . . . They felt that as Creek critics . . . if they abandoned their role as storytellers, something very significant would be missing from their criticism" (20–21). Storytelling, thus, enters the book both on an ideological and on a structural level, in the attempt to inscribe its own theories about its nature and various functions while generating a discussion of Native literature from an insider's point of view, a position that, in Womack's perspective, legitimates authenticity.

However, what separates the other theorists discussed in this study (Vizenor and Sarris in particular) from Womack is the way in which the oral tradition in their writing subsumes Western theoretical paradigms, reinventing and reimagining the language of authoritative discourse and turning it to its own advantage.[13] In Ashcroft et al.'s terminology, by "abrogating" the authority of English, Native American theorists creatively and imaginatively reappropriate this authoritative discourse as "(english)," that is, within their local framework and within a language "other" than the written, one capable in its dynamism and extraordinary vitality of infiltrating racial, cultural, and linguistic boundaries. Unlike these other theorists, however, Womack relies on the oral tradition in order to promote an (essentially) Native perspective, and, thus, despite his insightful reading and compelling discussion of the political nature of oral stories in the first part of the book, his approach inevitably risks fixing what he otherwise terms a "living literary tradition" (*Red on Red* 66).

As I argued at the beginning of this chapter, the term *Native perspective* is itself problematic and contradictory. Once the oral tradition enters into dialogue with the rhetorical systems of the Western tradition, once it forcefully enters a book such as *Red on Red*, a product of the conjunction of cultural practices and hybridized discursive modes, an authentic Native perspective, such as the one promoted by Womack, becomes an ironic contradiction. To insist, as Womack does, that seeking out a Native perspective is "a worthwhile endeavor" (*Red on Red* 4) amounts to a dismissal of the mutual interdependencies that more than five hundred years of history have thrust on the American continent. More significantly, it means turning Native identity into a textual commodity that continues to perpetuate fabricated versions of Indianness.

Like Allen's *The Sacred Hoop*, *Red on Red* begins in the oral tradition, with the Creek creation story that legitimates a sense of identity for the people. Womack writes:

> Through imagination and storytelling, people in oral cultures reexperience history. This concept of ancestral memory relates to nationalism in that sovereignty is an intersection of the political, imaginary, and literary. To exist as a nation, the community needs a perception of nationhood, that is stories (like the migration account) that help them imagine who they are as people, how they came to be, and what cultural values they wish to preserve. . . . Within the telling, the event is reexperienced so that the people are reconstituted as a nation as they hear about their origins in ancient stories of creations and journeyings. (26)

More critically than Warrior, Womack links the oral tradition to a nationalistic perspective and reappropriates the term *sovereignty* within a Native cultural and political matrix. The chapter "Reading the Oral Tradition for Nationalist Themes: Beyond Ethnography" contains a passionate discussion of the political nature of the oral tradition while vigorously responding to ethnographic and anthropological interpretations of tribal material.

At the beginning of his discussion, Womack argues that, as an intellectual idea, sovereignty is inherent in Native cultures and that, as a political practice, it predates European contact. Creeks, for example, had local representations in autonomous towns, and, more important, Creek storytelling articulated concepts of nationhood and politics (*Red on Red* 51). The Creek's creation story itself "combines," according to Womack, "emergence with Creek national concerns" (54). Whereas Warrior, Deloria, and the other critics mentioned earlier acknowledge the European theological and political origin of the term *sovereignty*, arguing that it has little to do with the original status of indigenous American realities, Womack goes back to the time before European treaty relationships with Native nations in order to claim sovereignty as a possession of Native communities. As does Allen in taking a gynocentric perspective, Womack appeals to a supposedly authentic past in terms of one shared culture, a sort of collective one true self to reinforce the idea of nationhood. While his intent is to demystify the notion of oral tradition as an ethnographic artifact and illustrate the crucial role of stories within the political life of a tribal culture, his position raises many doubts about the concept of tradition and cultural identity.

Again, Fanon's ideas on national culture offer us an apt critical lens through which to view Womack's argument. In *The Wretched of the Earth*, Fanon points out that, in postcolonial societies, the rediscovery of an authentic cultural identity is often the object of "a passionate research . . . directed by the secret hope of discovering beyond the misery of today, beyond self-contempt, resignation and abjuration, some very beautiful and splendid era whose existence rehabilitates us both in regard to ourselves and in regard to others" (210). Such observations undoubtedly validate Womack's reading of the oral tradition within a nationalist frame. In Womack's case, looking at the oral tradition as a deeply politicized body of work able to cultivate a political consciousness might serve, as Fanon argues, "as a justification for the hope of a future national culture" and might produce an important "change in the native" (210).

Womack's discussion in *Red on Red* of the problem of translation clearly responds to the idea of change suggested by Fanon. According to Womack, the dilemma over the performative aspects of oral stories that are "lost" in writing is part of the ethnographer's stance on the "static" nature of the oral tradition. He writes: "The problem with the 'translation problem,' with its skepticism and emphasis on literary diminishment, is that it places us within a 'pure versus tainted' framework that so much of Native studies gets cast in. . . . [T]his locks Native studies into a system that does not allow the discipline to evolve; it is the way in which we have inherited the vanishing mentality. I might argue that the translation controversy has as much to do with the vanishing notion as with linguistic realities" (*Red on Red* 65). To oppose this "vanishing mentality," Womack looks at the translation dilemma from a rather different perspective, claiming that, like the literatures of many other nations, Native literatures can and should be translated, that the idea of translation should be open, keeping in mind that the oral tradition is a "living literary tradition" (66) and, as such, should become central to Native political analysis and to the developments of Native literary theory.

Like most contemporary Native American authors, Womack suggests that the oral tradition can be reimagined and reexpressed owing to the living quality of language. By redirecting the language of the oral tradition, Native people concentrate, according to Womack, on "cultural survival rather than cultural disintegration" (*Red on Red* 66), proving that their culture is very much alive in the reality of contemporary America. However, what Womack seems to overlook is the danger that occurs when oral stories are used as an avenue to legitimate identity and authenticity. Given the ongoing transformation of stories, and given the extraordinary vitality and adaptability of the oral tradition, the attempt to fix traditions through the use of names conceived of as markers of authenticity inevitably leads to a perpetuation of the dominant discursive modes. In "Postindian Autoinscriptions," Vizenor articulates this risk: "Native American creation stories are in continuous translations, interpretations, and representations; *at the same time, postindian simulations and pretensions are abetted as lateral sources of identities*" (35; emphasis added). He claims that, when traditions and names are "fixed" in simulations of identities, these traditions serve the literature of dominance rather than the remembrance of tribal survivance (30).

Womack's approach to the Turtle story, a story central to Creek cosmology and ceremonial life, reveals some of the limitations and contradictions inherent in his position – at least as far as his idea of the oral tradition is concerned. Like Allen does when discussing "Kochinnenako in Academe" in *The Sacred Hoop*, Womack presents different versions of the story: the version told in Creek by the Creek elder Linda Alexander; Alexander's translation of the story in English and a poststorytelling conversation that she had with Womack; and the ethnographer John Swanton's two English versions of the story from his collection *Myths and Tales of the Southeastern Indians* (1929). Womack then offers his own interpretation. Despite his "crisis of faith regarding ethnographic work" (*Red on Red* 75) – in his opinion, ethnography turns people into objects of study instead of representing them as complex human beings – Womack nonetheless embarks on this interpretative journey in order to understand what Native people can learn from the oral tradition and how their interpretative strategies can differ from those of outsiders. Like Allen, Womack acts as a "Native informant," and, whether he acknowledges it or not, he is, to use Spivak's terminology (*In Other Worlds* 221), inevitably bound into a complicitous and parasitic relationship with his object of study. In other words, his analysis of the story turns the Native or subaltern into an object of investigation. More significantly, by constructing his interpretative theory, Womack inevitably silences the protagonists of the story.

According to Womack, "The Turtle story is a potent healing narrative that contains a medicine song that Turtle voices to sing himself back together after two women violently smash him to the point of near death" (*Red on Red* 87). Like many other Indian songs, the Turtle medicine song reveals the powerful healing power of language, the power to restore an inarticulate individual to a condition of speech. Womack traces parallels with the Navajo Night Chant in Momaday's *House Made of Dawn*, through which the protagonist, Abel, is restored to wholeness and voice. The Turtle story is also a trickster narrative with trickster patterns displayed throughout the narrative. In Linda Alexander's version of the story, Turtle is "hungry to the point of sickness"; he is "horny" and "wants to look up the women's dresses." As Womack explains, "The narrative begins to follow the trickster pattern because Turtle has ulterior motives; he begins to plan a way to meet his physical needs, his behavior involves a comic sexual element, and the trick backfires on him at the end" (*Red on Red* 89).

Whereas Paul Radin takes a Jungian approach and considers trickster to be an amoral figure (xxii–iv), Womack insists that the character of Turtle is humorous and poignant, the same qualities that, in Vizenor's words, make trickster "compassionate" (*Earthdivers* xii).[14] More significantly, comparing Alexander's English version to Swanton's, Womack notices how, in the ethnographer's "revision," the sexual material is edited out, the cultural context for the story is erased, and the aggregative style of oral storytelling has been completely replaced by phrases "common to writing, but not to oral speech" (*Red on Red* 96). Womack notices how, when compared to Alexander's Creek version (which he calls the "story version"), "Swanton's narratives seem encapsulated, paraphrased in the extreme" (96). In addition, "Swanton's narrators are completely erased leaving no tracks within the tellings. The effect of the erased narrator is a fragmenting one – the stories do not connect to a living human community. The tellings occur in a vacuum. They are artifacts; they have no bearing on contemporary concerns. The are self-fulfilling evidence amassed by the BAE [i.e., Bureau of American Ethnology] to prove the popular 'vanishing American' theory so widespread during Swanton's time" (98). By contrast, in presenting Alexander's version of the story and re-creating the moment when "the telling" actually occurs, Womack makes us feel the reality of the story, its rootedness in "real-life" experience and the physical world. He writes: "We felt the reality of the story that evening . . . because we started acting out its movement toward comedy ourselves. The end of our conversation consists of jokes about the inefficacy of Indian Health Service. And this, I would suggest, is also part of the Turtle story – its context that particular evening and relationship to the contemporary life of the people" (99).

Womack is quite right in pointing out the artificial construction of Indianness conveyed by the language of ethnography. What he fails to realize, however, is that his own analysis and interpretation of the story work in the same ethnographic mode, albeit with the terms reversed. He becomes the insider claiming to present the correct meaning of the story merely on the basis of an authentic Native perspective. Interrogating only his investigating tools when he should also be interrogating his position as a critic and subject of investigation, Womack voices simulations of tribal identity especially in referring to "a quintessentially Creek literary form [in the story], that of a persona writing, an author pretending to be someone else" (*Red on Red* 100). According to Womack the persona is "a literary technique Creeks have found useful for presenting Creek voices, maintaining Creek viewpoints, continuing Creek oral tradition, and speaking to a Creek audience. It is a Creek form that is identifiably Southeastern Indian in its contents and structure, as well as the forums where it has been presented" (101).

In his attempt to suggest ways in which the oral tradition can provide its own interpretative principles, Womack inevitably runs into the danger that, by appealing to the purity of this form (the Creek persona), and by arguing for a "quintessentially Creek" feature rooted in the oral tradition, he fixes that tradition as a cultural artifact. If the strength of the oral tradition is its ongoing vitality and adaptability, the same features that enable the survival of a culture, how can Womack advocate a "quintessentially Creek . . . form," the same one that legitimates a "quintessentially Creek" perspective? How would he define *Creekness* other than as a universal and transcendental category inside people on which history has made no fundamental mark? Even granted that the technique of the persona writing originated in the Creek oral tradition, how can he insist on its "quintessentially Creek" quality when the oral tradition itself has evolved into new cultural forms? In his anxious attempt to re-create a cultural feature through which to legitimate a nationalistic culture, Womack conveniently dismisses the fact that he is utilizing language and tools borrowed from the colonizer and that, by wishing to attach these instruments to some form of nationalism, he inevitably ends up exoticizing them. Womack's Creekcentrism runs the risk at best of repeating the errors pointed out by Fanon and other Third World intellectuals and at worst of turning into a reductionist Nativism.

Among the most significant representatives of postcolonial discourse theory, Kwame Anthony Appiah provides, in *In My Father's House*, a penetrating analysis of the Nativist discourse applied to the categories *nationalism* and *race*. From the position of a mixedblood identity (African on his father's side and British on his mother's), and as an intellectual who defines himself as the historical product of the encounter with the West, Appiah shares with Native American intellectuals the same ambiguous relation and cultural (dis)location between the world of his forefathers and the world of industrialized countries. Referring to African intellectuals in particular, he uses the term *europhone* to describe the product of cultural practices originating from the encounter between non-Western and Western modes, adding that neither Third World literature nor Third World literary criticism can escape this europhone reality.

Appiah's analysis of African cultural nationalism leads him to formulate his ideas on Nativism. Discussing the now-classic manifesto *Toward the Decolonization of African Literature* (1980), the work of the Nigerian authors Chinweizu, Onwuchekwa Jemie, and Ihechukwu Madubuike, all of them "encumbered with extensive Western university educations," Appiah claims that the authors' main goal is to "wrestle the critical ethnocentrism of their Eurocentric opponents to the ground in the name of an Afrocentric particularism" (*In My Father's House* 56, 57). While acknowledging the hybrid nature of the African novel, with its confluence of African oral tradition and imported European literate forms, Chinweizu et al. argue for the necessity of recovering African oral antecedents, which they conceive of as prototypes for the African novel and which make the novel something other than a purely borrowed narrative form. They write: "But African literature *is* an autonomous entity separate and apart from other literatures. It has its own traditions, models, and norms. Its constituency is separate and radically different from that of the European or other literatures. And its historical and cultural imperatives impose upon it concerns and constraints quite different, sometimes altogether antithetical to the European. These facts hold true even for those portions of African literature which continue to be written in European languages" (4).

Statements such as this display, Appiah maintains, a Nativist rhetoric in their recapitulation of nationalist ideologies, ideologies that, ironically, however, reproduce the Eurocentric bias of Western criticism. Crucial in the Nativist's topology is the view that true African independence requires a literature of one's own and that, in the debate between *universalism* and *particularism*, the latter defines itself in opposition to the former. But, as Appiah points out, "There are only two real players in this game: us, inside, them, outside" (*In My Father's House* 56). Operating with this inside/outside topology, African intellectuals mobilize a nationalistic rhetoric, one in which "the literature of one's own is that of one's own nation" (56), and appeal to particularist identities in order to theorize the principles of this literature. However, Appiah maintains, what "the apostles of nativism" naively fail to acknowledge is that their approach ironically establishes a "reverse discourse" (59). He writes that, in this cultural battle, "the terms of resistance are already given us, and our contestation is entrapped within [the] Western cultural conjuncture we affect to dispute. . . . Railing against the cultural hegemony of the West, the nativists are of its party without knowing it" (59). Appealing to an Afrocentric particularism amounts simply, Appiah posits, to appealing to a Western universalism – to the extent that the Nativists still utilize a rhetoric of defiance inevitably dictated by the parameters of Western discourse. Even though the nativists might think that they are attacking the Eurocentric bias of Western universalism, their critique still "inhabit[s] a Western architecture" (59).

Particularly significant in the context of a Native American theoretical discourse is Appiah's question as to whether it is satisfactory to read a literature by means of a theory drawn only from its own cultural and intellectual inheritance, in his case the African inheritance. The question fits neatly with Womack's argument. Is it indeed possible to read Native literature by relying exclusively on a theory originating from a Native cultural background? Unlike Womack, Appiah would say that it is not, claiming that insisting on this rationale would mean underestimating the cultural hybridity and multiplicity of heritages of the modern (Native) writer. He writes, "To insist on nativism on these grounds would be to ignore plain facts: to ignore the undeniable datum that Soyinka's references to Euripides are as real as his appeal to Ogub (and also to Brazilian syncretisms of Yoruba and Christian religions)" (*In My Father's House* 66). Translated into a Native American context, this approach would mean ignoring the possibility that Vizenor's poststructuralist stance is as real as his Anishinaabe trickster tales with the figure of Naanabozho at the center of the narrative or that the references to Creek cosmology in the poetry of Joy Harjo are as real as the influences of Western feminist theory. Indeed, to insist on this cultural separatism means, Appiah concludes, perpetuating the self/other binarism, risking becoming what Sara Suleri has termed "Otherness-machines" (*Meatless Days* 105). Appiah writes, "Nativism invites us to conceive of the nation as an organic community, bound together by the *Sprachegeist*, by the shared norms that are the legacy of tradition, struggling to throw off the shackles of alien modes and thought. 'Here I am,' Senghor once wrote, 'trying to forget Europe in the pastoral heart of Sine.' But for us to forget Europe is to suppress the conflicts that have shaped our identities; since it is too late for us to escape each other, we might instead seek to turn to our advantage the mutual interdependencies history has thrust upon us" (*In My Father's House* 72).

Appiah's reflections on Nativism lead him to theorize about the modern African novel. The first generation of African novels – Achebe's *Things Fall Apart* (1958) and Laye's *L'enfant noir* (1968) – seems, he claims, "to belong to the world of eighteenth- and nineteenth-century literary nationalism" (*In My Father's House* 149) insofar as these novels aim at a re-creation of a common cultural past that is crafted into a shared tradition by the writer. Written in the 1950s and 1960s, these novels are, thus, a "realist legitimization of nationalism" (150). On the other hand, the novels of the second generation, which Appiah refers to as "postnativist" and "postcolonial" – novels such as Yambo Ouloguem's *Le devoir de violence* (1968) – are novels of delegitimization. Rejecting the narrative of the nation, these novels appeal instead to an ethical universal, a certain simple respect for human suffering. They promote, not a national, but a "transnational" solidarity (155).[15] Appiah writes: "If there is a lesson in the broad shape of this circulation of culture, it is surely that we are all already contaminated by each other, that there is no longer a fully autochthonous *echt*-African culture awaiting salvage by our artists (just as there is, of course, no American culture without African roots). And there is a real sense in some postcolonial writing that the postulation of a unitary Africa over against a monolithic West – the binarism of Self and Other – is the last of the shibboleths of the modernizers that we must learn to live without" (155).

Appiah's discussion of the African novel helps us further analyze Womack's argument insofar as it raises the question of authenticity in literary works and, in Womack's case, the issue of what a Native American novel is or should be. If, as Appiah suggests, it is, indeed, problematic to postulate the existence of a unitary colonized culture against a monolithic West, can we, indeed, conceive of the Native American novel as the quintessential reflection of an Indian perspective? In the light of Womack's Creekcentrism, would an authentic Creek novel be a perfect exemplar of a Creek national literature?

In the fourth chapter of *Red on Red*, "Alice Callahan's *Wynema*: A Fledging Attempt," Womack discusses the first novel known to be authored by a Native American woman as problematic because of "its failure to engage Creek culture, history, and politics" (107). On the basis of the "novel's erasure of Creek voices, the characters' rejection of Creek culture, the many instances of cultural misrepresentation throughout, the lack of any depiction of the nuances of Creek life, the protagonist's repudiation of Muskogean/Creek matrilinearity, and the author's choice of a non-Creek and non-Indian viewpoint" (107), Womack considers the novel "assimilationist" (116) and "unCreek" (111).[16]

Wynema was published in 1891, at a time when the works of other Native women writers such as the Paiute Sara Winnemucca and the Sioux Gertrude Bonnin, themselves the products of a Christian education, were overtly critical of Christian institutions. According to Womack, Callahan "could have written a very different novel had she chosen to do so" (*Red on Red* 121). That is, despite the fact that the notion of resisting complicity with Western or Christian cultural traditions was current, Callahan chose to write an assimilationist novel. LaVonne Ruoff, however, takes a somewhat different approach to the novel. She writes: "Because of her mixed-blood heritage and education, [Callahan] was both part of and separate from the Muskogee people, culture, and issues she examines. In *Wynema*, Callahan uses a double-voiced discourse, which simultaneously expresses the direct intention of the character speaking and the refracted intention of the author. The speeches of Callahan's characters represent not only the intention of character and author but also two cultures, Indian and non-Indian, and two genders, male and female. *Wynema* demonstrates how Indian women authors used and departed from literary trends present in nineteenth-century women's literature" (Callahan xix–xx). While acknowledging the sentimental and stilted language of *Wynema*, the result of the influence of romance authors of the period, Ruoff reads the novel as a reflection of the author's own ambivalence as an acculturated Muskogee and focuses on the novel's emphasis on both Indians' and women's issues, issues that make *Wynema* "a significant contribution to the history of Native American and women's literature" (xliii). To a certain extent, Ruoff's interpretation here moves along the lines suggested by Appiah in his discussion of the so-called second generation of the African novel, in which a much more human impulse transcends "obligations to churches and to nations" (*In My Father's House* 155).

It is not within the scope of this chapter to engage in a thorough discussion of *Wynema*. My point in introducing Womack's discussion of it is, instead, to address the controversial issue raised by Womack of what a Creek work is or should be. More significantly, I will start with the question of whether there can be such a thing as a Creek perspective or a Native perspective in writing fiction. How is such perspective defined? By whom? On what basis? Womack himself acknowledges that "defining just what a 'Creek perspective' is remains problematic, since there are many Creeks with many different perspectives" (*Red on Red* 118). Nonetheless, he insists that "Callahan's failures might suggest that a sense of Creek land, Creek character, Creek speech and Creek speakers, Creek language, Creek oral and written literature, Creek history, Creek politics, and Creek government might be potential considerations in our growing understanding of what constitutes an exemplary work in a national tribal literature" (122). Womack's position here would appear to endorse the nationalist approach of Cook-Lynn, Forbes, and the other representatives of tribalist discourse discussed so far and, thus, to be in line with his own theoretical notions of literary separatism. In Appiah's terminology, Womack legitimates a nationalist position that makes a claim for a fully autochthonous *echt* Creek (Native) culture as a response to the monolithic West, a claim that, in the long run, legitimates a Nativist conception of Creek life specifically and tribal life generally.

Defining a Creek or Native perspective is, indeed, problematic; even more problematic, I argue, is insisting on an essentially Creek or Native perspective in novels when the novel itself is, Owens reminds us, a "'foreign' (though infinitely flexible) and intensely egocentric genre" (*Other Destinies* 10), a genre rising out of social conditions antithetical to whatever we might consider "traditional" Native American oral cultures. Critical of positions that legitimate authenticity and nationalism, Owens indicates that, "for the Indian author, writing within consciousness of the contextual background of a non-literate culture, every word written in English represents a collaboration of sorts as well as a reorientation (conscious or unconscious) from the paradigmatic world of oral tradition to the syntagmatic reality of written language" (6). Borrowing the vocabulary of Ashcroft et al. (in *The Empire Writes*

Back) as well as from that of Mikhail Bakhtin, Owens explains how the dilemma of a privileged discourse already "charged" with "value" and "alien" is the primary concern for Native American fiction writers and significantly "adds complexity to the overarching questions of cultural identity" (7). Given the "privileged" position of almost all Native American fiction writers, who, regardless of their mixedblood or fullblood status, possess a high level of education, almost always at least one college degree, it is almost impossible for Native American novelists to step back into an autochthonous, unitary tribal culture and claim legitimacy or authenticity for their work. According to Owens, the challenge of Native American novelists today is to move beyond this "'Rousseauist' ethnostalgia – most common to Euramerican treatments of Native American Indians – toward an affirmation of a syncretic, dynamic, adaptive identity in contemporary America" (12). Traditional stories, songs, and rituals are reimagined by contemporary Native American fiction writers in order to tell stories of who they are today, in order for them to continue to survive as indigenous people and living human beings.

Owens's understanding of the American Indian novel runs opposite to that of Womack and other representatives of tribalist discourse. Womack's insistence on Creek life, Creek culture, the tradition of Creek intellectualism, and the role of community and culture in forming Creek thinkers constitutes his response to works produced in the last thirty years by mixedblood authors, works in which, according to Womack, the primary focus is blood and marginalization rather than the ongoing life of the nation. These are the same authors discussed by Owens, who argues, in contrast, that this is a powerful literature of resistance created as a countervoice to the dominant discourse, the same discourse that keeps perpetuating images of Indians as cultural artifacts.

From his chapter on *Wynema* Womack turns to a discussion of two Creek intellectuals, Alexander Posey (1873–1908) and Louis Oliver (1901–91), whose work presents characteristics of "authentic" Creek literature. According to Womack, Posey's immersion in local politics as well as his Creekcentric philosophy make him a perfect model for modern writers. Similarly, the writing of Louis Oliver, with its emphasis on Creek landscape, stories, and spiritualism, provides significant image of Creek intellectualism.[17] By contrast a literature such as that produced by mixedblood authors in the past few decades – which departs from the body and the culture of the people, from the communities, and from a specific sense of landscape – inevitably fails tribalist concerns and appeals to sovereignty. Like Warrior, Womack is suspicious of a literature such as Vizenor's trickster fiction that embraces the jargon of postmodern theory since, in this specific case, Native authors fail to incorporate tribal realities. He writes: "If we are going to liberate words from fixed meanings and celebrate their amorphous shape-shifting qualities, might we need to recognize not only that tricksters shape-shift but that witches shape-shift also . . . ? Is there a balance called for here, an acknowledgment that sometimes fixed meanings are necessary, other times free play, as well as an honest recognition that both can be abused? . . . What happens to political struggles when a concept like identity is deconstructed? . . . I am waiting for the day when Native people will be addressed on *their* own terms" (*Red on Red* 205).

Statements such as these inevitably raise a series of questions. Can Womack's work still maintain, as the product of the University of Minnesota Press, its professed Creekcentrism? Does the fact that Womack holds a professorship at the University of Lethbridge (in Alberta) change the way in which he speaks to his own community? Can a book written, as *Red on Red* is, in response to the charge that only whites can "do theory" speak to Native communities in their own terms? Can Womack justify grounding his study in a notion of Creekcentrism when that study must, as it does, inevitably engage Western literary theory (even if only to attack it)?

Ultimately, Womack is writing from a privileged position within the academy, his audience largely other academics, not Native communities. *Red on Red* remains, therefore, a sophisticated work of literary criticism and, as such, inaccessible to those members of a Native audience who cannot approach it from a similarly privileged position. To a certain extent, and all the more ironically perhaps, Womack's position resembles that of the privileged diasporic Third World so often critiqued by fervent opponents of postcolonialism, people such as Aijaz Ahmad, who argues that postcolonial theorizing is a matter of class and institutional privilege and a flight from collective socialities into the abstraction of metropolitan theory.

Undoubtedly, Womack's observations raise important questions as to the role of the intellectual in relation to the Native community. However, by overlooking his own "strategic location" – his implication in the discourse of the metropolitan literate culture – he presents only one side of the picture. Returning to Womack's question of whether political struggles lose their value when identity is deconstructed, one might also argue that they lose their value when identity is fixed as a cultural artifact, much like the problematic Creekcentric perspective promoted in *Red on Red*. It is in the last two chapters of *Red on Red* – those on Joy Harjo and Lynn Riggs – that the contradictory nature of Womack's position becomes most clearly evident. While referring to these authors as authentic representatives of a rigid nationalism, Womack fails to acknowledge (as does Warrior with Mathews and Deloria) how the multiplicity of heritages out of which they emerge ironically makes them ideal candidates for Krupat's cosmopolitanism.

According to Womack, Harjo's poetry is grounded in Creek nationalism, culture, and sensibility. In it the Oklahoma landscape serves as a catalyst for the speaker's "tribal memory" (*Red on Red* 233), enacting a sort of pan-tribal feeling through which all Native people can come together. Womack's main purpose in discussing Harjo is to explore how nationalist motifs take on pan-tribal concerns, without the two necessarily contradicting each other; such issues he also hopes to apply to his own work. Despite its Creekcentrism *Red on Red* is envisioned by Womack as a theoretical approach that all tribal groups should imitate. And Harjo's poetry is used in it to illustrate how such pan-tribalism can effectively work.

Traveling in the Southwest, through places important to Creek history, Harjo is able to imagine and empathize with the legacy of oppression faced by all Native people in the Americas. The poem "New Orleans," for example, from *She Had Some Horses* (1983), exemplifies, according to Womack, ways in which "tribal specificity and pan-tribal experience intersect" (*Red on Red* 226). In it Harjo takes memories triggered by her presence in New Orleans – memories of the tragic episodes of Removal generally and of Creeks drowning during a forced crossing of the Mississippi in particular – and recasts them within the context of violence against Indian people generally. Womack writes: "Memory . . . is essential to Harjo's Creek philosophy. In addition to the positive aspects of ancestral memory, there are five hundred years of genocide that also haunt Indian memory, making escaping with Deer Woman, going off into the deer world – a world untainted by colonialism, a world where environment and community are restored – a real temptation. Yet, this is not . . . an evasion of human responsibility; this is a belief that the Americas will once again eventually return to some form of indigenous consciousness" (230).

Whatever our reading of Harjo's poetry might be, it would be difficult to ignore traces of a certain Rousseauist or Nativist "ethnostalgia" in Womack's observations. Pan-tribalist feelings call to mind the visions and shadows of the Ghost Dance religion, the doctrine of spiritual renewal that spread across the plains at the end of the nineteenth century. According to the ethnographer James Mooney, "The great underlying principle of the Ghost Dance doctrine is that the time will come when the whole Indian race, living and dead, will be reunited upon a regenerated earth, to live a life of aboriginal happiness, forever free from death, disease, and misery" (777). The ideological connection between nationalism and pan-tribalism as perceived by Womack should, in this light, be obvious. Both hope to recover a precolonial cultural purity, thereby creating some kind of national consciousness entirely independent of the European colonial enterprise. Like nationalism, pan-tribalism becomes a powerful ideological tool with which to "forget Europe," as Appiah puts it (*In My Father's House* 72) – to move beyond the hybridization that characterizes any cultural encounter. According to Womack, "the process of decolonizing one's mind, a first step before one can achieve a political consciousness and engage oneself in activism, has to begin with imagining some alternative. In other words, the pan-tribal meaning of [Harjo's poetry] is the belief that tribal consciousness is returning in a new unity that transcends old tribal boundaries" (*Red on Red* 230). Yet Womack's analysis of Harjo is in places doubtful and deserves attention.

Take, for example, his discussion of Harjo's "Deer Dancer," which Womack analyzes in terms of a "Creek specificity" (*Red on Red* 228). He writes: "Historically deer were central to Creek food supplies before contact, then important to the Creek economy through trade with the English. . . . In this context, deer can also be taken as a symbol of adaptability, survival in the face of change, shifting worlds, and the power to transcend boundaries" (229). How can something be a symbol both of "adaptability . . . in the face of change" and of "Creek specificity," in this case a precontact, indigenous consciousness? To further complicate the picture, in dealing with Harjo's work, Womack conveniently overlooks the non-Native aspects of her poetry, such as the influences – from, for example, feminist theory, surrealism, and imagism – that significantly reflect an attempt to balance the Muskogean world and the European. In an interview Harjo has explained how she cannot return to the simplicity of the tribal heritage because her heritage is not wholly tribal, not wholly Oklahoman: "I always see Oklahoma as my mother, my motherland. . . . [But] my return usually takes place on a mythic level. . . . There are many memories there for me. It's one of my homes" (Coltelli 56–57). She has also talked about the responsibility that she feels as "a woman of my tribe, who is also part of this invading other culture, and the larger globe" (Coltelli 60). Out of these shifting identities, then, Harjo's poetry becomes an avenue for reconciliation and healing, conveying the necessity of writing beyond cultural barriers, of embracing those "transformations" – as the title of one of her poems indicates – that guarantee survival.

According to Allen, Harjo arrived at her view of the permeability of all boundaries from reading the work of feminists (*The Sacred Hoop* 166). Even more significantly, critics such as Kathleen Donovan have detected strong congruences between Harjo's thought and the work of the French feminist Hélène Cixous. Whereas Harjo laments the materialistic and objective nature of English, its lack of a spiritual center, Cixous tries to restore the body in writing, to open up language to structures that are nonhierarchical and nonexclusive of sexuality. Trapped in a system of oppositional duality, Harjo and Cixous share, according to Donovan, a culturally imposed self-fear and self-loathing, the product of gendered colonialism, a parallel to nationalistic colonialism (156). For both women, Donovan maintains, language becomes the gendered creative power capable of changing fear and hatred into forgiveness and healing, "by questioning and ultimately rejecting the polarities implicit in phallocentric culture and its discourse" (143). In the light of these observations and of Harjo's own declaration concerning her multiple identities and the ways in which these identities are reflected in her work, it is obvious that a reading of her poems from a Creekcentric perspective alone is reductive and, therefore, inadequate.

Womack's discussion of Harjo's poetry becomes all the more questionable when dealing with the figure of Choffee (also known as Rabbit) – the Muskogee trickster. Every time Choffee is introduced in Harjo's poems, Womack notices, a discussion of love as a real force that holds the universe together follows close behind. The poet strives for a balance between chaos and order, following the Muskogean idea of the balance of opposites (*Red on Red* 239). While looking with a critical eye at Vizenor's idea of trickster, conceived as it is with a resistance to definition and with shape-shifting abilities (to use postmodern terminology), Womack nonetheless acknowledges the crucial notion of balance between oppositions as being for Choffee the key concept in Creek philosophy. Translating trickster's ideology into his own theoretical discourse, Womack strives for balance between Native American viewpoints and postmodernism, thus contradicting his previous assertions. He writes that contemporary theory should not be abandoned, only "examined critically as to its values in illuminating Native cultures" (242). Later on he claims: "The Muskogee world is not the opposite of the Western world, *it is a world that must be judged by its own merits, in its own terms. . . .* Native literatures deserve to be judged by their own criteria, in their own terms, not merely in agreement with, or reaction against, European literature and theory. The Native Americanist does not bury her head in the sand and pretend that European history and thought do not affect Native literature, nor does she ignore the fact that Native literature has quite distinctive features of its own that call for new forms of analyses [*sic*]" (242–43).

In the light of the literary separatism that Womack has advocated throughout *Red on Red*, such a position appears, indeed, contradictory. He claims that, as employed in Harjo's poetry, Choffee should help the Native Americanist decenter the assumption that things European are normative. He writes: "If one is already reacting against Eurocentrism, then Europe is still at the center" (242). What he does not notice, however, is that his own position is not that far from this reactionary mode, a mode that keeps one eye always on Europe. "Harjo's poetry is deeply Muskogean," Womack concludes, and its Creekness, he argues, is the cornerstone on which she builds her pan-tribalism. Creekness and pan-tribalism legitimate, for Womack, a Native American literary separatism that categorically excludes any possibility of encounter at the cultural crossroads.

Equally problematic is Womack's discussion of the Cherokee writer R. Lynn Riggs and his reading of what many consider to be Riggs's most important play, *The Cherokee Night*. Explaining why a study devoted to Creeks has expanded to include a Cherokee writer, Womack presents two main reasons: first, Riggs's homosexuality provides the context for a discussion of issues of sexual orientation, issues that a pragmatic Native theory cannot ignore; second, Riggs's theories regarding Oklahoma, what Womack calls "a Queer Oklahomo Indian theory" (*Red on Red* 273), relate perfectly to the situation of Native American studies and to the nationalistic literary approach developed throughout *Red on Red*.

According to Womack, while Riggs was in Paris, studying European theater on a Guggenheim fellowship, he formulated a theory of Oklahoma and Oklahomans as well. Responding (in a letter to a friend) to a review of his plays, Riggs explained this theory: [18]

And I know that what makes them [Oklahomans] a little special, a little distinct in the Middle West is the quality of their taciturnity. They are voiceless, tongueless; they answer the challenge "Who goes there?" only by a flash of a lantern so quick, so momentary, that none but the acute guard sees more than a shadowy figure retreating into the darkness. There are two reasons for this: one – faulty education (or none at all); the other, the people who settled in Oklahoma were a suspect fraternity, as fearful of being recognized by others as they were by themselves. Gamblers, traders . . . [m]en disdainful of the settled, the admired, the regular ways of life. Men on the move. Men fleeing from a critical world and their own eyes. . . . And so they don't speak. Speech reveals one. It is better to say nothing. (qtd. in *Red on Red* 274)

This theory reflects, in Womack's view, the internal terrain of a "closeted gay man" (275), a sexual frontier that in the 1930s could be rendered only in a "state of silence, of hanging out in secret places, of fear of being found out as well as fear of self-recognition" (275). In an attempt to give voice to these voiceless, oppressed Okies, Riggs is significantly searching for his own voice. Womack writes: "Riggs applies his own inner queer experience to Indians as a whole and gives up trying to talk about them" (279). Throughout his life, Womack continues, Riggs was allowed to examine his "queerness" only through "coded statement" (283) since the figure of the homosexual Indian did not fit the popular American stereotype of the brave warrior. Within this context, a play such as *The Cherokee Night*, with its portrayal of doomed Cherokees and its endorsement of the vanishing-culture mentality, reveals, Womack suggests, a further example of the "coded statement" (283) through which Riggs reflects his own suffering as a homosexual. By adopting the doom-and-gloom vanishing-culture mentality, Riggs presents his struggle with his homosexual identity and his struggle with his Indian identity at the same time.

An in-depth examination of Womack's reading of *The Cherokee Night* is beyond the scope of the present discussion. What is important to note, however, is that Womack relates queer concerns to Native American matters, particularly to the issue of identity, an analogy that he finds extremely useful in that it further substantiates his notion of a Native separatism. He writes: "Behind the use of the term [*queer*] is the argument that gay people are not the same as straight people, that a queer frame of reference causes one to see the world differently than a straight frame of reference does and that queerness, those things that make gays and lesbians unique, should be celebrated rather than assimilated" (*Red on Red* 300).

Womack's concern with such issues can, thus, be traced to his separatist approach, to the fact that Native American studies should, at least from his perspective, generate its own theory, exploring issues of identity and authenticity, developing aesthetic criteria that emphasize tribal viewpoints, and allowing Native people to explicate their own texts and cultures. He claims: "The term 'queer' works for me because it acknowledges the importance of cultural differences and the usefulness of maintaining those difference rather than simply submitting to dominant-culture norms. . . . Also, the thinking behind the term 'queer,' which seems to celebrate deviance rather than apologize for it, seems embodied with trickster's energy to push social bound-aries" (*Red on Red* 301). The queer experience and the Indian experience are both, Womack argues, conceived as marginal – at least from the viewpoint of the status quo, which always aims for assimilation, for the liberal "why can't we all just get along?" type of reasoning (300). The future of Native studies lies, for Womack, in challenging the status quo, in breaking down the hierar-chy of center and margin and claiming a space of its own. Native critics will in the future take a position that is closer to Choffee's, "leaping away with the very flames themselves, rather than [remaining] victims outside the campfire waiting for someone to invite them over for a little warming up" (303). Like Allen, Womack insists on a separatist approach, one that intends to build its own (theoretical) dwelling rather than dismantle the epistemological house of the master using the master's tools.

Clearly, Womack's overall critical stance is problematic in that, taken to its logical extreme, it results in a hierarchical reversal, moving the margin (the Indian) to the center and the center to the margin. Still, it is interesting that, at the end of *Red on Red*, Womack turns to queer theory to stabilize that stance. As critics have pointed out, the most conspicuous strain of queer the-ory draws heavily on the theories and methods of poststructuralism and de-construction. Viewed in this light, queer theory becomes "less a matter of explaining the repression or expression of a homosexual minority than an analysis of the hetero/homosexual figure as a power/knowledge regime that shapes the ordering of desires, behaviors, and social institutions, and social relations – in a word the constitution of the self and society" (Seidman 128). As an oppositional, resistant discourse, queer theory grounds its debunking of the notion of stable sexes, genders, and sexualities in a specifically lesbian and gay reworking of the poststructuralist notion of identity, identity con-ceived as a site of multiple and unstable positions.

Patrick Dilley writes:

Queer theory is a postmodern concept, an outgrowth of movements both political and personal. It seeks to invert the delineations and borders of our culture, the very concepts we use to create knowledge. Queer theorists attempt to show the structures and concepts created by those limits and borders, and how the people involved in creating the-ory affect and are affected by those concepts. They challenge – and sometimes reject – the notion of epistemological certainty, normal and abnormal, inclusion and exclusion, homosexual and heterosexual. And the questions, once posed and answered, must continue to be reexamined for, if nothing else, queer theory has taught us the inefficiency of language to convey so complex a notion as identity, especially an identity based on sexuality. (469)

While indicating the difficulty of defining exactly what queer theory is, of finding a boundary for a methodology that questions boundaries, Dilley's observations illustrate how queer theory's primary concern is with a notion of identity that is fluid, continuously evolving, in progress. This identity resembles the kind of identity embodied within Native American discourse by the trickster figure, an identity that, in Vizenor's terms, embraces contradictions and oppositions rather than retreating into separatism. In the light of these observations, Womack's use of queer theory to reinforce his notion of a Native American separatism is ironically contradictory. By dismissing the poststructuralist, Eurocentric matrix of queer discourse theory, by refusing to engage the hybridization and syncretism inherent in its very nature, Womack misses a very important point. More significantly, by looking at queer theory as an avenue to legitimate authentic definitions of Indianness, such as his Creek or Native perspective, he runs into the ultimate paradox since queer theory itself unfixes and destabilizes the very notion of identity.

At the end of the introduction to *Red on Red*, Womack writes: "Jim and Hotgun just clean didn't cotton to reading another dang work on *House Made of Dawn*, *Love Medicine*, *Ceremony*, *Winter in the Blood*, and *Darkness in Saint Louis Bearheart* . . . they just wanted to write something that was different and something that was fun" (21–22). Surely, I posit, Jim and Hotgun succeeded in their intent, and so did their author. They created a "different," even funny book, one that argues for a Native perspective, "untainted" by the "malaise" of Western philosophical thinking. Jim and Hotgun might not be aware, however, that, by celebrating an authentic Native difference, they ultimately end up perpetuating further versions of colonialism, colonialisms in which the Native is once again significantly Othered.

On an ideological level, Warrior's and Womack's positions regarding the nature and content of a Native American literary theory converge in significant ways. Both insist, for example, on authentic traditions of Indian intellectualism. Both argue for the necessity of creating discursive modes that mirror indigenous forms of thought. Both raise important issues concerning the responsibilities of intellectuals to their communities. Both provide interesting readings of the fiction of some of the most influential contemporary

Native American writers. And the list goes on. But, despite these similarities, Warrior's and Womack's theoretical approaches remain problematic insofar as they are intended to challenge the ideological assumptions of Western hermeneutics. Embracing literary separatism, and refusing to acknowledge their implication in the dominant discourse, Warrior and Womack end up, like Allen, perpetuating the discursive paradigms of Eurocentric thinking, thus further marginalizing Native American literature and theory, consigning it to the role of the Other of the Euramerican consciousness.

> . . . an appreciation for the boundless capacity of language
> that, through storytelling, brings us together, despite
> great distances between cultures, despite great distances
> in time.
>
> Leslie Silko

3

Crossreading Texts, Bridging Cultures
The Dialogic Approach of Greg Sarris and Louis Owens

In his pivotal work on the poetics of Native American oral traditions, Dell
Hymes reinterprets a Chinook story that he first analyzed in 1968. In this
story, a girl is trying to tell her mother unsettling but crucial news that will affect them both, but, intent on maintaining the status quo, the mother stub-
bornly refuses to listen. In the event, her daughter can only argue, "In vain I
tried to tell you."[1] As he reflects on his methodology, on his successes and
failures in using anthropological philology and structural linguistics in the attempt to restore voice to oral texts that have been little more than museum
specimens, Hymes writes: "If we refuse to consider and interpret the sur-
prising facts of device, design, and performance inherent in the words of the
texts, the Indians who made the texts, and those who preserved what they
made, will have worked in vain. We will be telling the texts not to speak. We
will mistake, perhaps, to our costs, the nature of the power of which they
speak" (*"In Vain I Tried to Tell You"* 5-6). While coming from the specific
field of ethnopoetics, Hymes's observations "speak" perfectly well to the
subject of this chapter: crossreading and crosscultural communication as
ways of opening up rather than closing down ideas in language. As critics involved in reading texts originating in differing epistemologies, in the narratives of Native American oral traditions, we might, Hymes suggests, listen
carefully to what these narratives have to say even when they are heavily hybridized, affected by contact with Western discursive paradigms; we might
consider both our and their different viewpoints and ultimately learn to see
things in new ways. As readers and critics of Native American literature, our

primary responsibility is to make sure that these texts will "tell" us something and that they will not speak "in vain."

In *Keeping Slug Woman Alive* (1993) and *Mixedblood Messages* (1998), respectively, Greg Sarris (Pomo-Jewish) and Louis Owens (Choctaw-Cherokee and Irish) explore the ways in which people read across cultures and what the aims and consequences of these readings can and should be. Crucial to both critics' work is the idea of dialogue within and between people in order to expose boundaries that shape and constitute different cultural and personal worlds. Elaborating on Bakhtin's formulations, Sarris and Owens apply concepts such as *dialogism* and *heteroglossia* to the idea of reading across lines of cultural identity, overcoming rigid binary oppositions between Western and Native perspectives and constructing a criticism that challenges old ways of theorizing. Unlike Allen, Warrior, and Womack, who argue for a "tribalcentric" approach to a Native theoretical discourse, Sarris and Owens argue for a hybridized, multidirectional, and multigeneric discursive mode, one that encompasses their mixedblood identity and, ultimately and subversively, redefines the boundaries of Euramerican discourse.[2] Unlike Allen, Warrior, and Womack, who take a Nativist stance, Sarris and Owens do not aim to recover authentic Indian traditions or to speak exclusively from or within a Native or tribal perspective. While acknowledging that, in the light of their strategic location within the mainstream academy, for them to be taking a "Native perspective" is problematic, if not downright impossible, they conceive of writing within and out of the metropolitan center as a powerful subversive tool, a tricksterish subversion of the authoritative discourse of Euramerica, through which Native Americans can survive as indigenous people and living human beings. In ways similar to those elaborated in the oral traditions of tribal cultures, in which words and narratives have the power to create and to heal, Sarris and Owens turn to language as the most powerful tool with which to ensure the life and vitality of Native writing and identity in opposition to the stasis and entrapments created by the stereotypes and clichés of the Euramerican imagination. As critics deeply committed to a discourse on hybridity and dialogism, Sarris and Owens explore new creative avenues in a language that will allow Native people to reimagine themselves.

In *Keeping Slug Woman Alive*, storytelling and theorizing overlap, thus creating a discourse that resembles a "kind of story" (131). Similarly, in *Mixedblood Messages*, autobiography, critical theory, film commentary, and environmental reflections are blended in order to come to terms with a mixed heritage while suggesting a different way in which Native American scholars can enter the theoretical debate in the Western academy. Both critics seem to embrace Trinh Minh-ha's notion of multilayered identity, summed up in the statement: "I/i can be I or i, you and me both involved. We . . . sometimes include(s), other times exclude(s) me. . . . [Y]ou may stand on the other side of the hill once in a while, but you may also be me, while remaining what you are and what i am not" (*Woman, Native, Other* 90). Both also seem to embrace her idea that theory can, indeed, be "a form of creativity," a way in which to convey this fluid notion of identity and to resist "closure and classifications" ("The Undone Interval" 4, 9).

In examining Sarris's and Owens's dialogic strategies, I will point out the characteristics that make Native American theory different from other contemporary theoretical discourses while also demonstrating the crucial ways in which this same theory is in dialogue with, relies on, and subsumes Western discursive modes. Whereas Sarris's storytelling approach embraces the discourse of contemporary social scientists and reader-response critics, Owens engages in a conversation with discourse analysis and postcolonial theory, attempting to come to terms with concepts such as "contact zones" and a "frontier" space for Native American writing. In addition, as my discussion of *Mixedblood Messages* will indicate, Owens's reflections in the recent "As If an Indian Were Really an Indian" provide interesting avenues through which to illustrate the condition of mixedblood authors as diasporic, a condition that, ironically, resembles the character of the trickster figure in Native American oral traditions. Like tricksters, Owens argues, mixedblood authors who write out of a consciousness of a hybrid cultural inheritance are in an unstable position, one from which "it is difficult and undoubtedly erroneous to assume any kind of essential stance or strategy" ("As If an Indian" 208). Shuttling back and forth between worlds and worldviews, mixedblood authors disrupt and unsettle while bridging distances between cultures and experiencing every conceptual encounter as a crosscultural one.

The eight essays that constitute *Keeping Slug Woman Alive* cover a range of topics related to American Indian studies, including orality, art, criticism, and pedagogy. These topics, arranged in four major sections, are explicated within a storytelling technique that appears on nearly every page as part of Sarris's strategy to revitalize discussion about crosscultural studies.[3] The narrative structure of the prologue, entitled "Peeling Potatoes," is our initial introduction to this process of defining and telling. A mixedblood author now teaching at UCLA, Sarris reflects on the differences between his encounters with his Indian aunts and his encounters with his Euramerican students

as well as on the differences between his several heritages: Kashaya Pomo,
Coast Miwok, and Filipino on his father's side, Jewish, German, and Irish on
his mother's.[4] Having been adopted by George and Mary Sarris, Sarris was
allowed by Mary to live with different families on farms and ranches around
Santa Rosa, California, when George became abusive. Mostly, however, he
lived with Mabel McKay, a Cache Creek–Pomo Indian basket weaver and
medicine woman. He writes: "Mabel McKay was one of the people who took
me in, and from her I learned what is most important to me today" (11). *Keeping Slug Woman Alive* grew out of Sarris's interest in McKay's life stories, and,
in the long run, the book became a statement on how we should interpret and
communicate narratives. As a reader, scholar, writer, and teacher, Sarris's
purpose is always to consider the effect that a certain narrative has on his life,
to find out how that narrative has affected his life. For example: "The written text becomes the story of my hearing her [McKay's] stories" (4).[5]

As the prologue begins, Sarris, along with several Pomo women, peels
potatoes in McKay's kitchen and listens to the beginning of her story about
an "old medicine man . . . who followed her around" (1). The story does not
proceed chronologically, a narrative strategy that, in his anxiety to get to the
end and discover the meaning, Sarris finds unsettling. Nevertheless, he
learns an important lesson: "Mabel once said: Don't ask what it means, the
story. Life will teach you about it, the way it teaches you about life" (5). He
realizes that it is important to remember his life, presence, and history as he
attempts to understand Mabel. The text, thus, becomes a kind of dialogue
that opens and explores interpersonal and intercultural territories. Within
this context, the potato-peeling episode becomes a metaphor for the significance of listening to different voices during crosscultural encounters. Looking at the peeled potatoes, Sarris realizes that "things are not always what
they seem" (3). Whereas he values only the end product, the peeled potatoes,
the women in the kitchen value both the end product and the process (the act
of peeling); unlike Sarris, they are not wasteful. As simple as this lesson is,
it provokes and informs the entire argument of *Keeping Slug Woman Alive*.
He asks: "How do people read across cultures? What are the aims and consequences of their readings? How are their readings located in a certain history, say that of American Indian and Euro-American interrelations? Is there
a way that people can read across cultures so that intercultural communication is opened rather than closed, so that people see more than just what
things seem to be?" (3).

Keeping Slug Woman Alive represents an attempt to answer these questions. Following the lead of McKay's nonchronological storytelling tech-

nique, the prologue takes off in all sorts of directions, resembling the spider-web motif of Pueblo expression celebrated by Leslie Silko and other con-temporary Native American novelists. As Silko writes: "I have intentionally not written a formal paper because I want you to *hear* and to experience En-glish in a structure that follows patterns from the oral tradition. For those of you accustomed to being taken from point A to point B to point C, this pre-sentation may be somewhat difficult to follow. Pueblo expression resembles something like a spider's web – with many little threads radiating from the center, crisscrossing one another. As with the web, the structure emerges as it is made, and you must simply listen and trust, as the Pueblo people do, that meaning will be made" ("Language and Literature" 48–49). Unlike a West-ern articulation of philosophy that depends on linear, sequential reasoning, crucial within the Native worldview (a worldview common, I would suggest, to most tribal people in North America, despite cultural and historical di-versity) is the notion of interconnectedness leading toward a holistic con-ception of the universe. Such a view makes the Western idea of cataloging and dissecting chunks of information almost meaningless. Envisioned as an ongoing story, the web becomes, Silko suggests, an organic whole that hu-man beings inhabit, their words, thoughts, and actions inextricably tied to-gether. In a rhetorical context this means that there are an infinite number of connections between the speaker and the listener since both are participants in the same story (web). In the context of a Native American discourse whose main goal is to articulate a critical voice deeply grounded in an indigenous rhetoric, Sarris's storytelling strategy becomes a feasible technique through which to convey a Native epistemology not traditionally articulated in con-ventional academic discourse.

Storytelling as a living, expressive form has often been adopted by Third World theorists. Trinh, for example, examines processes of cultural hy-bridization, multiple identities, and languages of rupture. Elaborating on Silko's formulations, she envisions storytelling as a powerful tool with which to disrupt the binary opposition of subject/object – or, as she puts it, "I/It; We/They" – so treasured in Western thinking. She writes: "S/he who speaks, speaks *to* the tale as s/he begins telling and retelling it. S/he does not speak *about* it. For, without a certain work of displacement, 'speaking about' only partakes in the conservation of systems of binary opposition . . . on which territorialized knowledge depends. It places a semantic distance be-tween oneself and the work; oneself (the maker) and the receiver; oneself and the other. It secures for the speaker a position of mastery . . . while the 'other' remains in the sphere of acquisition" (*When the Moon Waxes Red* 12). The notion of "speaking to the tale" rather than "about it" is crucial to Sarris's concept of intercultural communication. Anyone who attempts to reconstruct someone else's life story should, Sarris suggests, follow an integrative approach that collapses artificial subject/object and genre barriers while paying special attention to "who is telling the story and who is listening and the specific circumstances of the exchange" (4). Sarris's reflections here lead him to discuss the contested notion of subjectivity.

Interwoven within the narrative structure of the prologue of *Keeping Slug Woman Alive* are references to literary and social-scientific discourse. Sarris draws extensively from such theorists as David Bleich and Stanley Fish, who have engaged the issue of readers' responses to texts, as well as from such social scientists as Stephen Tyler, Renato Rosaldo, George E. Marcus, Michael M. J. Fisher, and James Clifford, who, according to Sarris, have described "a way of writing crosscultural experience where all facets of the encounter are revealed for the reader" (5). While recognizing the significant challenge that these scholars pose to traditional methodologies, a challenge that is particularly evident in the efforts of social scientists to employ multiple voices and narrative forms, Sarris also bridges these two fields of study, overcoming some of their limitations. For example, critics have pointed out that, despite its claimed opposition to formalist criticism, reader-response criticism still looks at the text as a self-contained object, having simply transferred the "locus of meaning from the text to the reader" (Tompkins 206), and still understands the reader's response conventionally, as a way of arriving at meaning, not as a form of political and moral behavior.[6] Following this lead, Sarris finds criticism to be a metadiscourse that works "to distance itself from the text and subjects it studies" (6). On the other hand, contemporary social science calls for reflexivity and demands that interlocutors be aware of their boundaries, both personal and cultural, so that they might know the limits of and possibilities for understanding one another in the exchange. Rosaldo, for example, argues that "social analysis must now grapple with the realization that its objects of analysis are also analyzing subjects who critically interrogate ethnographers – their writing, their ethics, and their politics" (21). Exposing the inadequacies of old conceptions of static, monolithic cultures, he calls for social science to acknowledge and celebrate diversity, narrative emotion, and the unavoidability of subjectivity. In a similar vein, Sarris invokes polyvocality and diverse forms of narrative that significantly defy genre boundaries and Western forms of discourse. He breaks down the distinction between personal narrative and scholarly argument, showing that texts are living entities, a myriad of voices that, in the case of *Keeping Slug*

Woman Alive, interweave with his own voice, the stories that he discusses thereby becoming his stories and, ultimately, his readers'.

Keeping Slug Woman Alive thus seems to represent the kind of critical discourse advocated by Krupat in *Ethnocriticism* – one located at various frontier points where "oppositional sets like West/Rest, Us/Them, anthropological/biological, historical/mythical, and so on, often tend to break down" (15). The critic who operates in this in-between space becomes, in Krupat's words, a "border intellectual" (124), engaged more in recognizing, accommodating, and mediating differences than in assuming the authoritative role of the traditional Western critic. Envisioning himself on the border of various discourses, Sarris describes his own "ethnocritic/border" position: "The book should not be taken simply as an insider's records of things 'Indian.' I am not privileging an Indian's point of view regarding the texts and topics considered. I am not interested in pitting Indians against non-Indians, insiders against outsiders, or in showing that any one group of people is necessarily privileged or better or worse than another. Instead, these essays try to show that all of us can and should talk to one another, that each group can inform and be informed by the other" (7). What distinguishes his method from Krupat's, however, is his privileging of the voice and thus of the telling of the story. Whereas Krupat's ethnocritical discourse runs the risk of erasing the Indian's voice, becoming just one more version of ethnocentric criticism,[7] Sarris's continual questioning of the reader's interpretative strategies aims at preserving that voice, at opening a dialogue with the text, telling further stories that, in turn, inform other readers' stories. In the attempt to preserve the text's *voice*, Sarris suggests, critics are forced to engage a text on its own terms rather than on theirs. Whether writing down McKay's stories or discussing literary texts, Sarris is always careful not to close discussion with the texts, not to silence their stories. By adopting a "performative" mode of expression along with an expository one, he hopes to convey the same kind of interaction between performer and audience that we find in traditional storytelling.[8]

To a certain degree, Sarris attempts to do in his criticism what Native American writers have been attempting to do in their fiction. Novels written by American Indian authors in the past decades represent, as Owens points out, "an attempt to recover identity and authenticity by invoking and incorporating the world found within the oral tradition – the reality of myth and ceremony – an authorless 'original literature'" (*Other Destinies* 11). By appropriating what is an essentially "other" language and entering into dialogue with that language itself, Native American novelists produce what

James Ruppert calls a "mediative" strategy, that of moving "from one cultural tradition to another as well as connecting the locutor to the listener" (9). The most significant result of such an approach is an invitation to readers to expand their own conceptual horizons by considering alternate epistemologies. As in the storytelling process, readers are called on to create their own meaning, and, in the process, they are reeducated, encouraged to embrace different traditions of discourse.

Following the narration and theoretical discussion of significant cultural, familial, and personal contexts, the prologue returns to the potatoes episode and to McKay's story of the man who followed her around. As Kenneth Roemer notes: "By now, the readers understand that the story 'means' that we should pay attention to voices that open up crosscultural dialogues" ("Indian Lives" 86). However, we soon realize that McKay's medicine-man story does not end in this section. According to Roemer, "The final telling is not final" (86). Rather, it is an introduction to other stories, to the endless spiderweb structure that characterizes traditional storytelling as well as *Keeping Slug Woman Alive*.

The only surviving member of the Long Valley Cache Creek Pomo tribe and the last of the Bole Maru Dreamers, Mabel McKay has for years been considered a source of valuable information by anthropologists, linguists, and people in general who want to know about her shamanism and dream world.[9] Until recently, Sarris notes, she traveled regularly, giving interviews, demonstrating Pomo basket-making techniques, and telling stories about her culture, always insisting, "It is important for people to know" (18). Yet, Sarris adds, "her responses to questions are maddening" (17) and force interlocutors to examine presuppositions that shape and are embedded in their questions. Examining the various speech categories that McKay uses in conversation – responses to questions, gossip, idle chitchat, and stories, all characterized as *talk* – Sarris points out the performative aspect of McKay's verbal art: it is aimed at exposing the chasms between the two interpretative worlds that the discourse must bridge. In his attempt to present "Mabel" as she presents herself to him, Sarris incorporates McKay's strategy into his own critical approach. In the essay in *Keeping Slug Woman Alive* entitled "The Verbal Art of Mabel McKay: Talk as Culture Contact and Cultural Critique," he provides an example of "textualized dialogue" by reporting a dialogue-cum-story, the result of an exchange with McKay. The story of "the man who poisoned the beautiful woman doctor," which McKay told Sarris as he was trying to solicit answers to questions raised by one of his Stanford professors, makes him realize that, in the study of American Indian cultures, as in the study of other cultures in general, we should always expose and interrupt our interpretative patterns, consider their limitations and inability to frame the whole truth – that we should, in other words, make ourselves vulnerable.

Sarris himself realizes this process as he writes "The Verbal Art of Mabel McKay," an essay that interrupts and disrupts while opening a conversation with the reader's life. The story of "the man who poisoned the beautiful woman doctor" does not end with the end of the particular exchange in which it is introduced. Later in the essay, Sarris reports another conversation with McKay, one that took place during a visit to the various places in which the story is set. During the drive, McKay resumes the story, which opens out to encompass a broader, historical context and even Sarris's personal life: "'Yes, them days was hard time. Killing. Raping time, how they [Europeans] done with the women. Starvation. People moving. . . . You know about people moving around, different people.' I took these last words as a direct statement about my life, about my living in different homes as I was growing up. In that way I had a small sense, on a personal level, of the displacement our ancestors experienced" (29–30). Sarris realizes that he cannot reconstruct McKay's story independent of his own experience with it. In this sense, McKay's talk initiates "a kind of internal dialogue where the interlocutors examine the nature of their own thinking" (30), a process that allows the dialogue to continue in new stories and conversations. In "The Verbal Art of Mabel McKay" Sarris's central concern is to demonstrate that McKay is not simply an informant reporting on the past and that he is not simply a "textualizer" or a "fieldworker" recording her words.[10] For Mabel McKay and her interlocutors, Sarris writes, "Talk itself initiates and sets the groundwork for collaboration. It is an art generating respect for the unknown while illuminating the borders of the known" (33).[11]

Sarris's unique, privileged position as cultural mediator, as well as his direct familiarity with the world of Mabel McKay, has prompted meaningful critiques. Gail Reitenbach, for example, observes: "One need not be Indian to undertake such criticism of Indian materials. . . . Nevertheless, it is hard to imagine a non-Indian critic or teacher experiencing the kind of mutual exchange with Indian cultural phenomena that Sarris enjoys, even though he challenges both Indian and non-Indian readers to question their critical practice constantly" (409). Along the same lines, Roemer writes: "Someone with . . . a less 'appropriate' life might make a (pretentious or forced) botch of Sarris's approach" ("Indian Lives" 86). Implicit in these observations is a reference to the complex and puzzling question of Indian identity, a question that has given rise to perhaps the most essentialist forms of discourse on Native American literature and that still dominates the current critical debate. To argue that Sarris's "Indianness" (or "mixedbloodedness," to be precise) allows him privileged access to the material that he presents is to miss the main point of his overall critical endeavor. Despite Roemer's and (to a lesser degree) Reitenbach's insights into the storytelling technique of *Keeping Slug Woman Alive*, their commentary suggests how difficult it is, for both Native and non-Native critics, to avoid the overarching question of authenticity whenever Native American texts are concerned. To such observations, Sarris replies: "In my case, familiarity with the landscape and certain people cannot presume an understanding of the landscape and people, at least not in Mabel's terms. While I might know some things, and continue to learn, the dynamic of the talk remains the same" (31–32). Sarris's strategy, in other words, works for him (a mixedblood operating at the border of various discourses) as it works for other readers, people of differing cultural backgrounds who want to broaden their conceptual horizons to include an understanding of other cultures. The fact that Sarris is part Indian does not make his reading more comprehensible or authoritative; quite the contrary, it raises still more questions concerning his position as an Indian academic reading Native American literary texts.

The essay entitled "The Woman Who Loved a Snake" provides further commentary on this insider/outsider issue. Sarris opens the essay with a personal anecdote that in turn opens to other forms of discourse. He tells us how one day he took his friend Jenny to meet Mabel McKay.[12] A Ph.D. candidate at Stanford University, Jenny is a student of British literature who is working on a dissertation on Shakespeare. McKay tells Sarris and Jenny a story about a woman who fell in love with a snake, a story without a "definite" ending. At the conclusion of the story, Sarris reports, Jenny asks, "What did the snake represent?" Sarris continues: "Jenny's response to the story, that is, her question, prompted in turn a response from Mabel that exposed what was different about their respective worldviews regarding the story. For Jenny the snake was symbolic of something and, in that sense, supernatural. For Mabel the snake/man was part of one coexistent reality, a reality that is located in historic time and subject to its strictures" (37). A few weeks later, Jenny tells Sarris how she had been thinking about McKay's story, how she had wanted to write it but also how the "story wouldn't stay put"; more important, she had been thinking that "there is so much more than just the story and what was said that *is* the story" (37). Jenny's response to the story, that of a (Western) analytically trained mind, a mind used to recording, gathering, sorting, and analyzing, was to attempt to impose a structure on it, *her* structure.

Interestingly enough, Jenny's approach to the story brings to it the same "anthropological creed" that Trinh discusses in *Woman, Native, Other*: "But it is particularly difficult for a dualistic or dualistically trained mind to recognize that 'looking for the structure of their narratives' already involves the separation of the structure from the narratives, of the structure from that which is structured, of the narrative from the narrated, and so on. It is, once more, as if form and content stand apart; as if the structure can remain fixed, immutable, independent of and unaffected by the changes the narratives undergo; as if a structure can only function as a standard mold within the old determinist schema of cause and product" (141).[13] In Trinh's formulation, Jenny's notion of reality, meticulously cultivated within Western universities, prevents her from perceiving the story as a living thing, an organic process, a way of life. In her attempt to impose a structure on the story, Jenny fails to acknowledge that what are taken for stories are, in Trinh's words, "fragments of/in life, fragments that never stop interacting while being complete in themselves" (143). Quoting Silko's *Ceremony*, Trinh writes: "[They see no life] / When they look / they see only objects" (140).

Many times in my work with Native American literary texts I have found myself asking the same kinds of questions that Jenny asked. Like Jenny's, my notion of reality is deeply embedded within an analytic mind-set, one used to dissect, to categorize, to fix. And, just as Jenny's literate instincts tell her, mine tell me that, if I can just write down the text, I can determine its meaning. However, unlike Jenny's experience with the oral tradition, mine has never been immediate, face-to-face with a storyteller; it has, instead, been intermediate, mediated by written texts, texts, moreover, that, despite a heavy reliance on the oral tradition, are still modeled after traditional Western genres.

My first approach to Leslie Marmon Silko's *Ceremony* raised the same kinds of problems that Jenny faced while listening to McKay's stories. Like Jenny, I tried to impose Western analytic thought processes on Silko's narrative, wondering about the meaning of specific events and characters as they appear in the poems/stories – the form taken by the oral material incorporated in the novel. As a Western reader, I took very lightly the words of the second framing "poem" of the novel, in which the reader is told that "stories aren't just entertainment" (2), and thus read the mythic material framing the main story (Tayo's story) as a metaphor for everyday reality. Whereas Jenny saw the snake in McKay's story as symbolic, I saw Thought Woman, the spider, and the other mythic figures in *Ceremony* simply as supernatural beings intended to lend an exotic touch to the narrative.

In my naive approach to *Ceremony* I underestimated the different epistemological orientation out of which the narrative originates, an orientation that, I now know, must be carefully accounted for through the exercise of a strategy that Owens calls *crosscultural reading*. In other words, I have learned that signs and semiotic systems are not necessarily universal, that things need not necessarily "mean" something. Over the years, I have become more and more conscious of the level of complexity that Silko's novel (as well as many other novels written by Native American authors) presents. Having become a more sophisticated reader, and having expended considerable effort to learn something about Pueblo mythology and culture, I have come to understand the novel's extraordinary capacity to question readers' ideological and epistemological boundaries while making them embrace new ones. I have finally come to understand what Carol Mitchell means when she says, "Silko's novel is itself a curing ceremony" (28). I can now identify with the confusion and the sense of alienation that Jenny's questions revealed, and I can understand why and where those questions originated. Yet more intriguing still is Sarris's use of Jenny's experience to illustrate his own response to the story, a rhetorical strategy perfectly designed to convey the idea of how stories and life merge, the idea of stories as living things.

Jenny's response reminds Sarris of the unspoken context of the story of the woman who fell in love with a snake – McKay's and Jenny's different world-views. Sarris writes: "[This] is a story not only about the woman in the story but about Jenny and, as I will show in this essay, about me" (38). Despite his mixed heritage and his familiarity with the world of McKay's stories, Sarris is in a position that is not that different from Jenny's. As a scholar, he too is "exposed" (38) and made vulnerable by his own understanding or lack thereof. He realizes that McKay's undermining of straightforward answers makes the oral exchange possible while continuing the life of the story.

Woven within the life of the snake-lover story is another story that McKay tells Sarris during one of their many road trips to Pomo villages. In front of Elem Rancheria, the old village site and present-day reservation of the Elem tribe of the Pomo Indians, on the south side of Clear Lake, McKay tells a story about "what the people of Elem saw" (45), a story about first contact between Natives and non-Natives, but also a story about dream, prophecy, McKay's grandmother, and McKay's life. McKay's story reminds Sarris of other stories and experiences while leading him to reflect on the nature of the oral exchange. As an interlocutor, Sarris is confronted with his prejudices and points of view and is made vulnerable by his limited understanding of McKay's world. Ironically, he finds himself in a position similar to that in which Jenny finds herself with regard to the snake-lover story. The world of the story "What the People of Elem Saw" is, however, largely alien to him; like Jenny, he finds himself at the margins.

Borrowing the concept *culture contact* from the anthropologist Gregory Bateson, Sarris claims that each story is to a certain extent a contact narrative, a dynamic dialogue that opens the territory of orality while engaging listener and teller in a mutual learning process.[14] McKay's words neatly summarize the point: "Remember that when you hear and tell my stories there is more to me and you and that *is* the story. You don't know everything about me and I don't know everything about you. Our knowing is limited. Let our words show us as much so we can learn together about one another. Let us tell stories that help us in this. Let us keep learning" (46). Responding to Jenny's question as to how he writes McKay's stories (46), Sarris presents an essay such as "The Woman Who Loved a Snake" (as well as the rest of *Keeping Slug Woman Alive*) as a model for writing what "Mabel says." McKay's narrative practice counters literate tendencies that would close the oral context in which communication takes place. While acknowledging that McKay's strategy is not the only way to "break open that immense oral territory" and that there is, moreover, no guarantee that "the territory will be opened" (47) – most, of course, depends on the interlocutor – Sarris nonetheless poses interesting questions, questions that have arisen out of his interaction with McKay. As he puts it, "Mabel's talk, which is oral, provides an opportunity to explore the territory for individuals who may in some ways share her territory, such as myself, and for those who do not, such as Jenny. The territory, after all, is not empty, unpeopled" (47). McKay's observations concerning the mutual exchange taking place in the oral context lead Sarris to further discuss the issue of crosscultural communication, this time in the context of revealing tribal knowledge to outsiders.

The Native American writer, who operates at the frontier site of various discourses, in a borderland zone in which identities are conceived as multiple, shifting, and fluid, is often uncomfortable with issues of allegiance. How does one balance academic life and community life, and how does the overall issue of "secrecy" affect this balance? In a consideration of the risks involved when moving from the sacred world of ritual and myth to the secular world of the novel, Owens discusses the issue of the "desacralization" of traditional material. He claims: "Ironically, for the novelist writing with a consciousness of responsibility as a member of a living Native American culture, this irreversible metamorphosis from oral, communal literature to the written commodity of published work may be an essential objectification" (*Other Destinies* 11). This transformation, Owens adds, can, indeed, be problematic, as Paula Gunn Allen has indicated, threatening in the long run to trap Native American writers in the slippery terrain of identity and authenticity.[15] Would a Native American author who deliberately incorporates material from the oral tradition into Western European forms be suddenly less authentically "Indian"? Is contemporary Native American novelists' use of tribal material in their fiction an act of exploitation, or is it rather a significant step toward an affirmation of a syncretic, adaptive, and dynamic identity, a reflection of the dynamic nature of the oral tradition itself?

The essay entitled "Telling Dreams and Keeping Secrets" is Sarris's attempt to come to terms with some of the issues discussed above, particularly that of the "desacralization" of traditional material. The essay begins with a personal anecdote: having been invited to speak at Stanford University on the occasion of a screening of the ethnographic documentary *The Sucking Doctor* and to bring members of his family with him to take part in a discussion of the film, Sarris and some family members are debating whether to take the trip. The documentary – which, according to Sarris, "covers the second night of a Kashaya Pomo healing ceremony" – shows a portion of the ceremony in which Essie Parrish, a leader of the Bole Maru religion, "sucks a pain out of her patient's body" (63). Sarris then shifts from matters personal to matters academic in order to evaluate some crucial questions: "In creating narratives for others about our histories and religions, in what ways are we not only compromising those histories and religions but at the same time compromising our identities, which are largely dependent upon these, as well as our resistance to the colonizer and dominant culture? How might my particular discussion of the Bole Maru from an insider's perspective be appropriated by outsiders for their purposes, political or otherwise?" (68).

For Sarris, discussing issues related to the Kashaya healing ceremony, as well as to the Bole Maru religion, becomes a way of meditating on and mediating among his various heritages; ultimately, it becomes a way of reinforcing the concept of crosscultural communication that he has been pursuing all along. As a critic belonging to what Rosaldo terms "multiple, overlapping communities" (194), Sarris realizes that his writing and speaking about the Bole Maru religion cannot help but be an act of mediation among different discourses. By acknowledging that his affiliation with the Kashaya Pomo religion is through Mabel McKay, Sarris is aware that he is not ideally positioned to be the "Native informant" since he risks compromising family members. He writes: "The position of having multiple identities at once as a result of belonging to multiple, overlapping communities may underscore the potential for new and inventive projects, but a borderland position often is not an easy or comfortable one to be in, nor does it guarantee a project or report agreeable and intelligible to all of the communities involved. I must think about the many communities where I live and work, and I must remember my allegiance to my Indian community" (69–70).

As a way of resolving this dilemma, Sarris argues that the academic life and the Indian community need not necessarily be in conflict. Academic discourse can be interrogated and integrated with other forms of discourse, collapsing what is essentially an arbitrary distinction between the academic and the nonacademic. More significantly, as a result of this integration, both groups – in this case, the Kashaya Pomo and the non–Kashaya Pomo – can arrive at some form of crosscultural communication.

Sarris's position here would seem to respond to Owens's observations on desacralization in contemporary Native American fiction. Rather than conceiving of the oral tradition as a static cultural artifact, one that, when "translated" into writing, loses authenticity, Native American fiction writers clearly illustrate, Owens suggests, ways in which such a tradition can be significantly reimagined and reinvented (see *Other Destinies* 12). The Bole Maru documentary functions, to a certain extent, like the fiction discussed by Owens insofar as it becomes a way in which to open communication and provide alternative views on Kashaya Pomo identity. Instead of looking at the Bole Maru religion merely as a cultural artifact, a remnant of the past, Sarris considers how the practice is changing and, more important, how it affects the Kashaya people today.

Sarris's essay concludes with a narrative account of the encounter between him and his family and the Stanford academic community. A student's response to *The Sucking Doctor* clearly sums up the point of the entire essay: "Well, that's what I have been bothered about all quarter. . . . We read all this American Indian literature, the folklore and everything, and I don't know what I am reading. I don't know anything about the Indians. I was hoping to know something after today. Like where to start" (74). Sarris relates how one of his family members, Anita, "jumps in" and, responding to the student, asks her, "Do you know who you are? Why are you interested? Ask yourself that" (74). Considered in the light of Sarris's overall argument, these questions cut to the heart of the matter under analysis here: Why do we "read" other cultures? What do we see when we do, and why are we interested? What are we looking for? Is it the exotic Other, what Trinh calls "the voice of difference likely to bring us what *we can't have* and to divert us from the monotony of sameness" (*Woman, Native, Other* 88)? Or is it, rather, a genuine attempt to share knowledge of who we are as human beings?

Coming from a writer working at the intersection of multiple identities and multiple discourses, Trinh's reflections fit well the question raised by Sarris. She writes: "Eager not to disappoint, i try my best to offer my benefactors and benefactresses what they most anxiously yearn for: the possibility of a difference, yet a difference or an otherness that will not go so far as to question the foundation of their beings and makings" (*Woman, Native, Other* 88). Ironically, however, Trinh's strategy does question the foundations of "our" beings and makings. In her ongoing attempt to dismantle monolithic notions of identity and authenticity, Trinh envisions a complex identity that is constituted by "infinite layers" (90), one in which the static essence of the "*Not-I*" is constantly fleeing. Similarly, Sarris's family members challenge the students' expectations about Indians and pose significant questions concerning the possibility of looking at other cultures in ways that foster crosscultural communication rather than perpetuating an us/them universe. Sarris writes: "I had brilliant answers to my questions about this trip. The Bole Maru had become in this instance at Stanford an interrogative text. It was a historic move; from a secret cult to one that facilitated crosscultural discourse about itself and other cultures and doctrines, the Bole Maru had again been reinvented, modified in a given historical context. . . . The Bole Maru was providing all of us a way to talk, to survive together, to understand. The dialogue it prompted exposed our differences and similarities, the bridges we had to cross in reading and knowing one another" (75–76). Like McKay's Pomo baskets, the Bole Maru documentary moves beyond the ethnographic and the anthropological. What would normally be considered a museum piece – a film documenting a healing ceremony – becomes a powerful tool with which to generate questions, and open a dialogue, and make people really think about their own lives.[16]

Later in *Keeping Slug Woman Alive*, Sarris turns his attention to the literary experience. Reading *Autobiographies of Three Pomo Women*, edited by the anthropologist Elizabeth Colson, as well as Louise Erdrich's novel *Love Medicine*, he readdresses the questions raised in earlier essays: How is his approach determined by his borderland experience, and what kind of dialogue can be opened? Sarris's reading of these texts becomes a crosscultural project, an attempt to understand how their narratives become a story, first, for him and, ultimately, for all potential readers.

As he begins reading *Autobiographies*, Sarris is caught in the middle of the insider/outsider debate: "My impulse as a critic was to say what was truly Pomo, so that I could show what Colson missed, how ignorant she was as an outsider to Pomo culture. But who am I to speak for and define the central

Pomo or any Pomo? To what extent would I be creating an Indian just as Colson had, albeit an Indian different from Colson? Who am I as a spokesperson for either the Pomo or Colson? Who am I as a Pomo Indian? Who am I as a critic? I am caught in the borderlands again" (83). A comparison of Sarris's approach with that of Allen and Womack is, at this point, illuminating. Whereas Allen and Womack insist that Native American literature can be approached properly only from a Native or insider perspective – that anything else is tantamount to cultural appropriation – Sarris constantly scrutinizes his borderland position and attempts to understand how he can open a dialogue with the text so that he can continue to inform and be informed by it.

Sarris's reflections here lead me to consider my own critical stance. As an outsider reading and studying Native American literature, I must continually scrutinize my own position. Rather than looking at these works as self-contained objects whose meaning only needs extracting, I open a dialogue with them and attempt to understand how their narratives speak to my own life experience, to the fact that my culture is different from theirs. And that dialogue does not stop when I stop reading. Like Sarris, I continue to inform and be informed by the stories. My interpretive strategy is one, not of cultural appropriation, but of crosscultural mediation, aimed at embracing differing discourses and worldviews.

Crucial to Sarris's mediative strategy is his continual questioning of his role as crosscultural critic. As he puts it, "An Indian, either as a scholar working in the university or as a nonuniversity tribal scholar working as a consultant for a non-Indian scholarly enterprise, is not an objective purveyor of the so-called truths of his or her culture" (91). In particular, Sarris continues, no Pomo Indian can take such an objective stance since Pomo cultural and religious practices vary "from group to group and even from family to family within a group" (91). In fact, no one reader can ever be a perfect lens into the life and circumstances of any culture. Similarly, reflecting on the nature and context of minority discourse, Abdul JanMohamed and David Lloyd argue that "becoming minor" is a question, not of essence, but of position, a "subject position" that can be defined only in terms of the cultural formation of minority subjects and discourses within the dominant culture (9). They write: "Because we, the critics of minority culture, have been formed within the dominant culture's educational apparatus and continue to operate under its (relatively tolerant) constraints, we are always in danger of reproducing the dominant ideology in our reinterpretations unless we theoretically scrutinize our critical tools and methods and the very categories of our epistemology, aesthetics, and politics. In the task of reevaluating values, our marginality can be our chief asset" (8–9). By reading *Autobiographies* from within such a critical stance, Sarris continues his ongoing project of opening a dialogue with the text, hoping that the text and the stories of his relationship with it in turn inform other readers' stories, "continually opening and exploring the *original bicultural composition* at hand" (92).

Drawing from Krupat's approach to American Indian autobiographies,[17] Sarris looks at these autobiographies as products of crosscultural contact, that is, as original bicultural narratives that are the products of the collaborative efforts of an Indian informant and a white editor, the latter employing different strategies for conveying point of view. Along with Krupat, Sarris scrutinizes scholarly approaches to narrated autobiographies – especially those of Brumble and of Bataille and Sands – pointing out significant limitations. According to Sarris, "What all these scholars do not seem to see is that while purportedly defending Indians and enlightening others about them, they replicate in practice that which characterizes not only certain non-Indian editors' manner of dealing with Indians but also that of an entire European and Euro-American populace of which these editors and scholars are a part. The Indians are absent or they are strategically removed from the territory, made safe, intelligible on the colonizer's terms" (90). By refusing to consider their position with respect to the texts that they analyze, these critics, Sarris suggests, close discussion with their narratives and prevent crosscultural communication. In their analyses, the Indian is still significantly silenced. Rather than opening up a dialogue with the text under analysis, they end up othering it by creating an unbridgeable gap between it and themselves.

Sarris, however, takes a different approach. He employs a variety of discursive styles and critical methodologies in the attempt to make his work a border product, a narrative situated at the crossroads of cultures. And interspersed with academic argument are personal anecdotes, recalling his interaction with the text. Moved by anger, frustration, and confusion – the products of his mixedblood existence – Sarris at first reacted to *Autobiographies* by privileging his own – Indian and, therefore, authoritative – perspective over Colson's. He writes: "For a long time I wanted to dismiss Colson. I wanted to show her as ignorant, arrogant, typically 'white.' I wanted to run her out of the territory. I wanted my anger. As an Indian that's what I know best. But that isn't exactly my case. My anger is also that of a mixedblood caught in the middle. . . . More denial. Rejection. Frustration and anger" (112). But he gradually overcame these feelings: "In the case of Colson and the three women and myself, we become a part of an old and vicious cycle.

One says what the other is. The other gets defensive and says what the one is. No one sees what we do to ourselves and one another. No one sees beyond themselves. Personal and cultural boundaries are rigidified. We don't see how our worlds are interrelated. We don't see our very real situations in both worlds" (113). He is reminded of his own story, his mixedblood existence, and of old stories, too. He comes to terms with his mixed identity, and, taking the advice of the old stories, he learns how to counteract the poison of hate and anger. In this sense, *Autobiography* has, indeed, become a story for him.

Given the bicultural nature of narrated American Indian autobiography, it is obvious that, when dealing with it, readers must pay careful attention to such issues as the translation, representation, and interpretation of the Other. That is, they must take into account, not only their own perspective, but also those of the Indian speaker and the recorder-editor. What happens, however, when we are dealing with what, following Sarris, I term *American Indian written literature*? [18] Do we need to be concerned with interpretative strategies, or can we dismiss the crosscultural elements that constitute these texts, concluding that, since these works are written in English, they are somehow "transparent"? What is the difference between, say, reading *Ceremony* and reading *Hamlet*? Do we approach both texts in the same way, or do we use different evaluative standards? Sarris's "Reading Louise Erdrich: *Love Medicine* as Home Medicine" attempts to clarify some of these issues while reinforcing the notion of the importance of crosscultural interaction between text and reader.

In the case of Indian written literature generally, it is crucial, Sarris notes, that readers take into consideration, not only the fact that the "Indian writer is both Indian speaker and cross-cultural mediator," but also "the Indian writer's specific culture and experience and how the writer has mediated that culture and experience for the reader" (130). Discussing the difficulties inherent in American Indian novels, Owens makes a similar point: without at least some knowledge of traditional mythology, readers cannot achieve an in-depth understanding of these complex texts and will find themselves confused and, perhaps, even frustrated by the reading experience (*Other Destinies* 15). (As I made clear earlier, my own personal experience with Silko's *Ceremony* bears out this point.) More important, however, ignoring the Native American writer's sociocultural context means engaging in what Sarris, quoting Murray, calls "one-sided communication" – which means "to 'circumscribe and totalise' the Others' cultures and worldviews in order to 'circumscribe and totalise' the Others' written texts" (128). [19]

Before turning specifically to Erdrich's *Love Medicine*, Sarris explores the difference between reading the canonical texts of English literature and reading contemporary American Indian literature, taking as his examples *Hamlet* and *Ceremony*. It should be noted here that Shakespeare has already figured in *Keeping Slug Woman Alive*. Discussing Jenny's confusion when faced with the unfamiliar cultural context of the snake-lover story, Sarris points out how that confusion spilled over into her work on Shakespeare, making her doubt that she could ever truly understand the world of Elizabethan and Jacobean England, a world so remote from her own. Returning in "Reading Louise Erdrich" to the subject of reading Shakespeare, Sarris suggests that the difference between reading a canonical work such as *Hamlet* and reading a text such as *Ceremony* goes beyond historical or sociocultural distance to embrace, instead, an epistemological orientation. He posits that "readers must interact with the world of the texts that are cross-cultural, comprised of many elements *foreign* to the worlds of the readers" (130; emphasis added). But let us consider the issue of historicism first.

Originating in the nineteenth century as a reaction to the Enlightenment, the historicist approach called attention to the sociohistorical dimension of literary works. Specifically, it assumed that it is possible to reconstruct the material and ideological circumstances of past cultures and, thereby, achieve a reliable understanding of the literary works produced by those cultures. The early phase of the historicist enterprise saw a complete faith in objectivity and univocal meanings, as critics asserted that it was, indeed, possible to recover the authentic culture of a specific literary work. Such a position would, inevitably, lead to controversies and future changes of direction. When, in the twentieth century, the historicist debate was resumed, critics began to question the processes and methods by which the past is constructed, thus shifting the focus of their attention from object to subject. As Stephen Greenblatt points out, "The earlier historicism tends to be monological . . . concerned with discovering a single political vision, usually identical to that said to be held by the entire literate class or entire population. . . . The new historicism . . . tends to ask questions about its own methodological assumptions and those of others" (5).

The application of a (new) historicist approach to the question of reading *Hamlet* should be obvious. Like Jenny in Sarris's text, twenty-first-century American readers will be troubled by historical and sociocultural difference. Thus, in mediating the text, they must find a continuity between Shakespeare's past and their present. More important, they must also recognize that the historical contexts within which *Hamlet* exists come to us through a variety of signifying practices that are subject to all the problematics associated with the interpretive process. The more important question, however, is whether the historicist approach can be usefully applied to the question of reading *Ceremony*.

As I argued earlier, a historical and cultural engagement with the Laguna world will clarify many of the issues that puzzle non-Native readers of *Ceremony*. Yet, as critics have pointed out, crosscultural reading requires a different kind of engagement. Specifically, it requires an engagement with a different epistemological orientation. Readers approaching any Native text must confront articulations of philosophies and worldviews quite different from those of the West. As Vine Deloria points out, "Tribal peoples are as systematic and philosophical as Western scientists in their efforts to understand the world around them. They simply use other kinds of data and have goals other than determining the mechanical functioning of things" (*Spirit and Reason* 41). The most significant difference between Native and Western articulations of philosophy is that, as Kimberley Roppolo puts it, the Native articulation is "accomplished by indirect discourse": "We are taught by story, and we explain by story, not by exposition" (268).

Crucial, then, to an understanding of a Native articulation of the world is the significance of stories as the essential creative power through which reality is ordered. In the case of *Ceremony*, Silko underscores such power by opening the narrative with Thought Woman (Ts'its'tsi'nako) thinking and, thereby, creating the narrative that we read. As Owens puts it, "By announcing in what amounts to textual superscript her own subordination as author to the story-making authority of Thought-Woman, or Spider Woman ('I'm telling you the story / she is thinking'), Silko effects a deft dislocation of generic expectations, placing her novel within the context of the oral tradition and invoking the source and power of language found in that tradition" (*Other Destinies* 169). Such a strategy is rarely employed in works from the Western literary tradition. Despite the sociocultural and historical differences out of which these texts generally originate, they are still cast within an epistemological framework to which Western readers can relate. The same is not true of works outside the Western literary tradition. These texts have a much more disorienting effect on Western readers. Yet, as Sarris convincingly points out in his discussion of *Ceremony*, Western readers will still find ways to relate these narratives to their own life experiences. He writes: "If readers don't hear the texts, if they don't notice and explore those instances where the texts do not make sense to them, where the texts might question, qualify, and subvert the readers' agendas, the readers systematically forsake the opportunity not only to gain a broader understanding of themselves, of their own historicity, but also of the text. . . . More often than not, *it is something strange and unfamiliar that can make us aware of our own boundaries*" (131; emphasis added).

In the final part of the essay Sarris switches to personal narrative, presenting his reading of *Love Medicine*. As he looks at Erdrich's dysfunctional Chippewa community, one in which drinking, bickering, and violence are the norm, Sarris is reminded of his own community and his own family. As he interrogates his reading, he writes: "Is Erdrich's Chippewa community really that similar to what I know of and read into my own Indian community? . . . What about the specific circumstances of Chippewa colonial history that may affect both the nature of Chippewa oppression and of Chippewa triumph over that oppression? How has Erdrich as a writer understood that history? How might I understand it?" (144). While not providing definite answers to these questions, Sarris reinforces the point that we should constantly interact with the world of the text, always keeping the discussion open. He argues that, as a reader who projects his own experience and ideas, his own community, onto the text and its community, he is unable to arrive at generalizations that apply to either community; he cannot, in other words, achieve closure. He can, however, start a conversation with the text. Like Lipsha, one of the characters in Erdrich's novel, Sarris has also traveled far to "find" (136) his father, to ask questions about his origins, his home. His narrative becomes, then, a story of this interaction with the novel, a story that other readers, readers who have different stories and come from different kinds of communities, can further explore. Sarris hopes that other readers can "travel home" (136), just as he has.

Keeping Slug Woman Alive ends with two essays detailing Sarris's attempts to put his theory into practice in the classroom, demonstrating how the concepts of crossreading and crosscultural communication are not merely theoretical abstractions. In one class, for example, Sarris asked predominantly white students to retell a Pomo story in their own words, his purpose being to make them see how cultural biases influence their interpretative acts. Drawing from the "Critical Thinking" movement, Sarris intends students to see Native American texts as something vital and relevant to their lives, not as something separate from their historical and social contingencies. He writes: "Understanding and not control is the goal of critical discourse, and this understanding is dynamic, dialogic in nature" (153). Storytelling in the classroom becomes, thus, a powerful tool with which to open a dialogue, talking back to material that is often foreign to students and engaging students despite their backgrounds. As he had pointed out earlier, stories can be used in any number of ways and for any number of reasons. They "can work to oppress or to liberate, to confuse or to enlighten" (5). All the more significant in the classroom environment is Sarris's role as mediator, scholar, teacher. While focusing on the students' response to a story, Sarris constantly scrutinizes his own position with regard to both the story and the students' response to it so that the story is always created anew, so that communication remains open and ongoing.

The final essay, "Keeping Slug Woman Alive: The Challenge of Reading in a Reservation Classroom," offers an interesting analysis of the surprisingly negative response of students on the Kashaya Pomo Reservation to a written, translated version of the Slug Woman story.[20] It also provides Sarris with a further opportunity to discuss his role as crosscultural "mediator." In his attempt to understand the students' reaction, Sarris considers all the key points that he has been discussing as fundamental to his theoretical approach – particularly the importance of considering the text as a living thing, not as a cultural artifact, and the necessity of taking account of the position and cultural background of the audience as well as of his own position and cultural background. He comes to the conclusion that the students reacted as they did because the story was presented to them in a "depersonalized" way, as a lifeless text that told them "what an Indian is" and that allowed no room for questions or discussions (193). He also goes on to show how the Slug Woman story can be made to come to life, released from the text in which it had been confined. He writes: "Slug Woman is alive on the Kashaya Reservation. In the writing of this book, both in telling my stories and in my academic analysis, I found her in us. I found her in our silence. She has lured us there, so we don't know what we are doing as a people where we are going, so we can't talk with one another about our confusion and pain. . . . This study is an attempt to doctor and to heal. Can it sing medicine songs? Can it lift Slug Woman up, singing, right before our eyes?" (199).

By constantly interweaving family, personal, and tribal stories, Sarris's critical approach aims at achieving in writing the same kind of interaction that we find in the oral exchange while challenging the traditional role of the master, rationalist critic. By constantly scrutinizing his position as a scholar and critic (as well as a person of Native ancestry), and by insisting on keeping the discussion with the text open, Sarris calls attention to the fact that the critic is, after all, telling a story, not just decoding a text. As is Mabel McKay's, Sarris's main intent in his critical endeavor is to keep the stories alive, to listen to what they have to say, to make of them a form of autobiography. In his consistent effort to cross boundaries and traverse frontier spaces of discourses, Sarris indeed performs trickster strategies, deconstructing rigid borders, embodying contradictions, ultimately becoming what Owens terms a "cultural breaker" (*Mixedblood Messages* 41), mediating and interpreting different cultures and teaching his readers to do so as well.

In *The Man Made of Words* N. Scott Momaday claims: "At the heart of the American Indian oral tradition is a deep and unconditional belief in the efficacy of language. Words are intrinsically powerful. They are magical. By means of words one can bring about physical change in the universe" (15–16). Similarly, in an interview with Joseph Bruchac, he calls attention to the power, beauty, and intrinsic magic that words convey: "Words come from nothing into being. They are created in the imagination and given life on the human voice. *You know, we used to believe – and I'm talking now about all of us, regardless our ethnic backgrounds – in the magic of words.* The Anglo-Saxon who uttered spells over his fields so that the seeds would come out of the ground on the sheer strength of his voice, knew a good deal about language, and he believed absolutely in the efficacy of language" (Bruchac 183; emphasis added).

Louis Owens's theoretical approach translates Momaday's ideas about language quite literally. At the heart of *Mixedblood Messages* is Owens's challenge to all of us to articulate through literature and other means messages of cultural survival and to share these messages by writing and reading across lines of cultural identities. Like Momaday, Owens believes in the primary, essential human need to order the universe with words, and he articulates the necessity, for all of us, of looking at language as a vehicle through which we can surmount our physical and cultural boundaries and continue to survive as living human beings. The fact that in such diverse cultures as the Anglo-Saxon and the Native American (and, I would argue, in almost any other living culture) can be found a belief in the efficacy of words to cure and to heal should be an indication that barriers among cultures can be overcome and that we can, indeed, communicate across lines of cultural identity. "We are all human," Owens writes, "and as humans we are astonishingly alike across great cultural and even temporal chasms" (15). As a form of art, an art that speaks to the human spirit, literature has the power to transcend the specific culture within which it is created. Thanks to the "boundless capacity of language," as Silko reminds us, art can bring people together to share their (human) stories of personal and cultural survival.

Owens's *Mixedblood Messages* is divided into four major sections, covering literature, film, family, and place. Owens explains:

> In *Mixedblood Messages*, I wanted to put together a book that looked at mixed identity and the construction of Indianness from as many angles as possible. Thus I included essays on literature, film, and environment. However, I also wanted to foreground the subjectivity of the critical posture, to write a book in which the critic is the subject as much as the subject is criticized. It becomes, then, a kind of metacriticism in which the usual subject position of the godlike critic is interrogated. In that sense, the criticism criticizes the critic, as well as the critic (writer) criticizing (analyzing) the subject. (Owens, "Re: Re: *Mixedblood Messages*")

Like Sarris, Owens brings to the text his identity as a critic, submitting that identity to severe scrutiny. Like Sarris, Owens explores the significance of his mixed heritage and produces a text that participates in various critical discourses. However, whereas, in the attempt to open discussion with the text and convey the performative aspect of storytelling, Sarris takes an autobiographical approach, constantly emphasizing his position as a reader, his own text becoming a story of *his* readings (hearings) of McKay's stories, Owens takes a different approach. He explains that, "in most autobiographical writing, the subject is narrowly the writer's self" (Owens, "Re: Re: *Mixedblood Messages*"), something that he avoids by balancing the tension between scholarly argument and personal narrative. Owens's strategy is similar to Trinh's critical stance: both "informal and personal," with a range of narratives that is "eclectic," resulting in a text in which "categories leak" (Trinh, *Woman, Native, Other* 94). Thereby the notion of a pure, authentic Native essence is significantly dismantled.

Owens begins his critical journey into "mixedblood messages" and crosscultural readings with "Crow Love," a personal narrative of his childhood, but also a story that symbolically reflects the colonial situation. As a child, Owens writes, he was friends with a boy whose father had made him believe that "to make crows speak human words it was necessary to split their tongues with a sharp knife" (*Mixedblood Messages* xii). In a similar pose, the colonizer "performs his surgery," "desperate to give his words to the 'other,' so that the whole world will ultimately give back the reflected self" (xii). For more than five hundred years, the tongues of Native American people have been split, silenced, reduced to "inarticulateness," a condition that Momaday's novel *House Made of Dawn* conveys brilliantly.[21] When Europeans arrived on the North American continent, they did not hear the Natives' speech since, as Owens relates in "Columbus Had It Coming," one of the admiral's first acts was to ship a handful of Taino Natives back to Spain so that they might "learn to speak" (3). Ever since, language has been used by the colonizers to conquer and to silence, to erase the indigenous people of the continent, to ensure that they are subsumed into what Owens calls "Euramerica." Quoting Henry Louis Gates, Owens recalls a similar dehumanization of African Americans, the victims of a "logocentrism and ethnocentrism" that deprived them of the potential "to create art, to imagine a world and to figure it" (4, quoting *Black Literature* 7).

Nevertheless, despite this ongoing project of physical and cultural annihilation, despite more than five hundred years of being uprooted, relocated, and even terminated, Native people have, astonishingly, survived. And their stories have been crucial in the act of cultural reappropriation and liberation. Using the language of Ashcroft et al., Owens writes: "The people he [Columbus] mistakenly and unrepentantly called 'Indians' have indeed 'learned to speak,' appropriating the master discourse – including the utterance 'Indian' – abrogating its authority, making the invaders' language our language, english with a lower case *e*, and turning it against the center" (*Mixedblood Messages* 4). From the outset, then, Owens situates the experience of Native American people within a postcolonial discursive mode, anticipating the complicated issue of whether the term *postcolonial* can be appropriately applied to the Native American condition, an issue that he explores in detail in the recent essay "As If an Indian Were Really an Indian," to which I will return.

The proliferation in the past few decades of texts by Native American authors is, according to Owens, an extraordinary sign of the "subversive survival" of indigenous people (*Mixedblood Messages* 4). Produced in English by mostly mixedblood authors highly educated in the Western tradition, these works nonetheless come from what D'Arcy McNickle has termed a different "map of the mind" (*Wind from an Enemy Sky* 125) and Owens, following McNickle, calls a different "conceptual horizon" (*Mixedblood Messages* 4). Attempting to convey in writing the world of the oral tradition, a world in which myths and ceremonies are indistinguishable from everyday reality, these works produce an "other" literature that nonetheless, Owens argues, "participates profoundly in the discourse we call American and World Literature" (56). That is, by appropriating a language other than the written and incorporating it within the structures of the colonizer's discursive modes,

Native American writers accomplish what Owens terms an act of *crosswriting*, a subversive maneuver that significantly challenges readers to reconsider their beliefs and worldviews. Parallel to crosswriting is, then, the act of *crossreading*, that is, crossing our own conceptual horizons in the attempt to understand different epistemologies. Owens writes: "More and more we will be required to read across lines of cultural identity around us and within us. It is not easy but it is necessary, and the rewards are immeasurable" (11). Other critics have commented on the dialogic nature of the crosscultural exchange, seeing the multiple narratives of contemporary Native American texts as a significant effort to achieve what Bakhtin calls "an ideological translation of another language, and an overcoming of otherness" (365). According to James Ruppert, these texts create multiple narratives of identity, an identity that is a dynamic force in the making. They are oriented toward "a restructuring of the reader's preconceptions and expectations." These texts, he argues, "maneuver the reader into . . . different ways of knowing" (ix).

While primarily referring to works of fiction, Owens clearly implies that the act of crossreading can be profitably applied to any kind of literary discourse, including a theoretical one. A text such as *Mixedblood Messages* (indeed, virtually any text analyzed in this study) might at first unsettle readers' expectations if they are not willing to move beyond their theoretical preconceptions and explore the differing cultural codes of the author's background. While heavily and inevitably drawing on Western hermeneutical discourse, *Mixedblood Messages* brings to our attention elements from a Choctaw-Cherokee epistemology, particularly the idea of words having the power to create but also to destroy the world. In a subtle example of his own crossreading, Owens writes how at an early age he learned the importance of stories and our inextricable relationship with the world we inhabit:

> I happen to be descended from a mix of Choctaw, Cherokee, Irish, and Cajun ancestors. Within all these cultures the oral tradition runs strong. Stories, I learned very early, make the world knowable and inhabitable. Stories make the world, period. Whether they tell of Raven or Coyote imagining the world into complex being or start by telling us that in the beginning was the Word and the Word was with God, stories arise from that essential and most human of needs – what the poet Wallace Stevens called the blessed rage for order, the Maker's rage to order words of the sea. Stories also arise out of our inescapable need to feel ourselves related to what John Steinbeck and Edward F. Ricketts . . . called "the whole thing known and unknowable." (210)

By translating an old but seemingly shared belief into a contemporary context, Owens posits that the only way for our global community to live is if individuals cross the lines of their own cultural identity, always remembering that language, as Silko reminds us, has the "boundless capacity that . . . brings us together" ("Language and Literature" 59). It is with this idea of crosscultural encounter that Owens invites us to approach Native American literature; rather than perpetuating stereotypical, romantic clichés of Indianness, cultural artifacts that have no reference to reality, we must come to terms, he argues, with the fact that Native American writers are demanding that "the world must enter into dialogue with that literature and make it profoundly a part of our own modern existence, just as Native Americans have for centuries made European literature a part of Native America. And they are insisting that rather than looking to this literature for reflections of what they expect to see – their own constructed Indianness – readers must look past beyond their mirroring consciousness to the other side" (*Mixedblood Messages* 23–24).

The essay "Mapping the Mixedblood: Frontier and Territory in Native America" is Owens's response to Euramerica's ongoing attempt to annihilate and erase the Indian, confining him to the safe territory of its own discourse. Borrowing Pratt's notion of "contact zones," Owens appropriates, in a tricksterish subversion, the term *frontier*, which "carries with it . . . a heavy burden of colonial discourse" (*Mixedblood Messages* 26), thus making the space that it signifies one of extreme contestation, fluidity, and multidirectional hybridization. He writes: "Frontier, I would suggest, is the zone of trickster, a shimmering, always changing zone of multifaceted contact within which every utterance is challenged and interrogated, all referents put into questions" (26).[22] As such, *frontier* for Owens stands in stark contrast to *territory*, conceived as a "place of containment, invented to control and subdue the dangerous potentialities of imagined Indians" (26). If in the year 1890 Frederick Jackson Turner proclaimed "the death of the frontier," with the Indians either dead (massacred) or "disappeared" (confined to reservations), Owens insists on the necessity of revitalizing the term *frontier* so that the utterance *Indian*, a further version of *territory*, is symbolically deconstructed. Against deadly stereotypes and clichés that aim at confining the Indian to the museum, Owens argues: "Native Americans . . . continue to resist this ideology of containment and to insist upon the freedom to reimagine themselves within a fluid, always shifting frontier space" (27).

Owens's frontier (territory) discourse assumes a role all the more significant in the discussion of Native American literature and literary theory. In the discursive field of Native American studies, it would seem almost legitimate, according to Owens, to avoid this new form of colonial enterprise known as *critical theory*. As discussed earlier, Allen, Warrior, and Womack all insist that, in order to promote an autonomous Indian tradition of intellectualism, it is necessary to reject categorically the master's tools and embrace the battle against colonialism with weapons different from those provided by the dominant discourse. However, according to Owens, such separatist sentiments are difficult to translate into practice since, whether we like it or not, Native American critics already function within the dominant discourse and "do not have the luxury of simply opting out" (*Mixedblood Messages* 52). More important, as previously indicated, such a separatist stance runs the risk of confining the Indian (once again) to the safe territory of Euramerican discourse. Instead of participating in the cultural struggle from within, appropriating the master's tongue and obligating him to listen to voices other than his own, and thereby challenging the very foundations of his own ethnocentric discourse, the Indian reverts to a Nativist mode. In the safe territory of Indian criticism, however, the parameters are still, ironically, dictated by Western categories. The binary us/them is merely reversed, the Indian now occupying a privileged position.

In "The Song Is Very Short: Native American Literature and Literary Theory," Owens explores the degree to which Native American authors are implicated in the theoretical discourse of the metropolitan center. As I argued in the introduction, various critics, including Owens himself, have relied recently on the instruments of postmodernist and poststructuralist theory to interpret Native American texts. In "As If an Indian Were Really an Indian," Owens suggests that critics have found themselves more and more using the language of postcolonialism as a viable tool with which to explicate the hybridization of Native American texts as well as the diasporic condition of their authors. Beginning with Krupat, it has been argued that the literature produced by Native American authors bears interesting parallels with the ideological perspective of postcolonial literatures. Notwithstanding cultural, historical, and geopolitical differences, Native American literature operates within the context of what Krupat, drawing on Asad, has termed "anti-imperialist translation" (*The Turn to the Native* 35), presenting an English powerfully affected by a foreign tongue, and adopting Western literary forms to convey, in writing, the rhythms and patterns of the oral tradition.

More significant, the concept of identity as permeable and multirelational – resembling the shape-shifting character of trickster as it is conveyed in the work of virtually every contemporary mixedblood author, but primarily that of Vizenor – would seem the most significant point of encounter between Native American literature and postcolonial theory. Yet, Owens points out, distinctions must be made and questions raised before labeling Native American productions *postcolonial*. As Krupat reminds us, it is not precisely correct to conceptualize Native American literature as postcolonial since the status of Native Americans remains colonial: "Call it domestic imperialism or internal colonialism; in either case, a considerable number of Native people exist in conditions of politically sustained subalternity" (*The Turn to the Native* 30).[23] Owens characterizes the general situation as follows: "A very real danger faced by the Native American, or any marginalized writer who would assume the role of scholar-critic-theorist, is that of consciously or unconsciously using Eurocentric theory merely as a way of legitimizing his or her voice – picking up the master's tools not to dismantle the master's house but simply to prove that we are tool-using creatures just like him and therefore worthy of intellectual recognition" (*Mixedblood Messages* 53). Particularly dangerous, Owens goes on to suggest, is the attraction of postcolonial theory, often conceived as an oppositional discourse.[24]

Both in *Mixedblood Messages* and in "As If an Indian Were Really an Indian," Owens interrogates the significant erasure of Native American voices from postcolonial discourse, voices ignored by all the major representative figures of postcolonial theory except Trinh T. Minh-ha. While referring to other minority voices, such as those of Hispanic and African American writers, critics such as Said, Spivak, and Bhabha in particular, Owens notices, constantly overlook "the existence of a resistance literature arising from indigenous, colonized inhabitants of the Americas ("As If an Indian" 210). By applying Dipesh Chakrabarty's concept of the "symmetry of ignorance" to the work of mainstream academic historians, Owens argues that this absence of reciprocity applies even more to postcolonial theory's ignorance of Native American studies than it does to the First World's ignorance of Third World history.[25] In other words, if they are to be taken seriously, Native American critics must be familiar with the work of Bhabha and Spivak, but Bhabha and Spivak need not be familiar with the work of Native American critics.

Yet I would argue that, self-consciously or otherwise, Native American theorists such as Owens and Vizenor take stances similar to those articulated within the discourse of postcolonialism. More significant, they even at times incorporate postcolonial terminology in a Native American paradigm, providing an example of how what often remains an overtly cerebral Eurocentric strand of theoretical discourse can, indeed, become a truly oppositional discourse. For example, if we consider Vizenor's trickster hermeneutics, in which the discursive modes are significantly dictated by the Chippewa/ Anishinaabe tradition, we might find how such a strategy translates into a Native American epistemology Bhabha's celebrated notion of the "third space." According to Vizenor, the marginal status of trickster becomes, much like Bhabha's realm of the "in-between," a position of power, enabling the construction of a new identity, one that exists at the intersections of cultures and survives only by constantly struggling to maintain balance. Similarly, Owens appropriates the concepts *mimicry* and *diaspora* and applies them to the Native American experience.

Critics might point out that, although such acts of translation are conceived as "anti-imperial," they rely, ironically, on the language of an *ambivalent* discourse of antiresistance. The question here is not simple and goes back to Owens's overarching argument that, whether we like it or not, Native American authors are already implicated within the dominant discourse of the metropolitan center. Any appeal to a pure or authentic Native American theory is utopian and absurd. Paralleling Gates, Owens suggests that, in the context of a Native American discourse, we should ask how it is possible to produce what Gates calls a "signifying difference" (*Black Literature and Literary Theory* 3) by repeating the paradigms of the mainstream academic discourse and simultaneously show the same discourse some of its significant limitations. By incorporating some of the postcolonial lexicon into his analysis of Native American literature while pointing out postcolonial theorists' blatant ignorance of Native American literatures, Owens accomplishes a subversive maneuver much like Bhabha's act of mimicry. Unlike Bhabha's, however, Owens's goal is to expose the ambivalence of both colonial and postcolonial discourses. Owens's discussion of Momaday's literary accomplishment, the Pulitzer Prize–winning novel *House Made of Dawn* (1968), significantly testifies to this subversive exposure.

In awarding the Pulitzer Prize to N. Scott Momaday, a member of the Pulitzer jury acknowledged " 'the arrival on the American literary scene of a matured, sophisticated literary artist from the original Americans' " (Schubnell qtd. in Owens, *Mixedblood Messages* 58). According to Owens, "These words indicate that an aboriginal writer has finally learned to write like the colonial center that determines legitimate discourse" ("As If an Indian" 224). Elaborating on Bhabha's formulations, Owens claims that Momaday's creative gesture was a superb, impressive act of mimic subversion, one requiring extensive education on the part of its author, a condition without which it would have been impossible to be heard at the center. Having earned a doctorate from Stanford, and having skillfully appropriated the literary techniques of modernist discourse, Momaday acts, in Owens's view, as the quintessential "mimic man" of anticolonial resistance, one who turns the "other" or "slippage" position, to use Bhabha's terms, into a powerful weapon of appropriation. While subversively and superbly employing the language of Euramerican modernism, *House Made of Dawn* relies on an intricate web of elements from the Pueblo and Navajo oral traditions, a complex layering that, although undoubtedly unrecognized by the Pulitzer jury (and, if recognized, probably considered simply a touch of exoticism), places the novel in that shifting, hybridized, and unstable position of anticolonial resistance. Owens writes: "Exoticism packaged in familiar and therefore accessible formulas, carefully managed so as to admit the metropolitan reader while never implying that the painful difficulties illuminated within the text are the responsibility of that reader – clearly *House Made of Dawn* is both 'inside' and 'outside' the West" ("As If an Indian" 225).

While recognizing Momaday's brilliant act of subversion, however, Owens suggests how such mimic maneuvers, such negotiations, "are never simple or free of cost" ("As If an Indian" 226). Himself a critic both "inside" and "outside" the metropolitan center, Owens shares with Spivak the sense of a certain complicity with the heritage of imperialism, what Spivak calls "the impossible 'no' to a structure which one critiques, yet inhabits intimately" (*Outside in the Teaching Machine* 281). Owens writes:

> Those of us working in the field of what we call Native American literature can and undoubtedly will chafe at the ignorance and erasure of Native American voices within the metropolitan center and within what at times appears to be the loyal opposition to that center called postcolonial theory. And we can, and undoubtedly will continue to try to make our voices heard – "to give voice to the silent." . . . However . . . it seems that a necessary, if difficult, lesson for all of us may well be that in giving voice to the silent we unavoidably give voice to the forces that conspire to effect that silence. ("As If an Indian" 226)

In the third section of *Mixedblood Messages*, entitled "Autobiographical Reflections, or Mixed Blood and Mixed Messages," Owens attempts to come to terms with his mixed heritage and explores the concepts *motion* and *diaspora* as means of understanding his ancestors' liminal experience as well as his own. The essay "Blood Trail" begins by looking at pictures of his mixed family and remembering stories of Oklahoma, a state with a Choctaw name, a significant link to Owens's past. Photographs assume an important role in this section, and Owens himself seems fascinated by these cultural artifacts. Elsewhere he has written that "all photographs of Native peoples tell more than one story, open themselves to different possibilities, different inventions" ("Their Shadows Before Them"). At the same time, photographs are also a means of finding out who we are. As he imagines the life of his ancestors in Indian Territory at the beginning of the twentieth century, Owens fills in the gaps in the story told by the photographs, re-creating or inventing a past that becomes more and more fluid with each imaginary journey.

In the essay "The Man Made of Words," Momaday writes: "We are what we imagine. Our own very existence consists in our imagination of ourselves. Our best destiny is to imagine, at least, completely, who and what, and *that* we are. The greatest tragedy that can befall us is to go unimagined" (167). From this act of imagination, Momaday wrote *The Way to Rainy Mountain*, a journey into his Kiowa past, into what he calls the "memory in the blood" of his ancestors (7). Elaborating on Momaday's formulations, Owens writes about his own "blood trails," his own Choctaw and Cherokee roots "sifted trough generational storytelling" (*Mixedblood Messages* 150). As he explains, behind the title "Blood Trail" lies, of course, the Trail of Tears, one of many forced relocations of Native peoples, this being the one that laid the foundations for the state of Oklahoma. To a certain extent, Owens writes, stories are "another sort of removal most American Indian people have experienced, another kind of trail that winds through generations and locations and finally leaves us sometimes in a kind of suspension. These are the blood trails that we follow back toward a sense of where we come from and who we are" (150). As he looks at family photographs, photographs in which "there were always automobiles," Owens reflects on how the migration stories that tell people who they are and where they came from reflect the sense of what he calls "indigenous motion," a quality that is "genetically encoded in American Indian being" and that has allowed Indian people to change and adapt to centuries of cultural displacement (164). Both in form and content, *Mixedblood Messages* conveys Owens's sense of indigenous motion. By creating a fluid, mixed-genre text, in which different discourses are woven together to give significance to his own liminal experience, Owens illustrates how the syncretic and adaptive nature of the oral tradition finds its way onto the written page, creating a shifting, hybridized space in which tribally based ideas can be creatively and effectively incorporated into a new, original creation.

In "Motion of Fire and Form," Owen writes: "I conceive of myself today not as an 'Indian,' but as a mixedblood, a person of complex roots and histories. Along with my parents and grandparents, brothers and sisters, I am the product of liminal space, the result of union between desperate individuals on the edges of dispossessed cultures and the marginalized spawn of invaders" (*Mixedblood Messages* 176). In "As If an Indian Were Really an Indian," this frontier-zone identity is further elaborated to embrace Stuart Hall's notion of diaspora. Hall writes: "The diaspora experience as I intend it here is defined, not by essence or purity, but by the recognition of a necessary heterogeneity and diversity; by a conception of 'identity' which lives with and through, not despite difference; by *hybridity*. Diaspora identities are those which are constantly producing and reproducing themselves anew, through transformation and difference" ("Cultural Identity" 235). Both "Uramerican" and "Euramerican," raised in most of his earliest years in Mississippi Choctaw country (albeit not within a traditional culture), a Ph.D. English professor, Owens defines his work, as well as that of other mixedblood writers, as the production of a migrant living and working in the Native American diaspora. He writes: "Today in the U.S., urban centers and academic institutions have come to constitute a kind of diaspora for Native Americans who through many generations of displacement and orchestrated ethnocide are often far from their traditional homelands and cultural communities" ("As If an Indian" 208). However, much like the contested term *hybridity*, the concept *diaspora* is easily exploited. Although I myself do not object to Owens positioning himself as a migrant in the diaspora – a strategy that, as I pointed out earlier, aims at reinscribing some of the concepts of postcolonial discourse theory within a Native American experience – other critics might.

Contemporary invocations of diaspora have been severely criticized, both politically and intellectually, by those people who claim natural or First Nation sovereignty. Such criticism is most likely inevitable since, as Clifford points out, the specific "cosmopolitanisms" articulated by diasporic discourses and identities often collide with nation-state ideologies and indigenous claims ("Diasporas" 308). Tribal assertions of sovereignty and First Nationhood usually stress continuity of habitation, aboriginality, and a natural connection to the land. More important, as we have seen in my discussion of Warrior and Womack, representatives of tribalist discourse aim, in the most extreme cases, at recovering a pure, original past, a precontact time that might legitimate nationalistic claims. What such a position does not take into consideration, however, is that Native cultures themselves experienced migration and hybridization even before the European invasions. Momaday's Kiowa ancestors, for example, migrated from the headwaters of the Yellowstone River south to the Wichita Mountains, acquiring along the way a sense of who they were as a people. Momaday himself undertakes a similar journey, albeit one of memory only, a journey "intricate with motion and meaning" in which legendary, historical, personal, and cultural experiences significantly converge (*The Way to Rainy Mountain* 4). It therefore seems appropriate to designate the experience of such writers as Momaday and Owens as that of *migrancy, transculturation, diaspora*.

One must, ultimately, recall Aijaz Ahmad's critique of contemporary post-colonial intellectuals. He writes: "People who live in the metropolitan countries for professional reasons . . . use words like 'exile' or 'diaspora' – words which have centuries of pain and dispossession inscribed in them – to designate what is, after all, only personal convenience" (85). Regardless of whether we agree with this position, which is not without its problems,[26] we find that we have come full circle, that we have returned to the haunting questions that Owens himself raises in his discussion of Momaday's mimic subversion. As both Uramerican and Euramerican intellectuals, Native critics inhabit, whether consciously or unconsciously, the very structure that they critique. They are, therefore, "distinctly migrant," Owens writes, in the sense that they "possess a mobility denied to [their] less privileged relations" ("As If an Indian" 224). Along the same lines, Rey Chow notices that "'diasporic consciousness' is perhaps not so much a historical accident as it is an intellectual reality – the reality of being intellectual" (15).

In "Blood Trails," Owens engages in a passionate, often humorous exchange with Elizabeth Cook-Lynn in order to demystify essentialist "blood-quantum" theories as signifiers of Indianness. The main thrust of Cook-Lynn's "American Indian Intellectualism and the New Indian Story" is an attack on the production of mixedblood authors, which she considers "a kind of liberation phenomenon" and a "deconstruction of a tribal-national past" (69). According to Cook-Lynn, as products of the university setting mixedblood authors – for example, Wendy Rose, Diane Glancy, Joseph Bruchac, Gerald Vizenor, and Louis Owens – express the Indian experience in assimilative and mainstream terms, promoting individualistic values that have no stake in First Nation ideology. In response Owens claims, first, that the fiction of mixedblood authors focuses on the recovery of a sense of identity, a recovery dependent on a rediscovered sense of place as well as community. He is even more critical of Cook-Lynn's notion of "tribal realism," a vague concept that may suggest Vizenor's notion of the "invented Indian." The authors mentioned by Cook-Lynn, Owens argues, do not live in reservation communities, but they "create art about urban or rural mixedblood experience" (*Mixedblood Messages* 158). They tell stories of who they are today, stories of survival in which the past is constantly reimagined in the present tense, not frozen in some distant, entropic time. Owens writes: "Should the stories of such people, the products of colonial America's five hundred years of cultural wars against indigenous peoples, not be told because they do not fit the definition of what one Lakota critic thinks is tribally 'real'? Are their stories not ones that 'matter' and have "meaning'? Contrary to what Cook-Lynn asserts, this is a powerful literature of resistance, a countervoice to the dominant discourse that would reduce Indians to artifactual commodities useful to tourist industries" (158–59).

Even more indicative in the context of my discussion – since it raises the question of the commitment of Native American intellectuals to Native communities – is Cook-Lynn's critique of mixedblood writing as insufficiently politically engaged. Quoting the Italian Marxist critic Antonio Gramsci, she argues that mixedblood authors who have become part of the elite American university scene are "failed intellectuals because they have not lived up to the responsibility of transmitting knowledge between certain diverse blocs of society," that is, the marginalized, subaltern classes ("American Indian Intellectualism" 70). They are not, in other words, what Gramsci would term *organic intellectuals* because they often write "in the esoteric language of French and Russian literary scholars that has overrun the lit/critic scene" (76). What Cook-Lynn overlooks is Gramsci's unfounded idealism, his faith in how effective the work of his organic intellectuals can ultimately be. Even more problematic is her tendency – shared by many Third World critics – to patch together out of Gramsci's work a notion of nationhood that is, not necessarily Gramscian, but simply useful to her argument.

Discussing the effects of Gramscianism on cultural studies, David Harris identifies the British Gramscians as "those writers who stitch together their stories using Gramsci's work at strategic moments" or those who use selected concepts to generate a sense of relevance within the theoretical debate (3). Harris is even more dismissive of the American Gramscians, people such as Lawrence Grossberg, among others, whose relation to Gramsci is, Harris claims, carried largely by a kind of "'hall of fame approach,' where Gramsci is merely a founding father of radical work" (28). Putting aside the piquancy of Harris's tone – a tone directed not so much at the authors themselves as at the issues they raise – and considering his observations in the light of Gramsci's central concepts, we see that Cook-Lynn has, indeed, joined the circle of American Gramscians. Dismissing – or heedless of – the complexity of Gramsci's thought, she extracts from it only those ideas that help her consolidate her notions of sovereignty and tribalism as they apply to the Native American experience.

Compounding the problem of selectivity is the problem of the difficulty of reading Gramsci. Stuart Hall, for example, has recognized that multiple readings of Gramsci, all plausible, are possible, partly because of the fragmentary nature of the *Prison Notebooks*, but also because of the context (personal and political) in which they were written (see Hall quoted in Harris 24). Other scholars have pointed out that our reading of Gramsci today is determined largely by the interpretation of his work propagated by the postwar Italian Communist Party (the PCI) – and Palmiro Togliatti in particular – which made Gramsci out to be a follower of Lenin. Harris, for example, indicates that the PCI appropriated Gramsci's writings to strengthen its own program of popular democratic Eurocommunism (25). And Pasquale Verdicchio claims that "to consider Gramsci solely as an Italian Marxist is a misprision of his subjectivity that supports the type of State power apparatus he unveils in his writing" (175). That is, as a Sardinian Gramsci belongs to the subaltern peasantry of southern Italy, a "subjectivity" that, given that region's centuries-old history of colonization and cultural dislocation, would account for his ambivalence regarding the role of the intellectual as it is articulated in the *Prison Notebooks*. Clearly, determining the intended meaning of Gramsci's political thought should be a primary concern for scholars engaged with his ideas.[27]

In Gramsci's thought, the intellectual is organically linked to the revolutionary class through membership in the political party that leads it. However, despite his concern that the masses participate in the party's political decisionmaking process, the practical and theoretical problems presented by the dialectical tension between leaders and led, party and masses, are nowhere worked out in detail in the *Prison Notebooks*. Although it might be true that the shape and content of the *Prison Notebooks* were determined largely by the fact that they had to pass the severe scrutiny of the prison censors and that Gramsci wrote without access to an adequate library, his ambivalence concerning the function of the intellectual might be best understood in the context of his own origins. As a Sardinian educated into Italianness, Gramsci naturally felt the impulse to overcome the backwardness that in the early twentieth century typified Sardinia and embrace a more sophisticated nationalism. While his becoming a socialist does not necessarily mean that he rejected his own past *tout court*, his inability to define his own role as an intellectual in relation to the subaltern classes, particularly the poor native in-

habitants of Sardinia, is indicative of the internal conflict of the transcultur-
ated immigrant who has been assimilated into the mainstream culture. As
Verdicchio points out, "The singularity of Gramsci's works is that they
are the product of a subaltern subject. As a Sardinian, Gramsci represents
the very subject construction that is engaged in the formation of nation-
states" (175).

Ironically, Gramsci's ambivalent position resembles the diasporic condition of many contemporary Native American writers and Third World critics alike, people who, from the privileged position of an academic setting,
consciously or unconsciously participate in the construction of the subaltern, Other culture of which they are also part. Gramscians who overlook this
fact will inevitably continue to misinterpret Gramsci's work, seizing on only
those elements of his thought that support their own positions. In the case of
Cook-Lynn, basing her attack on mixedblood authors in Gramsci – accusing
them of producing an art-for-art's-sake kind of literature – allows her to side-
step her own implication (as a Native American intellectual) in the discourse
of the metropolitan center. Yet, as Harris reminds us, more often than not,
"Gramsci's work is not coterminous with gramscianism" (24).

As I pointed out in the previous chapter, the question of how effectively
Native American authors working in the safe space of an academic institution
commit themselves to their Native communities is complicated and controversial. As Weaver rightly points out, the variety of Native communities existing today underscores the difficulty of identifying one kind of ideal Native
community to which all Native writers can relate ("Native American Authors
and the Communities" 53–54). Implied in the idea of community is also the
notion of writing as a social function, a notion that Native writers often share
with Third World authors. Reflecting on the "social function of art," Trinh
writes: "Commitment as an ideal is particularly dear to Third World writers." It helps alleviate the sense of guilt over having joined "the clan of lit-
erates," and thus the privileged classes, while the rest of community "stoop
over the tomato fields, bending under the hot sun (a perpetuation of the same
privilege)" (*Woman, Native, Other* 10). Commitment should also, Cook-
Lynn argues, be the primary concern of Native intellectuals, who should
"write in a vocabulary that people can understand" rather than in the esoteric language of imperialist discourse ("American Indian Intellectualism"
76). However, Trinh reminds us, this search for "clarity" or correct expression can also be a means of subjection, a quality of official, taught language,
since clarity itself "has long been the criterion set forth in the treatises on

rhetoric whose aim was to order discourse so as to *persuade*" (*Woman, Native, Other* 16).

Trinh's is a poststructuralist notion of writing, one in which rules are broken down and fixed ideas are continually dismantled. Similarly, Owens's formal experimentation – incorporating elements of the oral tradition in established Western literary genres – aims at destabilizing the master's discourse, abrogating its authority, and forcing readers to come to terms with new ways of reading and thinking. While representatives of the nationalist, separatist discourse might continue to critique Owens's work for employing academic jargon – the fruit of hegemonic theoretical dominance – irrelevant to those it purports to liberate, Owens's position still raises interesting questions about the "social" function of Native American intellectuals. Drawing from Robert Young, Owens writes that today Native Americans are helping reposition a "global point of view" (*Mixedblood Messages* 4), challenging us to come to terms with the fact that the so-called First World is not always in a privileged position with regard to the Second or Third World. More significantly, Owens posits, Native Americans are repositioning terms such as *First, Second*, and *Third World* "to signify not the cultural/historical hegemony of the Western World but rather those paradigmatic, mythic levels that underlie this present world in the origin myths" (4). Although Native American intellectuals cannot always speak to the economically, racially, and politically oppressed people on reservations, Owens suggests that they can speak about and against their dangerous and denigrated positions inside the dominant culture. More important, by conceptualizing the reality of indigenous people as something other than Other, Native American intellectuals might help decenter the very essence of subjectivity.

By demanding that the West begin to listen to voices other than its own, Native American intellectuals take a significant step toward those acts of crosscultural communication necessary, Owens posits, for the global community to survive. Those who argue that such a cosmopolitan position inevitably makes Native American intellectuals complicit with colonialist discourse – since it avoids the material and political realities of First Nation ideology – should be reminded that the domain of culture is a primary component in the struggle toward decolonization. Again, Chow's observations will be helpful at this point:

We need to remember as intellectuals that the battles we fight are battles of words. Those who argue the oppositional standpoint are not *doing* anything different from their enemies and are most certainly not directly changing the downtrodden lives of those who seek their survival in metropolitan and nonmetropolitan spaces alike. What academic intellectuals must confront is thus *not* their "victimization" by society at large (or their victimization-in-solidarity-with-the-oppressed), but the power, wealth, and privilege that ironically accumulate from their "oppositional" viewpoint, and the widening gap between the professed contents of their words and the upward mobility they gain from such words. (17)

By envisioning a "para-sitical intervention" (16), Chow cuts to the heart of the debate about how intellectuals struggle against a hegemony that already includes them and can no longer be clearly divided into national and transnational spaces. Putting it in Foucauldian terms, Chow raises questions of how intellectuals can resist the forms of power that transform them into its objects and instruments in the spheres of knowledge, truth, consciousness, and discourse. These same issues are a primary concern to Native American theorists.

According to Owens, by continuously interrogating their own critical position with regard to the dominant academic center of which they are inevitably a part, Native American writers and critics can, indeed, conduct a significant struggle against an ideology whose primary tenet is the systematic representation of the Indian as a romantic artifact, the inhabitant of an unchanging past. By refusing to be considered merely as a vanishing race, Native American writers and critics are significantly resisting the forms of power that have defined and confined them for more than five hundred years. Finding in writing the most appropriate tool to turn the language of the invader against the center, forcing him to confront differing epistemologies and ways of reading (listening), their works thus signify what Owens calls a "subversive survival of indigenous Americans" (*Mixedblood Messages* 4), one that is gradually transforming the profession, the job market, and the canon. The final cluster of essays in *Mixedblood Messages* puts these theoretical observations into practice.

Entitled "Words, Wilderness, and Native America," this last section enters the ongoing debate between intellectual activity and political engagement by focusing on environmental issues. The essays collected in this section are, in the author's words, "environmental reflections" (*Mixedblood Messages* xvi), inextricably related to the topic of the power of words with which the book began. According to Owens, inherent in the work of Native

American writers is a sense of responsibility to use words with care since, following many Native beliefs, "we can form and alter the world for good or bad with language, even with thought" (209). Words are related to the natural world, as the innumerable creation stories out of which Native people derive their sense of identity tell us. Owens writes: "Silence a people's stories and you erase a culture" (211). This is something that Euramerica's colonizing impulse knew far too well, considering that the first step toward appropriation and possession of the indigenous people on the North American continent was the silencing of their voices.

Further explicating the European impulse to erase indigenous voices, Owens invites us to consider the act of mapping, itself an act of appropriation and possession since "maps write the conquerors' stories over the stories of the conquered" (211). Owens refers specifically to the Glacier Peak Wilderness, in the state of Washington, and to the mountain named Glacier Peak. He writes that one of the names of the peak is "Dakobed," "a Salish word meaning something like Great Mother" (211), a place to which the local Indian people, the Suiattle, look to see where they came from. Owens's reference to the ideology of mapping is indicative of the radically different cosmographies held by the Natives and the Europeans. Whereas the former see the natural landscape as an invaluable source of knowledge (providing them with stories that tell them who they are), a place to be respected and honored, the latter see it as a resource to be exploited until it is used up. Since the battles that writers and critics fight are battles of words, Owens reminds all of us of the enormous responsibility that we have to use words with care if we intend to alter the world for good. As writers, Owens suggests, it is our responsibility to make people understand that the only way that we as humans can survive on this planet is to arrest our self-destructive impulse as far as the environment is concerned.

While the "environmental reflections" of this last section might at first suggest a further reenactment of stereotypes of Indianness, Owens is particularly careful to free his message from any kind of romantic appeal to "mother earth," instead bringing Native American epistemology into play in an analysis of First World ideology. Framing his reflections in terms of the current debates surrounding ecocriticism, Owens suggests that the move toward a more biocentric worldview – extending notions of ethics and broadening conceptions of global community to include nonhuman life-forms and the physical environment – should be made by first listening to the voices of indigenous people, whose relationship with the environment is quite different from that of the Eurocentric West. His dialogic theory suggests how ecocriticism's rejection of the subject/object division of anthropocentric ideology overlaps with a Native American conception of a universe of relationships that constantly mediate and translate each other. If, as critics have pointed out, ecocriticism is testing the boundaries of academic discourse, requiring that the "voice" of the physical environment be heard, Owens makes a case, I believe, for a "transformative ecocriticism," one that employs the perspective and worldview of the indigenous people who managed to live on the North American continent for many of thousands years, developing an ethic of respect for the land.

Joni Adamson Clarke argues that any satisfactory ecocritical discussion of nature or nature writing must be conducted from a multicultural perspective.[28] Focusing on the works of Simon Ortiz and Leslie Marmon Silko, Clarke suggests that the ways in which Native American literature defies traditional conventions of nature writing raise some important issues that should be taken into serious consideration by scholars involved in current ecocritical debates (11). To a certain extent, Owens's environmental reflections in *Mixedblood Messages* aim toward what Clarke calls a "transformative ecological theory and practice." Quoting passages from Momaday's *The Way to Rainy Mountain*, McNickle's *Wind from an Enemy Sky*, and Luther Standing Bear's *Land of the Spotted Eagle*, Owens emphasizes Native Americans' "sophisticated, holistic understanding of the ecosystems they inhabited" (225), an understanding in which there was no place for the word *wilderness*.[29] Drawing from McNickle, Owens reminds us that "we inhabit a world that is ecosystemic and not egosystemic, a world in which everything is interrelated and humanity is connected with the natural world through social relationship" (227).

Such a relationship between the Indian and the social world is, according to Owens, perfectly conveyed in Momaday's notion of "reciprocal appropriation," "appropriations in which man invests himself in the landscape, and at the same time incorporates the landscape into his own most fundamental experience" (Momaday qtd. in Owens, *Mixedblood Messages* 226). Momaday conceives of this appropriation as primarily an "act of imagination," one in which man explains the world through stories and survives in it by transmitting the culture that these stories convey. A journey through the storied landscape resembles, thus, an interior journey of awareness and imagination in which the traveler comes to terms with his or her cultural identity.

Weaving together bits and pieces of Native cosmologies and epistemologies, then, this last section of *Mixedblood Messages* reaches out to rewrite dominant ecocritical discourses that exclude the indigenous worldview, ultimately enfolding this seemingly Western theoretical approach within a reimagined Native orientation. In order for us to see the intricate, indigenous network of connections conveyed, for example, in Silko's *Ceremony*, it is imperative, Owens suggests, that we move beyond our current conceptual horizons and embrace the traditional knowledge of indigenous people. Instead of perpetuating the asymmetrical relationship whereby minority cultures must master the dominant culture in order to survive, we should, according to Owens, reverse the direction of the exchange. Only by crossing physical and cultural boundaries can we arrive at the understanding that "as humans we are astonishingly alike" (15), as Owens puts it, and that the rewards of such crosscultural approaches can, indeed, be immeasurable.

Both *Keeping Slug Woman Alive* and *Mixedblood Messages* can be considered excellent examples of these crossreading and crosswriting strategies as they have been theorized throughout this chapter. By focusing on the dialectical quality of the oral exchange, Sarris requires his readers actively to participate in his text: in his reading of Mabel McKay's stories and in his reading of other theorists' "stories" as well. As readers, we are implicated in this unique storytelling strategy by continuously questioning our own position and cultural background and evaluating carefully our response to a specific text. In a more subtle and indirect way, Owens's multigeneric text challenges us to expand our own preconceptions and worldviews and to embrace the differing conceptual horizons of a Native cosmology and epistemology. Arguing for a dialogic approach, Sarris and Owens envision a Native American critical theory as a constant and delicate balancing of Western and Native forms out of which people can, indeed, cross boundaries and explore differing cultural worldviews. Given the hybridized nature of Native cultures, and given the adaptive and syncretic nature of the oral tradition that has allowed these cultures to survive, Sarris's and Owens's theoretical approaches respond well to a Native theory conceived, much like the related literature, as a vital instrument of survival for indigenous people today.

We can be prisoners, and we are, in our bodies. But we
can liberate our minds. Tribal people were brilliant in
understanding that a figure, a familiar figure in an imaginative
story, could keep their minds free.

Gerald Vizenor

4

Liberative Stories and Strategies of Survivance

Gerald Vizenor's Trickster Hermeneutics

In Vizenor's secular version of the Anishinaabe creation story, Wenebojo, the
earthdiver (and trickster figure), brings up five grains of sand from the water
to form the earth, which is made on the back of a turtle: [1]

> When he found these five grains, Wenebojo started to blow on the
> muskrat, blew on him until he came back to life. Then Wenebojo took
> the grains of sand in the palm of his hand and held them up to the sun to
> dry them out. When the sand was all dry, he threw it around onto the
> water. There was a little island then. . . . Then animals at the bottom of
> the water, whoever was there, all came up to the top of the water and
> went to the island where Wenebojo was. They were tired of being in the
> water all that time, and when they heard about the earth that Wenebojo
> had made, they all wanted to stay there.
> Wenebojo kept on throwing earth around. (*Earthdivers* xiii–xiv)

In *Earthdivers: Tribal Narratives on Mixed Descent,* Vizenor identifies contemporary mixedbloods as the new earthdivers, trickster personae who
"dive into unknown urban places now . . . to create a new consciousness of
coexistence" (ix). He also implies a crucial association between the function
of tricksters and that of writers: "Earthdivers, tricksters, shamans, poets
dream back the earth" (xvi). Contemporary mixedblood trickster writers
"speak a new language," Vizenor claims, "and in some urban places the
earthdivers speak backwards to be better understood on the earth" (xvi).

Like the earthdivers, mixedblood writers must create a new space, a new urban "turtle island" on the written page in order to articulate a new Native American personal and literary identity. From the outset, then, Vizenor's notion of mixedblood functions as a metaphor for cultural hybridity and cross-cultural encounters rather than for ethnic or racial mixing. Crucial in *Earthdivers* is the idea of tribal people in cities trying to understand how their mythic traditions apply to their everyday lives. "Must we be severed from the dreams and tribal visions to survive in cities?" Vizenor asks, a question that spawns his entire creative process. Only by engaging with the mythic and the metaphoric as they are articulated in tribal stories will Natives escape, Vizenor argues, the conceptual inventions that trap them as they search for the sacred in the city.[2]

"My pen was raised to terminal creeds." This line of Vizenor's (from *Interior Landscapes* 235) is often quoted as characterizing the revolutionary project that he has been pursuing in his writing since the beginning of his career: deconstructing the most destructive stereotypes of Native Americans created by the Euramerican imagination, those "terminal beliefs" that have prevented and still prevent Native Americans from imagining themselves as contemporary, living human beings. In *Wordarrows: Indian and Whites in the New Fur Trade*, Vizenor envisions a contemporary "cultural word war" in which Native people will survive only if they disassociate themselves from the deadly rhetoric of "Indianness." Vizenor himself enters the conflict by using language as a way of removing, relocating, reimagining the sign *Indian*, a Euramerican invention that has no referent in tribal languages. Like Sarris and Owens, Vizenor turns to language as the most powerful tool with which to deinvent the invention and find a new creative space in which to reinvent mixedblood identity.

In the introduction to *Gerald Vizenor: Writing in the Oral Tradition*, her groundbreaking study of Vizenor's work, Kimberley Blaeser writes:

> Gerald Vizenor, mixedblood Anishinaabe, comes from a storytelling people. Of the crane clan, he descends from the orators of that people. Stories form the foundation of his being, words the foundation of his career. . . . "You can't understand the world without telling a story," he claims. "There isn't any center to the world but story."
>
> Before he ever conceived of his own power to create, young Vizenor had experienced the liberating power of oral culture, the wonderful imaginative freedom inspired by storytelling. He says, "The thing I remember mostly about stories – whoever was telling them: my grand-

mother, my uncles, the kids, even my mother – the thing that I remember most vividly is the idea of being set free." (3–4)

Blaeser's observations help us establish, from the outset, the essentials of Vizenor's life and writing.

As I argued in the introduction, Vizenor's writing begins in traditional Chippewa (Anishinaabe) tales, in which words have the power to create, alter, and even destroy the world. Recognizing the vitality of the oral, Vizenor's lifelong effort is to "write in the oral tradition" (Blaeser's term; see her *Gerald Vizenor*), to require the same imaginative response that he finds in the oral exchange, and to bring the reader beyond the restrictive boundaries of the written page. When asked about the possibility of translating the oral tradition into the written text, he says: "Well, I don't think it's possible, but I think people ought to interest themselves in trying to translate it. . . . I think it can be reimagined and reexpressed and that's my interest" (Bowers and Silet 48–49). Much like the earthdivers and the tricksters, who create a new space on earth, Vizenor intends to create a new space on the written page, a new "turtle island" in writing, someplace where his tribally based ideas can be creatively and effectively incorporated into a new, original creation.

Employing strategies that often parallel both Sarris's and Owens's approaches, Vizenor intends to find his own path in theory, one that ultimately pushes back the boundaries of theory itself while subverting the monologic, totalitarian structure of Western hermeneutics. Suspicious of the strategies of realism as a fictional mode, with its objective, positivist analogues in criticism, Vizenor employs an analytic framework that is open rather than authoritative, one in which language opens up infinite possibilities to imagine. To accomplish these goals, Vizenor relies both on Native American traditions and contemporary critical theory since the two, for him, ultimately converge in important ways. He claims that "trickster stories, oral or written, and contemporary theories are not developmental ideas" since "the pleasures of tricky language have always been with us" (Vizenor in Lee, *Postindian Conversations* 59). As acts of imagination, trickster stories have always aimed at liberating people's minds, forcing them into self-recognition and knowledge, and keeping them alert to their own power to heal.

Similarly, as he looks at contemporary theories of language, Vizenor is particularly attracted to notions of infinite play, indeterminacy, manipulation, and creative escape, concepts that play a crucial role in postmodernist and poststructuralist discourse theory. Drawing from these theories, Vizenor conceives of language as deception, something that applies perfectly well to the ideological intent of trickster stories. "Deception," he says in a personal interview, "is one good, ironic theory on the origin of language; that is, the prompt and inspired, primary purpose of language was to deceive by direction and metaphors the listener, who was a stranger. . . . Why else would humans have a need to create a language? Similarly, and in the context of language theory, trickster stories are openly deceptive, but the difference, of course, is that everyone is aware of the pleasures of illusion, transformation, and deception in trickster stories" (Pulitano, interview). As with oral narratives, Vizenor's writing invites us to join the dialogue, encouraging us to participate in the "tricky" act of the exchange by finding our own answers. "Trickster tales," he says in an interview with Blaeser, "are discussion in the best sense of the word. It's engagement. . . . It's imaginative. . . . It's a discourse . . . It's liberation. . . . It's life, it's juice, it's energy. . . . But it's not a theory, it's not a monologue" (*Gerald Vizenor* 162).

Vizenor's most recent collections of critical essays, *Manifest Manners* (1994) and *Fugitive Poses* (1998), are the most radical, the most innovative, and definitely the most subversive examples of what, in this study, I have taken to be Native American critical theory. While heavily and inevitably drawing from Western hermeneutical discourse, Native American theory possesses, I would argue, unique characteristics, characteristics that allow the Native oral tradition to speak for itself about its nature and various functions, providing the tools, concepts, and languages necessary to a discussion of Native American literature, and, ultimately, adding to the rhetorical systems of Western critical theory. As I argued earlier, Allen, Warrior, Sarris, and Owens in particular, each in different ways, adopt storytelling strategies that, with varying degrees of success, produce a criticism that reflects the highly hybridized and dialogic nature of Native texts.

Despite their differing approaches to defining the parameters of a Native American critical theory, crucial in all these authors – even in those who take an overtly separatist stance – is the idea of the dynamic nature of the oral tradition, of stories that continue to evolve and change, much as Native cultures have for more than five hundred years. Crucial in these authors too is the idea of the performative nature of the oral tradition, a concept that they transfer to the written page, with the reader becoming an active participant in the dialogue. In Vizenor's case, these strategies become even more evident as he crosses – more forcefully and more radically than the others – the boundaries of the written text and makes his writing what Elaine Jahner, quoting Dell Hymes (*"In Vain I Tried to Tell You"* 79), calls "a specific kind of 'mythic breakthrough into performance,' one that parallels but does not and should not attempt to substitute what happens in oral performance" ("Heading 'Em Off at the Impasse" 2).

Drawing from the work of Walter Ong and that of other scholars (e.g., Sledge; Ramsey; and Standiford), Blaeser applies what Ong terms the "psychodynamics of orality" to Vizenor's style. According to Blaeser, among the characteristic features of Vizenor's work we find

> a fixed grammar of themes such as the invented Indian, the new urban reservation, and trickster liberation; a spectrum of stock characters such as the various reincarnations of the evil gambler, the tribal entrepreneur, and Naanabozho, the tribal trickster; dialectical discourse such as the numerous question-and-answer scenes between a Vizenor persona and a representative of the social sciences, or between reincarnated historical figures and a contemporary trickster figure; and riddles in the form of neologisms, or English words written backwards. We even find, for example, Vizenor's own special brand of formulaic diction, repetitive phrases, and epithets (used in oral cultures to aid memory and for amplification). (*Gerald Vizenor* 31)

Although representing only a small part of Vizenor's impressive literary production,[3] both *Manifest Manners* and *Fugitive Poses* display all the features that Blaeser lists, as is typical of his writing. In *Fugitive Poses* especially, Vizenor's "performative" technique finds a higher degree of sophistication, interwoven, as it is, with Derrida's ideas concerning language and signification.

Elaborating on Blaeser's formulations, the present discussion will indicate how, regardless of genre, Vizenor's main goal in his writing is to find ways to write in the oral tradition of the Anishinaabe while exploring the resultant tension with the written form. In *Manifest Manners* and *Fugitive Poses*, Vizenor explores such tension by experimenting with the nature of the essay itself. Owing to its open nature, the essay, for Vizenor, becomes an excellent medium through which to convey the dialogic context of the oral tradition on the written page. In *Fugitive Poses*, then, Vizenor adopts Theodor Adorno's ideas of the essay as a "critique of ideology" to show how this medium becomes "a dialogic context of survivance" (26).[4] According to Adorno, instead of reducing cultural phenomena, the essay as a form immerses itself in them as in a "second nature," a "second immediacy," in order to reject any form of objective representation (20). As does a trickster story, "the essay opens," Vizenor argues, "with an argument based on the idea of chance and imagination as a source of meaning, rather than going for causation, closure, and authority. . . . The essay and trickster story both arise by chance, imagination, and by metaphors of conversion, or survivance" (Pulitano, interview).

Both *Manifest Manners* and *Fugitive Poses* display the ubiquitous presence of the trickster figure conceived, as it is for Vizenor, in a semiotic sense, "a semiotic sign" in a language game ("Trickster Discourse" 192). While discussing Vizenor's notions of language, especially in terms of the influence of the oral tradition, I pay particular attention to the influence that contemporary theory – deconstruction and poststructuralism in particular – has had on his work in order to illustrate the characteristics of his "trickster hermeneutics." Terms such as *simulation, hyperreality, trace, play*, and *différance*, among many others, have become part of the standard vocabulary of Vizenor's discourse on the Native American experience. By incorporating the terminology of poststructuralist and deconstructivist theory into a Native American paradigm, Vizenor creates a mediational discourse with an intensely political message. He writes: "English, that coercive language of federal boarding schools, has carried some of the best stories of endurance, the shadows of tribal survivance, and now that same language of dominance bears the creative literature of distinguished crossblood authors in the cities. . . . The shadows and language of tribal poets and novelists could be the new ghost dance literature, the shadow literature of liberation that enlivens tribal survivance" ("The Ruins of Representations" 163).

As one of the "wordmakers," as one who "shapes his words in the oral tradition" (*Wordarrows* vii), conscious that language bears responsibility for the formation and sustenance of community, Vizenor "shapes his words" on the written page knowing that language creates the self and defines culture.[5] By using the language of colonial discoveries to deconstruct the various representations of *Indianness* invented by the dominant culture, Vizenor seems to move within ideological parameters similar to those articulated within postcolonial discourse theory while providing further opportunities to discuss Native American theory in the context of postcolonialism. In Ashcroft et al.'s terminology, he "unlearns" the authoritative power of English by creatively appropriating it within the local framework ("english") (38). Yet his strategies of resistance significantly challenge and move beyond the often Eurocentric grid of postcolonial discursive modes.

In Vizenor's novel *Darkness in Saint Louis Bearheart* (1978; reprinted in 1990 as *Bearheart*), one of the characters, Belladonna-Darwin-Catcher, is asked to talk tribal values. Her response: "We are tribal and that means that we are children of dreams and visions. . . . Our bodies are connected to mother earth and our minds are parts of the clouds. . . . I am different than a white man because of my values and my blood is different" (*Bearheart* 194). As Belladonna continues her "tribal sermon," a hunter interrupts her by asking: "What does Indian mean?" On her reciting in reply additional essentialist romantic clichés, the hunter himself replies: "Indians are an invention. . . . You tell me that the invention is different than the rest of the world when it was the rest of the world that invented the Indian. . . . Are you speaking as an invention?" (195).

Vizenor's harsh satire is relentless. In sentence after sentence, question after question, the hunter destroys Belladonna and her deadly views of the static *Indian*, the same views that Vizenor explores in *Manifest Manners*.[6] Regarding those views Vizenor has said:

> About Indian identity I have a revolutionary fervor. The hardest part of it is I believe we're all invented as Indians. . . . So what I'm pursuing now in much of my writing is this idea of the invented Indian. The inventions have become disguises. . . . There is another idea I have worked in the stories, about terminal creeds. . . . It occurs, obviously, in written literature and totalitarian systems. It's a contradiction, again, to balance because it's out of balance if one is in the terminal condition. This occurs in invented *indians* because we're invented and we're invented from traditional static standards. . . . Some upsetting is necessary. (Bowers and Silet 45 – 47)

In *Manifest Manners*, Vizenor's idea of the "invented *indian*," as well as his tricksterish deconstruction of it, begins on the very cover of the book, which features an Andy Warhol silk-screen portrait of Russell Means labeled "This is not an Indian."[7] A perfect Indian-looking warrior, braided, silentwise, and painted pastel brown-red from forehead to chest, Means is, however, out of time, a simulation from a New York studio. Inspired by René Magritte's *Les trahisons des images*, the cover conveys the idea that a certain image, a word, a name, a simulation, can take the place of the real. With an additional twist on Foucault's *This Is Not a Pipe*, in which the French critic suggests that the dialectic of discourse and vision is a fundamental figure of knowledge as power, Vizenor pronounces, "This portrait is not an Indian" (18), a phrase that functions almost as a refrain throughout the entire collection. As he explains to Robert A. Lee, "There is a double irony and an allegorical absence of natives in the portrait. The *indian* is a discoverable museum absence. Clearly the stoical image of the warrior is one simulation, and the other ironic simulation is that the actual artistic production of the silk screen was only supervised by Andy Warhol. Means, the warrior image, is teased by the absence of the artist and natives, teased by line and color" (Lee, *Postindian Conversations* 83).

Vizenor's insistence that the word *indian* be spelled lowercase and italicized reflects his dissatisfaction with the problem of identity among tribal people, who have been burdened with names invented by the dominant society. He says: "You see, *indians* are simulations of the discoverable other, and only posers or the naïve dare stand with an ironic name. That is to say, the simulations of the other have no real origin, no original reference, and there is no real place on this continent that bears the meaning of that name. The *indian* was simulated to be an absence, to be without a place. The reference of the simulation is a weak metaphor of colonialism, and, of course, manifest manners" (Lee, *Postindian Conversations* 85). To contravene the invention, Vizenor presents the idea of the *postindian*, the Native presence after the simulation who represents both resistance and survival, reinvented as *survivance*. Postindian warriors of survivance thus become, for Vizenor, the embodiment of a Native presence, those who overturn the tragic notion of Manifest Destiny and eternal "victimry." "Postindians," he says, "create a native presence, and that sense of presence is both reversion and futurity" (Lee, *Postindian Conversations* 84). Rather than direct opposition aimed at reversal of the dominant discursive modes, Vizenor adopts contiguity and infiltration of the dominant symbolic orders and systems as the most effective political stance to take in what he calls the contemporary "Cultural Word Wars" (*Wordarrows* viii).

By alluding to Foucault even before the text begins, Vizenor hints at his theoretical agenda. Vizenor's tribally based ideas on language and signification find interesting points of convergence with the French poststructuralist critics. According to Jahner, Vizenor recognizes these French intellectuals as "kindred spirits, asking the same questions in comparable ways" ("Heading 'Em Off at the Impasse" 3).[8] Vizenor himself points out that "Natives have an equal perception of reality and could just as well be the kind of dazzling interpreters of the contradictions of our experience as French philosophers" (Pulitano, interview). Since language has been the most successful instrument with which the Euramerican imagination has defined and confined Indians, denying them the status of living, human beings, and turning them instead into cultural artifacts, Vizenor turns to deconstructivist theories of language (woven, of course, within the mythic structure of Native oral traditions) as a way in which to liberate the invented Indians and restore Natives to their affirmative presence.

Vizenor's journey into the various simulations of Indianness begins with him invoking, as Lee points out, a "two-way exchange of journeys" ("The Only Good Indian" 270): Meriwether Lewis and Captain William Clark's expedition westward, in 1804–5, and Luther Standing Bear's step eastward in 1789. Whereas Lewis and Clark hoped to be seen by tribal people, Luther Standing Bear, the first enrollee in the Federal Indian School at Carlyle, Pennsylvania, would have seen whites. The metaphor of seeing establishes the nature and content of Vizenor's argument. According to Lee, seeing and being seen – or, to put it another way, "the sign as against the signal" – have been at the heart of almost all Native-white encounters ("The Only Good Indian" 271).

Analyzing Victorian discovery rhetoric, Mary Louise Pratt argues that "the act of discovery itself . . . consisted of what in European culture counts as a purely passive experience – that of seeing" (204). The individual whom Pratt identifies as "the seeing man" is the one who is doing this seeing, "the European male subject of European landscape discourse – he whose imperial eyes passively look out and possess" (7). It would seem that, in the context of European expansion, including the discovery of America, a particular interaction takes place between aesthetics and ideology, an interaction legitimated by a rhetoric of presence and absence. Vizenor comes to the rhetoric of presence and absence as it is applied to the Native-white encounter through the work of the historian Larzer Ziff, according to whom, "The greatest danger the Indians could pose for Lewis and Clark arose from their absence rather than their presence. Without them the party could not have survived the Great Plains winter or have found the routes that permitted them to proceed without the losses of life and time that could have forced an end to their venture" (165–66). Vizenor expands on Ziff's work by bringing into play contemporary poststructuralist and deconstructivist theories on language (Derrida in particular) in order to comment on the literary annihilation of the Native reality.

Vizenor writes: "The simulations of manifest manners are treacherous and elusive in histories. . . . The pleasures of silence, natural reason, the rights of consciousness, transformations of the marvelous, and the pleasure of trickster stories are misconstrued in the simulations of dominance; manifest manners are the *absence* of the real in the ruins of tribal representations" (*Manifest Manners* 8; emphasis added). Vizenor's statements here perfectly respond to Derrida's definition of *metaphysics* as "the white mythology which reassembles and reflects the culture of the West: the white man takes his own mythology, Indo-European mythology, his own *logos*, that is, the *mythos* of his idiom, for the universal form of that he must still wish to call Reason" (*The Margins of Philosophy* 213). In the name of this so-called Reason, the West has created an ontological imperialism in which the Other is assimilated into the self. It is in this context that Derrida sets his forceful critique of the West's logocentric *ethnocentrism* and its authority and assumed primacy. Elaborating on Derrida's formulations, Vizenor extends that critique to European colonialism as it has constructed and misconstructed the category *indian*, "a colonial enactment," as he puts it, that "has superseded the real tribal names" (*Manifest Manners* 11).

Writing about Vizenor's strategy in *Manifest Manners*, Lee argues that "Postindian Warriors," the opening chapter of the collection, "confirms how the book will operate overall, a collage of observation and example rather than some single line of chronological argument" ("The Only Good Indian" 270). Indeed, from the very beginning the reader is confronted with Vizenor's habit of quoting bits and pieces from an extraordinary number of theorists in order to advance his argument. Following the opening observations on Lewis and Clark's expedition, Vizenor briefly discusses *Dances with Wolves* as "postindian simulation";[9] from Costner's movie, he plunges into Baudrillard's and Eco's theoretical landscape in order to emphasize his idea of *indians* as "simulations of the 'absolute fakes' in the ruins of representation" (*Manifest Manners* 9). Consider the following example:

> "Simulation is no longer that of a territory, a referential being or a substance," wrote Jean Baudrillard in *Simulacra and Simulations*. "It is the generation by models of a real without origin or reality: a hyperreal. The territory no longer precedes the map, nor survives it."
>
> Americans, moreover, pursue a "more to come" consumer simulation, wrote Umberto Eco in *Travels in Hyperreality*. "This is the reason for this journey into hyperreality, in search of instances where the American imagination demands the real thing and, to attain it, must fabricate the absolute fake." Indians in this sense, must be the simulations of the "absolute fakes" in the ruins of representation, or the victims in literary annihilation. (9)

While this magpie strategy of gathering attractive fragments might at first appear sterile or "opaque to the point of sheer meaningless," as Ward Churchill characterizes it (313), it is, in fact, the most effective way in which Vizenor could convey his message of Native survivance. Blaeser summarizes the point neatly: "Vizenor's . . . method becomes more than a literary exercise in subversion; it becomes a mode of tribal survivance, a way in which Native peoples can assert and create a new identity, one not contained by tragic or romantic visions of a vanishing race nor threatened by 'literary annihilation.' It becomes the voice of a new social consciousness, one destined to liberate and to heal" (*Gerald Vizenor* 107). Whereas the literature of dominance keeps treating living Indians as sources for a literary construction of a vanished way of life rather than as members of a vital, continuing culture, Vizenor responds by engaging the intellectual elite on their own ground, using their own tools to his advantage, gathering bits and pieces from various theoretical discourses only to subsume them into a Native context, into the visual and performative qualities that he feels are essential in tribal oral tradition.

While mainly indebted to Derrida and poststructuralist theorists, Vizenor's elusive style is also the result of a searching examination of his own Ojibway-Anishinaabe tradition, of visual thinking and mythic metaphors. In order to suggest the open, unresolved quality of the oral tradition and the possibility of a discourse that is liberating and healing, Vizenor coined the term *word cinemas*. According to Jahner, "[Vizenor's] 'word cinemas' are stories within stories within stories all written with as precise a set of references to visual, sensual detail as possible. The meaning lies between the stories, or in the way any one of them plays off against its enclosing frame" ("Allies in the Word-Wars" 67).

Vizenor prefaces the section in *Earthdivers* (165) in which he outlines the importance to his work of such cinematic techniques with a quotation from Derrida's *Writing and Difference*:

> Between the too warm flesh of the literal event and the cold skin of the concept runs meaning. This is how it enters into the book. Everything enters into, transpires in the book. This is why the book is never finite. It always remains suffering and vigilant. . . . Every exit from the book is made within the book. . . . If writing is not a tearing of the self toward the other within a confession of infinite separation, if it is a delectation of itself, the pleasure of writing for its own sake, the satisfaction of the artist, then it destroys itself. . . . One emerges from the book, because . . . the book is not in the world, but the world is in the book."

This passage establishes, according to Jahner, the primary connection between Vizenor and Derrida.[10] Whereas Derrida insists on the infinite quality of writing, Vizenor reminds us how, within Native epistemology, a sense of the sacred governs the view of language and how participation in the sacred is essential to human existence. Aware that language cannot capture meaning, Vizenor acknowledges, Jahner suggests, that "it keeps us within a life-giving and ultimately meaningful network of relationships" ("Heading 'Em Off at the Impasse" 23).

On the other hand, Vizenor's distance from Derrida appears evident in the context of a deconstructivist methodology. In a brief description of his overall agenda, Derrida writes: "To 'deconstruct' philosophy would be . . . to determine – from a certain exterior that is unqualifiable or unnameable by philosophy – what this history has been able to dissimulate or forbid, making itself into a history by means of this somewhere repression" (*Positions* 6). As Jahner points out, Vizenor's writing provides alternatives to Derrida's idea that "the exterior permitting deconstruction is necessarily 'unqualifiable or unnameable by philosophy'" ("Allies in the Word-Wars" 68). By bringing the mythic quality of the oral tradition onto the written page, Vizenor introduces an alternative way of knowing that is implicit in the mythic system of tribal people. Within this context, Jahner argues, "the mixedblood who belongs in both worlds at once is the natural deconstructionist" (68).

"Shadow Survivance" effectively explicates Vizenor's theory. At the beginning of the essay, Vizenor states: "The postindian turns in literature, the later indication of new narratives, are an invitation to the closure of dominance in the ruins of representations. The invitation uncovers traces of tribal survivance, trickster hermeneutics, and the remanence of intransitive shadows" (*Manifest Manners* 63). Once again, through a cryptic gesture, Vizenor relies on inversion, subversion, and "shadow words" as working strategies leading to the emergence of what he calls the "hermeneutics of survivance" (*Manifest Manners* 68).

Perhaps the best explanation of Vizenor's elusive style comes, however, from a passage in *Fugitive Poses*. Quoting from George Steiner, Vizenor writes: "The best acts of reading are acts of incompletion, acts of fragmentary insight, of that which refuses paraphrase, metaphrase; which finally say, 'The most interesting in all this I haven't been able to touch on.' But which makes that inability not a humiliating defeat or a piece of mysticism but a kind of joyous invitation to reread" (34). To those readers, including myself, who have been often frustrated by Vizenor's tricksterish maneuvers, this statement might, indeed, provide an answer to some questions. In it Vizenor opts for a discourse that is open and dynamic, one in which the reader's mind explores infinite possibilities, and one in which closure is infinitely deferred. On the syntactic level, for instance, Vizenor adopts a declarative, nonsubordinate style, refusing to make any kind of connection. Sometimes he even fails to complete thoughts or sentences, leaving the reader to make the necessary connections.

In an interview with Joseph Bruchac, Vizenor talks about his revolutionary intentions as far as language is concerned. He says: "I want to break the language down, I want to re-imagine the language. It's the same as breaking out of boxes. . . . I try to dissolve all grammar, any interruptions in the imagistic flow" (Bruchac 293). As I have already explained, part of this agenda has to do with his continuing attempt to explore the tension between the oral and the written and to incorporate the oral into the written. Regardless of the genre in which he is working, Vizenor's main concern is the primary role of language, which, as in the oral context, should set people free. Similar to the notion of moving beyond the rules of grammar is Vizenor's idea of blurring the boundaries between genres and between differing ways of knowing. A reader familiar with Vizenor's eclectic production will find a significant thematic continuity between his fiction and his criticism as well as a certain continuity in style and writing strategies. Whether reading his novels, short stories, autobiography, poems, or critical essays, we cannot escape the constant experimentation and astonishing imagery. To a certain extent, Vizenor's fiction is metacritical, arising out of the ideological matrix of his theoretical work and complementing his critical apparatus in significant ways. Therefore, even though the main focus of the present study is critical theory, the occasional brief digression into the realm of Vizenor's fiction, as in the discussion of "Almost Browne" that follows, will help explicate his writing strategies.

The short story "Almost Browne," for example, is a perfect illustration of Vizenor's attempt to mediate between the oral and the written discursive modes. Born *almost* on the White Earth Indian reservation (he was actually born on the road), Almost Browne taught himself to read from "almost whole books" (112), books whose edges have been burned. "He read the centers of the pages and imagined the stories from the words that were burned" (109). He pictured the rest of the words, and they "became more real in [his] imagination" (112). As Almost Browne says:

> Listen, there are words almost everywhere. I realized that in a chance moment. Words are in the air, in our blood, words were always there, way before my burned book collection in the back seat of a car. Words are in snow, trees, leaves, wind, birds, beaver, the sound of ice cracking; words are in fish and mongrels, where they have been since we came to

this place with the animals. My winter breath is a word, we are words, and the mongrels are their own words. Words are crossbloods, too, almost whole right down to the cold printed page burned on the sides. ("Almost Browne" 112)[11]

Clearly Blaeser is correct to point out that the story "comments on the origin and existence of the words outside the static written tradition, on the authenticity of the oral and the actual, on the presence and power of sound and language, on the 'almost' quality of mere words" (*Gerald Vizenor* 160).

Vizenor's interest in a living oral as opposed to a static written tradition is also one of the primary motifs in *Bearheart*. In the chapter entitled "The Bioavaricious Regional Word Hospital," Vizenor portrays a group of scientists attempting to find the cause for a national breakdown in communication. By using a "dianoetic chromatic encoder," they attempt "to code and then reassemble the unit values of meaning in a spoken sentence" (163). A further example of Vizenor's fascination with language, the name of the Bioavaricious Word Hospital clearly reflects Vizenor's feelings about the inability of the written word to liberate our imagination. At the hospital words are confined by static definitions and meaning nailed down, limited to a single sentence. Any attempt to reformulate and re-create the world by means of language is repudiated. At the hospital, words serve only to confine. To such strategies of containment Vizenor opposes strategies of liberation, the same that he finds in the oral and mythic traditions of the Anishinaabe culture.

To bring the oral and the written traditions closer together, Vizenor employs in *Manifest Manners* the metaphor of shadow to convey the multiple referents of imaginative language performance. Such a metaphor, therefore, becomes essential in explicating Vizenor's theoretical language.[12] He writes: "The shadow is that sense of intransitive motion to the referent; the silence in memories. Shadows are neither the absence of entities nor the burden of conceptual references. The shadows are the prenarrative silence that inherits the words; shadows are the motions that mean the silence, but not the presence or absence of entities. The sounds of words, not the entities of shadows and natural reason, are limited in human consciousness and the distance of discourse. Shadows are honored in memories and the silence of tribal stones" (64). In Vizenor's agenda, this notion of shadow becomes a powerful tool of resistance against the limiting and limited rules of language. As Blaeser points out, "It is this shadow presence or referent that the 'dead voices' lack; it is this shadow presence that Vizenor tries to bring into being with his writing" (*Gerald Vizenor* 77).[13]

In "Shadow Survivance," Vizenor weaves the metaphor of shadow within the poststructuralist notion of the infinite play of signification and within the Derridean concepts *trace* and *différance*. Crucial to poststructuralist thought is the concept of the *text* as a web-like complexity of signs in which, as Eagleton puts it, meaning is not immediately present but depends instead on the traces in and through them of all the other significant signs that they are not (*Literary Theory* 114). According to Derrida, "Whether in the order of spoken or written discourse, no element can function as a sign without referring to another element which itself is not simply present. This interweaving results in each 'element' – phoneme or grapheme – being constituted on the basis of the trace within it of the other elements of the chain or system. This interweaving, this textile is the *text*, which is produced only in the transformation of another text. Nothing, neither among the elements nor within the system, is anywhere simply present or absent. There are only, everywhere, differences and traces of traces" (*Positions* 26). Interestingly enough, Derrida's formulations here help explain the odd juxtaposition of many fragments of other texts in Vizenor's nonfiction, a technique that he does not explain.

Arnold Krupat links Derrida's infinite deferral of signification to the oral tradition of tribal people, a tradition that seems wholly unconcerned with fixed meaning. "So far as research has been able to determine," Krupat argues, "the audiences for oral performances . . . are very little concerned with interpretative uniformity or agreements of any exactitude as to what a word or passage *meant*" ("Post-Structuralism and Oral Literature" 118). Quoting a crucial passage from Silko's *Ceremony* in which the old singer Ku'oosh talks about the intricacies and entanglements of language, Krupat concludes that the Native approach to language is not so far from the poststructuralist, particularly from the notion of *trace* (123).[14] The only Native American writer consciously to incorporate poststructuralist thought into a traditional mythic system, Vizenor is attempting to forge a hermeneutics of survivance for Native people. He writes:

Jacques Derrida turns his *différance* to overread the dash, variance, and indeterminate traces that misconstrue the past representations of presence and absence in written literature. The casual compromises of objectivization in transitive actions are the terminal poses of presence and the past. Shadow and oral stories arise in tribal silence and are heard in that aural distance to the chance concept, that reach of lonesome silence between the signifier, the signified, and their signs. . . . Shadows are that silence and sense of motion in memories; shadows are not the burdens of conceptual references. . . . The shadows of tribal memories are the active silence, trace, and *différance* in the literature of survivance. (*Manifest Manners* 70–71)

To those critics such as Warrior and Womack who have been arguing for an authentic, tribalcentric tradition of Indian intellectualism, Vizenor's theory undoubtedly sounds too Western and too French, too abstract, simply another version of Western imperialism. According to Warrior, Vizenor's theory "offers very little at the level of program" ("Intellectual Sovereignty" 17). Churchill writes: "The construction of such impenetrable prose is meant not to illuminate and explain but the precise opposite. Its function is mainly to cast an aura of profound importance over thoughts that are trivial at best, or, more usually, utterly barren" (315). Other critics have been similarly unsympathetic to what they see as his linguistic idealism (see, e.g., Berner; Hills; and Wiget, review). To these accusations Vizenor responds by quoting Derrida on how "*différance* instigates the subversion of every kingdom" (*Manifest Manners* 71). More significantly, perhaps, it instigates the subversion of traditional ways of understanding identity, belonging, and origins.

When asked about his audience and, more specifically, about his ambition to educate his readers so that he can write for them, Vizenor declared: "I have no interest in passive readers. . . . I write to readers who are imaginative, and who are open to change. I write out of the energy of ideas that visionaries and philosophers pursue, you know, a different kind of thinking. So what am I doing? Well, on the surface what I am doing is trying to find readers who can imagine the presence of natives by imagination and understand the absence of *indians by critique*. . . . I write for people who would rather imagine the world rather than subscribe to the lessons of anthropology" (Pulitano, interview). It is this act of imagination that primarily informs Vizenor's strategies. With his method of writing Vizenor has discovered that he can also teach a method of reading and thinking; he can teach readers to liberate their minds, help them to subvert the simulations of Indianness.

According to Lee, "'Shadow Survivance,' like all of *Manifest Manners*, does more than simply exhort. While ending with a call for a remedy, at the same time it is itself 'the very embodiment of remedy'" ("The Only Good Indian" 274). Similarly, Blaeser points out how, by employing what Chris

Anderson calls a "rhetoric of process," Vizenor involves his readers "in the act of thinking or writing as it happens. He displays the process itself; his writing becomes the process" (*Gerald Vizenor* 168, 180).[15] Vizenor's style puts into practice his theoretical agenda, that of breaking down language in order to reimagine and, thereby, create a new way in which to conceive a Native identity, one that, trickster fashion, exists at the junctures of differing epistemologies.

In "Trickster Discourse: Comic Holotropes and Language Games," Vizenor conceives of the trickster figure as a semiotic sign, in contrast to anthropological views that see it as an individual, an amoral figure who, in the words of Paul Radin, "knows no good or evil yet is responsible for both" (xxiii). In response to what he sees as inaccurate academic theories about trickster, Vizenor resists any attempt to classify trickster energy, arguing that "trickster is not representational" (Blaeser, *Gerald Vizenor* 138). In the prologue to *The Trickster of Liberty*, he writes: "The Woodland trickster is a comic trope; a universal language game. The trickster narrative arises in agonistic imagination; a wild venture in communal discourse, an uncertain humor that denies aestheticism, translation, and imposed representations" (ix–x).[16] Vizenor's idea of trickster runs contrary, then, to the prevailing static views. While academic theorists tend to separate readers and tricksters, Vizenor's understanding of trickster involves engagement and dialogue. Writing that "the most active readers become obverse tricksters" (*The Trickster of Liberty* x), Vizenor imagines a trickster consciousness that becomes an ideal healing force, one that disrupts and confronts while creating the possibility for a discourse that is communal and comic.

The essay "Ishi Obscura" represents perhaps Vizenor's most vigorous repudiation of an authoritative anthropological discourse that confines Indians within the enclaves of academic surveillance.[17] In tackling its subject – Ishi, the last "wild man" in America, captured, placed in the care of the anthropologists Waterman and Kroeber, and put on display in a museum, the quintessential "invented *indian*," a simulation, a sign that has no referent in reality[18] – the essay employs Vizenor's usual magpie strategy, relying this time on the language of anthropology, Waterman and Kroeber's "explanations" of Ishi. For example: "Kroeber pointed out that 'he has perceptive powers far keener than those of highly educated white men. He reasons well, grasps an idea quickly, has a keen sense of humor, is gentle, thoughtful, and courteous and has a higher type of mentality than most Indians'" (*Manifest Manners* 131). Ultimately, the essay reverses the language of anthropology, creating a discourse of presence, not absence: "Ishi is not the last man of stone. He is not the obscure other, the mortal silence of savagism and the vanishing race. The other pronoun is not the last crude measure of uncivilization; the silence of that tribal man is not the dead voice of racial photographs and the vanishing pose" (126).

At the same time the essay subsumes anthropological discourse within Vizenor's own trickster discourse. Whereas anthropological discourse has fixed Ishi, identified him as a wild man, a primitive, an *"indian,"* Vizenor's trickster discourse frees him, underlining the fact that he survived in spite of and alongside the invention. By claiming that, when living in the museum, Ishi never revealed "his sacred tribal name" (*Manifest Manners* 128) and that "he never learned to slow his stories down to be written and recorded" (136), Vizenor underscores the ability of storytelling to liberate and to create. Whereas Euramerica uses words to contain and constrain, to pin meaning down in a single definition, Natives envision words as opening up infinite possibilities of signification. Whereas Euramerica uses written statements and records as markers of tribal identity, Natives affirm their presence in the telling and retelling of stories. It is these stories that have allowed them to adapt, change, and, ultimately, survive. To the anthropologists who "defined" Ishi within the strictures of a name, Ishi responds by presenting his stories as evidence of a *real* tribal character. Humorously defying the language of anthropology by employing visible strategies of orality, such as, for example, balanced oppositions of verbal contexts between Ishi and the people of the museum, "Ishi Obscura" becomes a perfect instance of the tribal imagination trumping academic invention.[19] Vizenor's observations elsewhere neatly summarize this point: "Traditional people imagine their social patterns and places on the earth, whereas anthropologists and historians invent tribal cultures and end mythic time. The differences between tribal imagination and social scientific invention are determined in worldviews: imagination is a state of being, a measure of personal courage; the invention of cultures is a material achievement through objective methodologies. To imagine the world is to be in the world; to invent the world with academic predicaments is to separate human experiences from the world, a secular transcendence and a denial of chance and mortalities" (*The People Named the Chippewa* 27).

Interestingly enough, Vizenor's strategy in "Ishi Obscura" calls to mind Trinh's witty deconstruction of what in *Woman, Native, Other* she calls the "language of nativism" (47). Engaging in a conversation with the anthropologist-Nativist, Trinh argues that, as a system of interpretation, anthropology should be treated in semiological terms, the foundations of its discursive and critical methodologies questioned. She writes: "Interpretative anthropology does not offer any important change of venue as long as negative knowledge about the constituted authority of linguistic utterance is made available in the very process of meaning and interpreting. Such critical practice necessitates a questioning and shifting (in anthropology) of the very notion of 'science' as objective understanding or study of systematized knowledge" (72). Twisting and spinning anthropology's worn codes in the attempt to devalue them and question the identity of the speaking/writing subject, Trinh joins Vizenor in the enterprise of devaluing and subverting an authoritative discourse, one in which the subject of knowledge has always been represented as the Other.

Discussing the trickster strategies of Vizenor's narratives, Owens posits that Vizenor's fiction arises out of the kind of laughter that Bakhtin envisions in the modern novel (*Other Destinies* 225); more precisely, he argues, Vizenor's trickster discourse "resembles Bakhtin's definition of Menippean satire" as an art form aiming at stripping down reality, "laying bare the hypocrisies, false fears and pieties," and bringing people to face themselves as they really are (226). According to Bakhtin, "The liberty to crudely degrade, to turn inside out the lofty aspects of the world and world views, might sometimes seem shocking. But to this exclusive and comic familiarity must be added an intense spirit of inquiry and utopian fantasy. . . . In Menippean satire the unfettered and fantastic plots and situations all serve one goal – to put to test and to expose ideas and ideologues. . . . Menippean satire is dialogic, full of parodies and travesties, multi-styled, and does not fear elements of bilingualism" (*The Dialogic Imagination* 26). By adopting the humor and method of the Native American trickster, the polyedric figure who overturns all laws, governments, and social conventions, only "to put to test and to expose ideas and ideologues," Vizenor challenges readers to liberate themselves from ideological confinement and to engage in a dialectic relationship with their larger experience. As he explained to Blaeser, in using trickster consciousness he is "drawing a configuration of an old idea in a different way, through a tribal literary practice" (*Gerald Vizenor* 137). According to Blaeser, "The culture hero appears in Vizenor's work in origin stories, and long told tales . . . as well as in recast and contemporary versions of those older stories. Nanaabozho and his pan-indian counterparts also appear as ethos, as persona, and as fictional characters of Vizenor's own imaginative tales" (*Gerald Vizenor* 137). However, Vizenor's trickster consciousness goes beyond these physical manifestations. As Blaeser puts it, "It arises from a certain state of mind, an anarchical energy, a liberating humor" (137).

In his theoretical works especially, Vizenor's "trickster signature" is enacted in his style, in his mingling of his ideas with the words of others, especially deconstructivist theorists, often placing them in the narrative frame or presenting them in the playful, contradictory fashion that embodies trickster consciousness. Like trickster consciousness, Vizenor's style is not linear, progressive; it does not follow the logic of cause and effect. Rather, it embraces chance, celebrates play, relishes ambiguity, breaks rules, confounds expectations, invites involvement. In Blaeser's terms, Vizenor's "dialogic style" becomes itself a "political act," a tool of liberation from any form of linear, monologic style, and universalizing theory (*Gerald Vizenor* 195).[20]

The essay "Eternal Haven" provides a very good example of Vizenor's revolutionary stylistic intentions. With playful humor, and in typically convoluted language, Vizenor takes satiric aim at Christopher Columbus. Envisioning Columbus as a "deverbative trickster," he writes that "the Admiral of the Ocean Sea" "landed in two pronouns, the he and you" – the pronouns of colonial Manichaean discourse – and that "he endures as the pronouns in trickster stories" (*Manifest Manners* 107). Given Vizenor's resistance to pronouns as signifiers of identity,[21] his repetition of the signifier *you* to refer to Columbus is clearly conceived as a challenge. Vizenor writes: "*You* are the discoverer of histories; *you* are the pronouns, the absence of the nouns in simulations. . . . *You* land and discover marvelous shamans. . . . *You* discover mother earth and the eternal havens of simulations" (107–8; emphasis added). By imposing pronouns on the indigenous peoples, Columbus was the first, Vizenor suggests, to simulate "*indians*" and render Natives as absences. By burdening Columbus with the second-person pronoun, Vizenor takes his tricksterish revenge, turning the language of the colonizer against itself and showing that language can liberate as well as enslave.

Vizenor also takes aim in "Eternal Havens" at Columbus's journal, appropriating its authoritative discourse.[22] Twisting the admiral's words, he writes: "'In order to win [the Natives'] friendship, since *you* knew they were a people to be converted and won to our holy faith by love and friendship rather than by force, *you* gave them red caps and glass beads which they hung around their necks,' *you* wrote in the journal. *You* are the discoverer in trickster hermeneutics" (*Manifest Manners* 108; emphasis added). Indeed, Columbus's methods of winning the Natives' friendship might have resembled the behavior of the trickster figure; yet, Vizenor suggests, he is no trickster since he "heard no solace in tribal memories" (108). More significantly, Vizenor adds, "his stories were denatured adventures, the translations of simulations into discoveries" (119). As the product of Manichaean discourse, Columbus is trapped in the confining and confined nature of language, in its static definitions and simulations of pronouns. Vizenor suggests, however, that language is much more than that. As tribal people well knew, language is power, force, vitality, liberation. It awakens creative powers; it brings about change; ultimately it undermines the existing social paradigm, always challenging us to reformulate ourselves.

Since the 1893 Columbian Exposition in Chicago, the nation has celebrated and honored the admiral's discoveries, as the extravagant and expensive quincentenary commemorations have clearly indicated. Yet, Vizenor writes, "Columbus is a commemorative curse not a communal tie; his names are the same as disease and death in the memories of the tribes on the island" (*Manifest Manners* 110). Moreover, since no birth records exist for him, since no authentic portraits of him survive, since even the original copy of his journal has been lost, the Columbus who has been celebrated for five hundred years is, in fact, a simulation. Columbus, as Vizenor imagines him, is a tragic man, a man trapped in the terminal creeds and moral determinism of the Old World, the complementary opposite of the playful comic tradition of oral narratives.[23]

A trickster consciousness is also manifested in the way in which Vizenor structured *Manifest Manners*. A number of critics have commented on the episodic nature of Vizenor's fiction, tracing it back to trickster tales (see, e.g., Velie; Owens, *Other Destinies*; and Jahner, "Allies in the Word-Wars"). And Blaeser has pointed out how such traditional tales often constitute cycles, "with both formal or causal relations between episodes as well as informal connections stemming from themes and motifs" (*Gerald Vizenor* 137). Despite the apparent disjuncture among the various essays, on close reading it becomes obvious that what ties these pieces together is the recurrent motif of the "invented *indian*," a notion that is explored in different terms in each. Within the context of the "invented *indian*" theme, the essays included in *Manifest Manners* address such diverse topics as the politics of contemporary casinos and the simulations of the American Indian Movement in the late 1960s. While the quality of the pieces included in the volume varies – at least with respect to how effectively they apply Vizenor's theories – they all nevertheless nicely exemplify its main theme, overturing the simulations that have been imposed on Native people by the manifest manners of colonialism.

Manifest Manners ends by returning in the epilogue to the notion of survivance and to the crucial role of the postindian in outdoing the invention. Vizenor begins the epilogue with an epigraph taken from Emerson's journals, an entry from 1837 that reports seeing "the Sacs & Foxes" at the Boston statehouse and then remarks that "it is right & natural that the Indian should come & see the civil White man" (*Manifest Manners* 163). Vizenor continues in his own voice: "Emerson was a spectator, *unseen* at an overture of a chief who had come to *see* civilization" (163). Nothing could be more appropriate than for Vizenor to invoke Emerson at the end of *Manifest Manners* and, in the process, to return to the metaphor of seeing, related as it is to imperialist ideology. By Emerson's day, the tribes had been decimated by disease, and they had had most of their land stolen. Both assaults can be attributed to the putting into practice by the young American nation of the notion of Manifest Destiny. We find a similar ideology in Emerson, a similar desire to dominate, albeit this desire is directed at the natural world: "I become a transparent eye-ball; I am nothing; I see all; the currents of the Universal Being circulate through me; I am part or particle of God" (Emerson 1584). Subsuming everything that it sees, Emerson's "I" perfectly reflects the Euramerican colonizing impulse, an impulse originating in the Cartesian celebration of the infinite epistemological possibilities of the human subject.

Emerson's "I" calls to mind another universalizing subject, the "inquiring child" of Whitman's "Facing West from California Shore," a text that, according to Owens, "brilliantly and efficiently illuminates America's self-imagining" ("As If an Indian" 214). Owens writes: "The Euramerican 'child' of Whitman's remarkable poem claims possession of the womb of humanity in a great, universalizing narcissism that subsumes everything in its tireless, inquiring quest after its own image, thereby excluding heterogeneity from the very womb, and is pleased and joyous about the whole endeavor" (216). Quoting Fanon, Owens argues that European America reflects in a tricky mirror that presence of the Other that is nothing but its own image reflected back at itself. Much like blackness, then, Indianness becomes a mask, a mask significantly constructed by white America, a mask that the Native must adopt in order to obtain recognition (217). Such a mask, Vizenor would argue, is the simulation of Indianness that the literature of dominance has imposed on Native tribes. It has not, however, been universally adopted – "some postindians," he notes elsewhere, "renounce the inventions and final vocabularies of manifest manners" (*Manifest Manners* 167), thus advancing a hermeneutics of survivance.

The metaphor of seeing as a reflection of imperialist ideology leads Vizenor once more to Foucault and to his notion of surveillance, this time via Michel Serres. In "Panoptic Theory" Serres writes about the conservative nature of surveillance and observation. He argues: "The human sciences are surveillance; the exact sciences are an observation. The first are as old as our myths; the others, new, were born with us, and are only as old as our history" (qtd. in *Manifest Manners* 168). The objective methods of observation of the social sciences have, Vizenor argues, contributed to the separation of tribal imagination and humor. To counteract surveillance and observation, the main methodologies of the human sciences, Vizenor presents trickster narratives as "contradictions" and not as "representations of culture" (*Manifest Manners* 170). He writes: "Naanabozho would mimic but never concede the coherence of other worlds, and so trickster continues the casual contradictions of presence and absence in a narrative that has no mechanisms of representation" (172). Against the innumerable European representations of Indians, representations in which the tribes have always been *seen* as absent, Vizenor advances a theory of survivance through stories, stories that affirm the presence of the people.

Published in 1998, *Fugitive Poses* takes up, in a more challenging way, many of the issues explored in *Manifest Manners*. In *Fugitive Poses*, the practice of Native American critical theory reaches a higher level of sophistication, as strategies and patterns from the oral tradition make the transition into contemporary theories of language. Adopting Adorno's ideas concerning the essay as a hybrid form, Vizenor presents "five essays on academic surveillance, simulations, resistance, natural reason, survivance, and the *transmotion* of native sovereignty" (*Fugitive Poses* 1), essays in which firm distinctions between fiction and nonfiction are blurred. None of these essays begin with first principles, and none end with definite conclusions, but each proceeds with an immersion in cultural phenomena – what Adorno defines as "second nature" ("The Essay as Form" 20) – that challenges the idea of indubitable certainty. As in all Vizenor's writing, form and content serve the same purpose, each equally significant.

Vizenor's main concern in *Fugitive Poses* is the ideology of European Enlightenment thought, out of which grew objective, rational, scientific methods of explaining reality. Once science positioned itself within a linear and temporal hierarchy of knowledge, any other systems of explanation, particularly non-European systems, were naturally dismantled as inferior. Out of the objectivity of science came the confined and confining knowledge systems of anthropology and social science, the same systems of thought that invented "*indians*" and then positioned these "invented *indians*" as simulations and as absences.

As defined by Jean Baudrillard, the term *simulation* implies "the generation by models of a real without origin or reality: a hyperreal" (2). In a passionate attack on ethnology, Baudrillard condemns Western civilization for driving the Indian "back into the ghetto, into the glass coffin of virgin forest," making him the "simulation model" for all conceivable Indians before ethnology (15). "For ethnology to live, its object must die," he claims, a statement that best conveys the notion of the Indian frozen in time, "cryogenized," "sterilised," protected to death and in death (13, 15).

Elaborating on Baudrillard's observations, Vizenor claims that what is labeled *real*, what is conceived as the one absolute or certain method of making sense of the world, simulates the real experience of people or, in the case of Natives, distinct groups of people, who are then labeled *indians*. Simulations such as *indians*, he argues, celebrate the absence of the people, not their presence, fixing Natives, making of them static museum specimens, denying them authentic existence in the present. According to Vizenor, Natives can avoid the simulations created by the Euramerican imagination only if they are willing to affirm their presence by means of humor, irony, and the liberating power of Native stories.

Vizenor's revolutionary project in *Fugitive Poses* begins in the introduction to the volume, in which the elusive figure of trickster is invoked. Influenced by Adorno, Vizenor does not proceed in a linear fashion but, instead, immerses his ideas in the "second nature" of the trickster universe, discussing the importance of trickster stories as liberating and creative acts of imagination. Consider the following: "Native American Indians are the storiers of presence, the chroniclers in the histories of this continent. There are no other secure stories that tease the creation of a Native presence, that actuate the sovenance and totemic observance of nature. Native stories are the traces of natural reason, not the spoils of surveillance. Native stories are communicative, autonomous creations, and the traces of a 'second nature' in these essays of *Fugitive Poses*" (1). Unlike the language of social-scientific discourse, which fixes Indians, makes of them static artifacts, what Vizenor elsewhere calls the "manifest manners of scriptural simulations" (*Manifest Manners* 17), the language of trickster stories aims, he insists, at liberation, at the disruption of such static definitions. In the furtherance of this goal, not only does Vizenor categorically refuse "*indian*" as a simulation of identity, but he also offers no alternative to it. He might use the term *Native*, but he avoids defining it, thereby avoiding fixing Native people yet again. "The native, an inscrutable persona," he writes, is "the trace of ethical transmotion and sovereignty" (*Fugitive Poses* 33), suggesting the idea that, much like trickster, Natives are not "representational" (Vizenor qtd. in Blaeser, *Gerald Vizenor* 138).

"Liberative Stories," the introductory essay, is structured as are trickster tales – as a series of episodes connected in an associative rather than a linear fashion. Vizenor begins by mining his experience as a visiting professor at the University of Tianjin in China in 1983. This allows him to pair Naanabozho, the trickster figure in the Anishinaabe oral tales, with the Monkey King, "the tricky cousin in the east" (*Fugitive Poses* 1), suggesting how trickster imagination cuts across ethnic allegiances and worldviews.[24] He moves next to a discussion of censorship as "institutive dominance" (10), in this case how the university censors would feed the students their assigned reading a few photocopied pages at a time and how, when that reading contained objectionable material (sex or violence), the photocopier would "break." He then alludes to the reelaboration and transformation in the translations of trickster tales by Christian missionaries and social scientists, who silently wrote out the scandalous character of trickster. Under "these masters of moralist and causal translations" (10), Vizenor claims, trickster became a tragic representation of Native cultures rather than a representative of creative, liberative experience. Finally, he turns to the American academic scene, specifically California in the 1990s, and the practice of a different form of censorship, for example, the way in which his students read his novels as representations of the real, a *real* that is, Vizenor argues, only an "*indian* simulation" and "a fugitive pose" (7) that his works consistently evade and deconstruct.[25] "The manners of censors are terminal creeds" (8), he concludes, and an obstacle to creative and liberative stories.

More than any other form of misrecognition of Natives as "*indians*," stories are, according to Vizenor, the creation of a sense of self and presence. He writes: "Native survivance is a sense of presence, but the true self is visionary. The true self is an ironic consciousness, the cut of a native trickster. Stories of truistic selves tease the originary" (*Fugitive Poses* 20). By categorically rejecting any form of pure origin and authentic self, Vizenor envisions Native identities in dialogic relation with many Others, including nature and those "who must bear the *indian* simulations of dominance" (22). Within this context, Derrida's notion of *trace*, intended as "the radically other within the structure of difference that is the sign" (*Of Grammatology* xvii), fits neatly with Vizenor's project of dismantling any form of pure origin and lost presence. Vizenor explains: "The simulation of the *indian*, lowercase and in italics, is an ironic name in *Fugitive Poses*. The Indian with an initial capital is a commemoration of an absence – evermore that double absence of simulations by name and stories. My first use of the italicized *indian* as a simulation was in *The Everlasting Sky*. The natives in that book were the *oshki anishinaabe*, or the new people. Since then, natives are the presence and *indians* are simulations, a derivative noun that means an absence, in my narratives" (*Fugitive Poses* 15).

Following through on this agenda, Vizenor provides a list of neologisms that he will use in the book, derivative words that are, however, never clearly defined. Vizenor's vocabulary in *Fugitive Poses* includes terms such as *transmotion, varionative, penenative, postindian,* and *interimage.* He explains: "There are two categories of words for which I provide a sort of phrase or paragraph, not definition, but discussion: Native words, usually in italics, in commas, and . . . words I made up" (Pulitano, interview). As discussed earlier, Vizenor's main goal in writing is to break down the rules of language and grammar and to open up new creative possibilities for the reader. Considering writing as a revolutionary gesture, a disruption of social and cultural values, Vizenor finds an interesting parallel between the activity of writers and trickster consciousness. Like tricksters, writers must constantly unsettle, contradict, and unglue the creeds of authoritative discourse. Like tricksters, writers have as their ultimate goal raising people's consciousness by calling for their direct participation in the dialogue.

"Penenative Rumours," the first of Vizenor's essays on academic surveillance, is an exploration of various theoretical landscapes within which Natives appear always as presence, not absence.[26] Echoes of Adorno and Derrida are heard from the very beginning, establishing, thus, the parameters of the entire essay. Vizenor writes: "Native American Indians actuate the stories of this continent, and natives are the *traces* of natural reason, the aesthetic fugitives of the originary. Native stories are the canons of survivance. . . . Natives have resisted empires, negotiated treaties, and . . . embraced the simulations of absence to secure the chance of a decisive presence in national literature, history, and canonry. . . . Natives actuate the '*second nature*' of the essay" (*Fugitive Poses* 23; emphasis added). This succinct formulation of his rhetorical strategy recalls Adorno's definition of the essay as a form evoking intellectual freedom and a critique of ideology. Adorno writes: "The essay does not play by the rules of organized science and theory, according to which, in Spinoza's formulation, the order of things is the same as the order of ideas. Because the unbroken order of concepts is not equivalent to what exists, the essay does not aim at a closed deductive or inductive structure. In particular, it rebels against the doctrine, deeply rooted since Plato, that what is transient and ephemeral is unworthy of philosophy" (10). Adorno's observations concerning the rebellious nature of the essay in turn recall Derrida's critique of logocentrism, an attempt to break down the binary oppositions that characterize the discourse of logocentric reason – oppositions such as speech/writing, presence/absence, origin/supplement – by exploring their mutual crossings and involvements.[27]

Translated into a Native American context, Derrida's ideas help us understand, Vizenor suggests, how colonial dominance has applied the discourse of logocentric reason to Natives, who have become the absent Others in the Euramerican hierarchy of *white/indian* or *civilized/savage*. Vizenor's goal is similar to Derrida's: break down these oppositions by showing their mutual crossings and interchanges. Instead of reversing the hierarchy granting *"indian"* a privileged position, Vizenor insists that it is a simulation and that the opposition *white/indian* itself is untenable. In a tricksterish gesture, he envisions the postindian as the figure who, with good humor and compassion, "must waver over the aesthetic ruins of *indian* simulations" (*Fugitive Poses* 15). In Derrida's terms, Vizenor positions the *"indian"* as a Native absence that has become a logocentric presence. Vizenor writes in *Crossbloods*: "More than a million people and hundreds of distinct tribal cultures were simulated as Indians" (xxiii). The invention has, he continues, become a disguise, an instrument that has allowed and still allows colonial domination to exercise surveillance over Native cultures.

According to Derrida, the metaphysics of presence is challenged by the notion of *différance*, a concept that sets the word in motion toward other meanings so that language cannot be fixed for the purposes of conceptual definition. As Christopher Norris puts it, "[*Différance*]. . . remains suspended between the two French verbs 'to differ' and 'to defer' [postpone], both of which contribute to its textual force but neither of which can fully capture its meaning. Language depends on 'difference' since, as Saussure showed . . . it consists in the structure of distinctive oppositions which make up its basic economy. Where Derrida breaks new ground and where the science of grammatology takes its cue, is in the extent to which 'differ' shades into 'defer.' This involves the idea that meaning is always *deferred*, perhaps to the point of an endless supplementarity, by the play of signification" (*Deconstruction* 32).

In Vizenor's agenda, the notion of *différance* becomes more a Native trickster, a character subverting "every kingdom" (*Fugitive Poses* 34) in stories, always deferring Native identities to other Native stories. He writes: "Native identities are traces, the *différance* of an unnamable presence, not mere statutes, inheritance or documentation, however bright the blood and bone in museums. Native identities must be an actuation of stories, the commune of survivance and sovereignty" (37).

Derrida's critique of the logocentric system of priorities converges, interestingly enough, with Adorno's observations on the nature of the essay. Writing of the essay that it "abandons the royal road to the origins, which leads only to what is most derivative" (11), Adorno indicates how it becomes a sort of heresy. Vizenor's position on the rebellious nature of the essay is similar. As do stories, essays disrupt, he argues, any form of linear structure and proceed by the association of ideas. In the essay's episodic movement and rejection of objectivity, it becomes, indeed, a critique of ideology.

Both in theory and in practice Vizenor translates almost literally Adorno's theories. As bits and pieces from various European theorists are woven into a discourse on Native experience, a reader familiar with Native American oral cultures immediately recognizes the structure – or, better, "antistructure" – of trickster tales, in which, as I suggested earlier, relations between episodes, as well as connections stemming from themes and motifs, are often informal. According to Blaeser, a "deep mythic structure" characterizes Vizenor's writing, one that, inspired by trickster tales, significantly and deliberately "subverts the formal Western ideals of literary aesthetics" (*Gerald Vizenor* 138). Blaeser writes: "Trickster identity is itself a subversion of the Western mode of classification, resisting singularity (and therefore becoming in Vizenor's work a perfect metaphor for the mixedblood)" (138). Responding to Andrew Wiget's critique of Vizenor's concept of trickster as inadequately theorized (see Wiget, review), Blaeser points out that such failure in theory is actually success in practice since "in [Vizenor's] conception trickster energy cannot be captured in academic theory" (*Gerald Vizenor* 142).

Similarly, responding to Wiget's observation that Vizenor's postmodern notion of trickster portrays "the palpable void beyond signification" (review 478), Owens has seen in Vizenor's "trickster pose" something more significant than a postmodern linguistic maze. He writes: "Embodying contradictions, all possibilities, trickster ceaselessly dismantles those imaginative constructions that limit human possibility and freedom, allowing signifier and signified to participate in a process of 'continually breaking apart and reattaching in new combinations'" (*Other Destinies* 235). Similar to the dismembering of trickster's body in traditional stories, Owens notices how "the self deconstructs [itself] schizophrenically" (235). At the same time, however, "trickster shows by negative example the necessity for humankind to control and order our world" (235). Through language – more specifically, through stories – a new sense of identity is created, an identity that, in Owens's terms, is syncretic, adaptive, and coherent, that contrasts static definitions and terminal conditions.

The dynamics of Vizenor's trickster strategy, as well as his use of deconstructivist theories, will be further illuminated by a consideration of Spivak's notion of "catachresis." Catachresis is, as envisioned by Spivak, a tactical maneuver, one that involves wrenching particular images and concepts out of their place within a specific narrative and using them to open up new areas of meaning. As Moore-Gilbert points out, it is in this way that Spivak has, for example, radically redefined Gramsci's concept of the subaltern (84). Her intention is always that of "reading against the grain" of the ostensible logic of the text in question, showing the "ruptures" of the text itself while disclaiming, in a perfect deconstructivist gesture, any intention of providing a formula for correct "cognitive moves" (Spivak, *In Other Worlds* 202). In Vizenor's case, the catachrestic maneuver takes a more radical turn. It involves wrenching concepts and rhetorical ideas out of Western discourse and bringing them into a Native context, into the oral strategies of Native epistemology with the ultimate goal of breaking down the boundaries between the oral and the written and challenging the reader to learn new ways of reading and thinking.

Along with his invocation of Adorno and Derrida, in "Penenative Rumours" Vizenor brings into the discussion of the Native experience Jung's ideas on alien abduction stories in *Flying Saucers* and Foucault's observations on the will to knowledge in *The Archaeology of Knowledge*. As in a trickster tale, in "Penenative Rumours" the argument proceeds, not logically or linearly, but by means of associative leaps and attempts to mediate between contradictory elements. The image of the "*indian*" as a demon, the fierce savage of Mary Rowlandson's Indian captivity narrative, shares interesting parallels with the figure of the alien in contemporary abduction stories. Vizenor writes: "The aliens and *indians* are simulations of the other in stories and narratives. The abductees and captives are pioneers in their stories, and they encounter the other in adverse dimensions: the savage, an awesome renunciation of modernism; and aliens, the small grays of technocracy and futurity" (47). However, Vizenor goes on, neither "pioneer" has a referent or presence in tribal stories, originating instead in a rigidly Western logocentric thinking.

The concept of the "*indian*" as an alien brings Vizenor to reflect on his own family history.[28] Interpreting that history from the perspective of the "*indian*" as absence, he points out that, whereas "in an earlier national census" (*Fugitive Poses* 50) his grandparents were asked to indicate tribe and proportion of Indian blood, in the 1930 census his father was not. Vizenor writes: "My father [Clement William Vizenor] was *anishinaabe* by reservation ancestors and an *indian* by simulation; the census counted him as an *in-*

dian, the absence of a native presence in the city" (50). In Foucauldian terms, Clement Vizenor's sense of identity has been determined by a will to knowledge, that which underlies the urge to observe, measure, and classify and exercises a "power of constraint upon other forms of discourse" (Foucault, *The Archaeology of Knowledge* 219). Nevertheless, Vizenor concludes: "Clement, his brothers, and other natives in urban areas were *indians* by simulation, transethnic by separation, but native in their stories of survivance" (*Fugitive Poses* 51). Once again we see Vizenor insisting on the affirmative presence of the Native in order to counteract the absence constructed by the Euramerican imagination.

As Blaeser points out, "a fixed grammar of themes" is a characteristic of orality that, in the attempt to narrow the distance between the oral and the written, Vizenor adopts in his writing (*Gerald Vizenor* 31). "Wistful Envies," the second of the five essays in *Fugitive Poses*, represents something of a variation on the theme of the "invented *indian*" and the series of tragic poses that have rendered Natives museum artifacts. In the process of exploring various Indian poseurs and other "wannabe" Indians, he introduces the term *varionative*, referring to that "uncertain curve of native antecedence" (*Fugitive Poses* 15) that triggers the nostalgia for lost origins. The discussion that follows ranges over the nineteenth century – such famous travelers as Charles Dickens, Giacomo Beltrami, and Alexis de Tocqueville who, in their journals, deploy the rhetoric of the vanishing American – and the twentieth. Reflecting Adorno's "second immediacy," however, the essay is neither passive nor objective. Rather, Vizenor playfully "immerses" himself in the issues at hand, opening up a dialogue with his subjects. Consider the following: "Dickens was certain to announce, unwearied of natural ruins, the romantic extinction of natives, a common treason of adventurers in the nineteenth century, and he did so with a curious aesthetic dominance. . . . V. S. Pritchett, in his essay on *The Mystery of Edwin Drood* by Dickens, notes that his 'natural genius is for human soliloquy not human intercourse.' *The omniscient novelist scarcely ever recounts the actual words of natives in his journal; the presence of native is a romantic soliloquy of their absence*" (77; emphasis added).

Vizenor is, however, most "immersed," most personally engaged, with the figure of Jamake Highwater, perhaps the most well-known of the twentieth-century Indian poseurs, notable for having invented much of the background that made him famous.[29] Despite Highwater's intense pride in being Indian, he was nevertheless, Vizenor argues, a simulation, the absence of the Native: "The reminiscer turned out to be the absence of the *real* in his own varionative poses and stories" (*Fugitive Poses* 68). Yet, Vizenor suggests, Highwater's impostures, clearly self-constructed, were ironic, definitely more artistic and creative than the eugenic blood-quantum theory and "other fascist certainties of identity" (69). As a result of scientism – what Tzvetan Todorov defines as "the use of science to establish ideology" (Todorov qtd. in Vizenor, *Fugitive Poses* 75) – modernity created, Vizenor claims, the objective simulations of racialism in order to document "authentic" Indian identities.

At this point in the essay Vizenor might seem, ironically, firmly entrenched in the declarative, objective style of social-scientific discourse, elaborating as he does on the idea (already advanced in *Manifest Manners*) of what he calls the eight "native theaters" that served scientism as sources of Native identity.[30] Nevertheless, he avoids the pitfalls of mimetic theories by relying on trickster's metaphoric language. Consider, for instance, his explanation of "native by victimry," the last of his eight categories: "The last native theater is the most wearisome, and one of the most common connections, or sources of varionative identities and historical condolences. This last estate is the pervasive autopose of victimry. The natives in this theater are cast as representations, the racialist tropes of vanishment; the historical measure of dominance, concessions, desistance, and the vectors of durative victimry" (*Fugitive Poses* 91). Here, even when mimicking a discourse fond of explanation and definition, Vizenor refuses to pin meaning down, ever committed to the notion that "*indians*" cannot be represented. He reverts to ambiguity and indeterminacy in order to maintain the open-ended nature of his narrative.

Discussing the controversial issue of blood-quantum theories in an interview with Laura Coltelli, Vizenor claims:

> To try to come up with a single idealistic definition of tradition in tribal culture is terminal. Cultures are not static, human behavior is not static. We are not what anthropologists say we are and we must not live up to a definition. . . . We are very complex human beings, all of us, everywhere, but especially in America and especially among tribal groups, and especially mixedbloods. Mixedbloods represent the actual physical union of the binary of tribal and Western. In my case it would be the premiere union between the French and the Anishinabeg or Chippewa. And I didn't have any choice in that, but I'm not a victim. (Coltelli 172)

Elsewhere, Vizenor has written that "mixedbloods loosen the seams in the shrouds of identity" (Swann and Krupat, *I Tell You Now* 101), suggesting a categorical rejection of the notion of blood as a marker of identity. By adopting the trickster figure (whose very identity reflects contradiction) as a metaphor for the mixedblood, Vizenor indicates that the existence of the mixed-blood resists any absolute definition. Mixedbloods exist in a sort of contact zone between age-old tribal traditions and contemporary adaptations. As Blaeser aptly points out, "The metaphor of the mixedblood itself represents a confluence in Vizenor, standing as it does not merely for the condition of race but also [primarily, I would argue] for the mixed conditions of culture, spiritual values, and traditions, sites of knowledge and truth, and personal and social motives, as well as for the mixed conditions of literary traditions" (*Gerald Vizenor* 156). Rather than adopting the victimizing pose of the mixed-blood trapped between two cultures, the pathetic, helpless, and hopeless figure of the Euramerican imagination, Vizenor finds ways to celebrate what he humorously calls "a torsion in the blood" (Pulitano, interview), conceiving of mixedbloods as a metaphor for tricksters. Like tricksters, mixedbloods mediate between worlds and worldviews, embracing contradictions, and surviving in a delicate, balancing act of mediation.

As I pointed out earlier, Vizenor's theoretical agenda parallels to a certain extent that of postcolonial critics. Mediating between the oral and the written traditions, his texts perfectly embody the cultural syncretism of postcolonial literatures as envisioned by Ashcroft et al. in their discussion of those poised on the border of two worlds. They write: "Post-colonial culture is inevitably a hybridized phenomenon involving a dialectical relationship between the 'grafted' European cultural system and an indigenous ontology, with its impulse to create or recreate an independent local identity. Such construction or reconstruction only occurs as a dynamic interaction between European hegemonic systems and 'peripheral' subversion of them'" (*The Empire Writes Back* 195; see also Blaeser, *Gerald Vizenor* 155–56). In the light of these words, I maintain that, despite the limitations of postcolonial theory itself as an approach to Native American literature,[31] the validity of that approach as far as Vizenor is concerned cannot be denied, at least in the sense that his works constitute what Ashcroft et al. would call "complex hybridized formations." As my discussion has so far illustrated, Vizenor's works do represent a considerable degree of hybridization between "the grafted European cultural system and an indigenous ontology" (Ashcroft et al., *The Empire Writes Back* 195). Shifting back and forth between Anishinaabe oral tradition and French high theory, they become the embodiment of counterdiscursive form.

When asked about the postcolonial phenomenon, Vizenor himself has admitted that he does not "see general postcolonial ideas or theories working easily to explain the native experience"; he does, nonetheless, acknowledge similarities between the strategies adopted by Native American authors and those of postcolonial writers and critics (Pulitano, interview). As we have seen, Native American writers and critics appropriate – consciously or otherwise – key terms from postcolonialism, adapting them to fit the Native experience. Appropriating Bhabha's notion of mimicry, and using it to describe Momaday's experimentation with Western literary techniques, allows Owens, for example, to get at the subversive nature of *House Made of Dawn*.[32] At the same time, however, Owens applies the concepts of hybridity and diaspora to the situation of Native American writers, questioning the significant erasure of Native American voices from the field of postcolonial theory, an erasure that makes postcolonial theory itself complicit with the kind of Eurocentric, imperialistic discourse that it purports to critique (see "As If an Indian" 224–26).

Unlike Owens, Vizenor does not consciously appropriate terms or strategies from postcolonial discourse theory in order to explicate the complex nature of his trickster universe. However, despite the fact that the postcolonial critics are, significantly, not among the extraordinary number of contemporary theorists from whom Vizenor borrows, a closer look at his trickster hermeneutics reveals a significant parallelism with postcolonial theory nevertheless. More important, that Vizenor moves – presumably unconsciously – along the lines of postcolonial formulations further illustrates some of the limitations of postcolonial theory itself, particularly in its attempt to position itself as a counterdiscursive form of resistance. Comparing Bhabha's notion of third space with Vizenor's concept of trickster as a metaphor for mixedblood identity bears out the point neatly.[33]

Drawing on the Benjaminian notion of translation, Bhabha argues that no culture is autonomous and authoritative in itself, not only "because there are other cultures which contradict its authority," but also because "its own symbol-forming activity" always underscores the claim to an originary moment. In other words, "Cultures are only constituted in relation to that otherness internal to their own symbol-forming activity which makes them decentered structures" (Bhabha in Rutherford 210). From this, Bhabha elaborates the notion of hybridity as an "act of cultural translation" that "denies the essentialism of a prior given original or originary culture.[34] He writes: "The importance of hybridity is not to be able to trace two original moments from which the third emerges, rather hybridity to me is the 'third space' which enables other positions to emerge. This third space displaces the histories that constitute it, and sets up new structures of authority, new political initiatives which are inadequately understood through received wisdom" (211).[35] As a liminal figure, inhabiting the space "between" two worlds and two cultures, Vizenor's trickster would seem to embody Bhabha's notion of hybridity, dismantling, as it does, essentialist notions of identity and pure origins. Within this context, then, the marginal status of trickster becomes a position of power from which to construct a new identity, an identity that, in Vizenor's formulation, exists at the intersections of cultures and survives by means of a constant struggle for balance.

Bhabha's notion of hybridity is fully elaborated within a semiotic context. In a catachrestic gesture Bhabha interrogates, (mis)appropriates, and transforms the terms or symbols of Western discourse. Thinking "outside the sentence," he wrenches words and concepts, tropes and ideologies, from their usual context, retextualizing them in a postcolonial, antidiscursive practice (*The Location of Culture* 180). In other words Bhabha becomes what Ashcroft et al. would consider the anticolonial appropriator who challenges the cultural and linguistic stability of the center by twisting old, authoritarian words into new, oppositional meanings. Yet critics have questioned whether Bhabha's style, dense and overblown, is appropriate to his subversive agenda, whether such opaque discourse can effectively convey the notion of hybridity, whether it is truly transnational and translational or ultimately Eurocentric at heart. Clearly such questions are beyond the scope of my project. They do, however, offer insight into Vizenor's writing strategies.

Like Bhabha's notion of hybridity, Vizenor's trickster is conceived within the realm of language, challenging in fundamental ways the accepted conventions of Western academic discourse. Unlike Bhabha's philosophical creed, however, Vizenor's is realized in both theory and practice, Vizenor ironically becoming, thus, one of the preeminent postcolonial (or not so "post") theorists of our time. Vizenor's mediational discourse has, however, a significant advantage over Bhabha's: a reliance on the patterns and rhythms of a discourse other than written in order to subvert the monologic structure of Western theory. Vizenor's trickster hermeneutics negotiates between two different epistemologies, and within this context it functions as the perfect embodiment of Bhabha's third space. By conceiving the mixedblood as a metaphor for the hybridized trickster, Vizenor has, indeed, found a new space out of which Native Americans can carve a new consciousness of coexistence. Verging in his work on a mixed identity, and, more important, perhaps, straddling the oral and the written traditions, he has found ways in which to engage readers (Natives and non-Natives alike) and thereby encourage them to reconsider their values and worldviews. Even the idea of a Native epistemology, which could be conceived as essentialist (think of

Allen's notions of tribal thought and a tribal universe), is, in Vizenor's formulation, not static or predetermined, but dynamic, acted out in the syncretic, adaptive nature of oral stories. As he puts it in *Earthdivers*, "Creation
myths are not time bound, the creation takes place in the telling, in present-
tense metaphors" (xii).

A Native epistemology is significantly reflected in the third essay of *Fugitive Poses*, "Literary Animals." Overturning the romantic pose that "sees" the
Indian as close to nature and to the animal world, Vizenor discusses the presence of animals in Native American literature and worldviews as, instead,
tropes of creation in the literature of survivance. Quoting from the Anishinaabe writer William Warren, he writes: "The *anishinaabe* are named in
'several grand families or clans, each of which is known and perpetuated by
a symbol of some bird, animal, fish, or reptile'" (*Fugitive Poses* 119). *Oodo-
demi*, Vizenor adds (with his usual twist on Derrida), the Anishinaabe term
meaning "totem" or "to have a totem," is "that native presence and trace of
the originary" (119), a definition quite different from the one provided by anthropologists. As in the other essays in *Fugitive Poses*, Vizenor presents his
dialogic strategy by engaging in a tricksterish exchange with social-scientific
discourse. For example, he contrasts the sacred version of the Anishinaabe
creation story as it is recounted by Warren, according to which five beings in
human form created the original five totems to which the Anishinaabe are related, with Lévi-Strauss's view that "the myth explains that these five 'original' clans are descended from six anthropomorphic supernatural beings who
emerged from the ocean to mingle with human beings" (Lévi-Strauss qtd. in
Vizenor, *Fugitive Poses* 122).

According to Blaeser, "By weaving his own works into a web of active connections, Vizenor invests them with a network of critical subtexts that add
richness and vitality to the written text" (*Gerald Vizenor* 190). In "Literary
Animals" Vizenor's "critical subtexts" allow him to cross the boundary between the oral and the written while writing back to the language of scientism. He adopts the notion of metaphor and metaphoric knowledge as
liberation and strategic indeterminacy to contrast with what he considers
Lévi-Strauss's deadly objectivism and rhetoric of absence. He writes: "Metaphors are crucial in the interpretation of native literature, and metaphors
are comparable as native traces, totems, shamanic visions, action, and con-
science of survivance" (*Fugitive Poses* 122). Vizenor had earlier – in the preface to *Earthdivers* – discussed the dialogic quality of metaphor – metaphor
as a means of transcendence – linking his ideas with those of theorists such
as Karsten Harries and Donald Davidson. In "Literary Animals" he elabo-

rates on these ideas, offering additional theoretical formulations meant to convey the idea of metaphor as a tool facilitating the comprehension of emotion, aesthetic experience, and spiritual awareness. In his ongoing attempt to escape from language into the realm of experience, Vizenor "uses metaphor," Blaeser suggests, "to create those moments when 'language falls apart and, falling apart, opens us to what transcends it'" (*Gerald Vizenor* 188). More important, she adds, "This understanding of metaphor has obvious similarities to Vizenor's philosophy of haiku and to his understanding of myth, in that all three – metaphor, haiku, and myth – operate within one realm of reality, the physical, with the express intention of providing an access to another, primal or spiritual realm" (188).

There is in Native epistemologies no separation among the various realms of existence, the universe being conceived of as a balanced equilibrium of forces. A tribal perspective thus views things very differently than does a Western scientific perspective. Take human-animal relations as an example. Far from attributing anything akin to human consciousness to animals, science clearly separates animal behavior from human reasoning (see Vizenor, *Fugitive Poses* 125). Vizenor, however, envisions animal-human relations in a tribal perspective. His novel *Bearheart*, for example, is set, he says, in "a time when humans, and animals, and birds got on pretty well, including language, and sex." He continues: "In some of the best natives stories, humans were related to bears, the creation of crossbloods. So the stories of human and animal unions created the first crossblood bears, wolves, eagles, and other creatures" (Vizenor in Lee, *Postindian Conversations* 100). Thus tribal traditions metaphorically represent primal connections, and, as Blaeser suggests, metaphoric language "points not to the words themselves, but to what lies beyond them" (*Gerald Vizenor* 190).

Considered from a tribal perspective, then, the problem with anthropology is that it relies, not on metaphoric knowledge, but on abstraction and depersonalized theories to objectify natural reason and the contingencies of humor.[36] In response to Lévi-Strauss, for example, Vizenor writes: "The native world is actuated in *anishinaabe* totems and stories of survivance. The totem is a native metaphor, a literary connection with creation, shamanic visions, a natural reason. Social science theories have reduced native myths, metaphors, and creation to the categorical representations of human development and comparative culture; these objective simulations have served dominance, not native survivance, and the perverse distinctions of savagism and civilization" (*Fugitive Poses* 123). Despite nostalgic perceptions of Natives as being in close association with nature and the natural, Native authors must, Vizenor points out, be ironic in their creations, their literary animals "traces of native transmotion and survivance" (133), in order to counteract the effect of the social-scientific view. Among those authors who effectively muster what he calls the "tropes of survivance" are Momaday, Silko, and Owens, authors who in their works give life to "metaphorical bears, wolves, mongrels, totemic cranes, and other creatures" (*Fugitive Poses* 133).

In the modernist aesthetic of romantic victimry, tragedy, and nostalgia, pictures are, Vizenor argues, the quintessential instruments of a rhetoric of surveillance whereby a Native presence is transposed into the spectacle of dominance. With the essay "Fugitive Poses," Vizenor returns to the theme of "*indian*" simulations, exploring in detail the representation of Natives in pictures and in what he calls "interimage simulations" (*Fugitive Poses* 147).[37] Ethnographic "interimages," Vizenor writes, have always fascinated explorers, Indians having been captured in paintings and engravings long before the invention of photography. In the sixteenth century, for example, Théodor de Bry created engravings of Indians that "were secured in museums, in academic service and as historical evidence" (151). The tradition continued into the nineteenth century in the work of such painters as George Catlin, Karl Bodmer, and Charles Bird King, who have been praised for "their exotic portraits of natives" (161–62). The camera only gave the colonizer yet another instrument with which to appropriate the Indian, capturing and, thus, imprisoning him in the fugitive poses of Occidental surveillance.

In "Fugitive Poses" Vizenor parallels the strategy that he employed in the previous essays, weaving his argument into a web of connections that open up the discussion in various directions while refusing, once again, to conform to the dictates of Western, analytic discourse. Susan Sontag, Roland Barthes, David Freedberg, Robert Brilliant, and W. J. T. Mitchell are some of the critics whose work he employs to discuss the interimage simulations of "*indians.*" Never commenting conventionally on any of the material that he quotes, Vizenor instead leaves the reader to make all the connections and critical evaluations. Consider the following "play" with Barthes's *Image-Music-Text*: "Roland Barthes argues that 'all images are polysemous.' The interimage of the *indian* is the absence of the unnameable native. The *indian* is not a connection to the real, a sense of presence, or crease of natural reason. Underlying the semiotic signifiers of the image, or the actual perception, are 'a "floating chain" of signifieds,' or the concepts, and the reader 'is able to choose some and ignore others.' . . . The interimage is polysemous, a dysfunction of meaning; the *indian* is a polyseme of tragic victimry" (*Fugitive Poses* 146). As is usual in Vizenor's strategy, Western language theories are subsumed within a Native discourse since language is, for Vizenor, the most imprisoning but, at the same time, and all the more ironically, perhaps the most liberating tool with which to escape the signifier "*indian.*"

Elaborating in *Picture Theory* on Foucault's characterization of our age as one of "surveillance," W. J. T. Mitchell envisions a "pictorial turn," a culture (usually identified as postmodern) totally dominated by images, something that has now become "a real possibility on a global scale" (15). Similarly, in *On Photography* Susan Sontag writes that "humankind lingers unregenerately in Plato's cave, still reveling, its age-old habit, in mere images of the truth" (3). Echoing Foucault, she adds: "To photograph is to appropriate the thing photographed. It means putting oneself into a certain relation to the world that feels like knowledge – and, therefore, like power" (4). As a tool of power, photography, then, aptly reflects the imperialist ideology of dominance over Native people. "After the opening of the West in 1869, by the completion of the transcontinental railroad came the colonization through photography," Sontag writes, adding that "the case of the American Indians is the most brutal" (64). More significantly, Vizenor writes, "At the same time that colonial nations dominated much of the world and many native communities were removed to federal exclaves, the new technologies of photography captured the fugitive other in the structural representations of savagism and civilization. The 'pictorial turn' of cultural surveillance, the desires of objectivism in the new social sciences, became the manifest manners of the time" (*Fugitive Poses* 152).

Objectivism, desire for the Other, visibility, scrutiny – all are metaphors for ways of knowing through which Euroimperial ideology has legitimated dominance for several centuries. "Occidental surveillance, not observation," generated, Vizenor argues, the "fugitive poses" of the camera, interimage simulations that erased Native stories and the presence of Natives who, ironically, "were observers, more mature in their humor, tease of causes, and tragic wisdom than their 'discoverers'" (*Fugitive Poses* 157). To the innumerable representations and simulations of Natives in "portraitures," Vizenor opposes the ironies of postindian literature, ironies that, through trickster stories, transmute these contradictions and "closures" into a continuous presence of Native people.

Stories as affirmative presence and survivance inform the nature and content of Vizenor's last essay, "Native Transmotion." The essay begins with a discussion of a 1968 court case: specifically, Charles Aubid's testimony in his dispute with the federal government over the right to regulate the wild rice harvest on the Rice Lake National Refuge, near the East Lake Reservation in northern Minnesota.[38] The engagement with legal themes that we see in *Fugitive Poses* is, however, not new to Vizenor's work. Neither does it take his work in an entirely different direction. Rather, the law figures prominently in all his work since, historically, almost every aspect of tribal life has been determined by U.S. law. From tribal identity to territorial rights, from casinos to the Indian Arts and Craft Act of 1990,[39] court cases are, for Vizenor, cultural definitions, a further attempt by Euramerica to establish and define "*indians*" as absence.

In his play *Ishi and the Wood Ducks*, for instance, Vizenor explores the issue of establishing a tribal identity by bringing Ishi to court. Charged with violating the Indian Arts and Crafts Act – since "he sold objects as tribal made, and could not prove that he was in fact a member of a tribe recognized by a reservation government" (327) – Ishi is trapped by the Euramerican legal system, his tribe having been ruled extinct and he himself, therefore, being ruled not an Indian. Despite the court's ruling, what is truly important, Vizenor argues, is that Ishi's character and identity are established in his endless wood duck stories, those that the actual Ishi liked to tell in his museum home and that took seven hours in the telling. Vizenor's point here is that Natives reveal their living character in the creative moment that is the telling of their stories. In that moment, Vizenor insists, the world is imagined in its eternal mutability and a Native sense of identity reshaped.

This is also the point of introducing the story of Aubid. Speaking in Anishinaabemowin, the language of the Anishinaabe, Aubid testified in court that he had been present years earlier when government agents had declared that the Anishinaabe would always have control of the wild rice harvest. Vizenor writes: "Aubid told the judge that there was once a document, but the *anishinaabe* always understood their rights in stories, not hearsay" (168). Just as Ishi created an Indian presence is his stories, Aubid created an Anishinaabe presence in his testimony. In this sense, Vizenor writes, "he was a virtual cartographer, because he mapped a visual representation, a native criterion of transmotion and sovereignty" (*Fugitive Poses* 169).

Whereas Euramerica uses maps to resolve issues of sovereignty, Natives rely on creation stories, which, even when incised on birch bark or cedar (pictomyths), testify more, Vizenor suggests, to creative connections and natural reason than to a sense of possession and ownership. Thus the story of Aubid brings Vizenor to the issue of indigenous versus colonial law as a metaphor for the clash of distinct and often irreconcilable worldviews. Elaborating on Norman Thrower's discussion of the Hereford Cathedral *mappamundi* as a "thirteenth-century map of the world," containing pictures, trade routes, secular histories, myths, and other information, Vizenor writes: "There is no commensurate *mappamundi* of the native world; however, the native stories of creation, totemic visions, and sacred documents are comparable to the spiritual inspiration of cathedral windows" (*Fugitive Poses* 175). Within a Native epistemology, stories are, in a sense, maps, whether they convey information about specific trails or, more significantly, make sense of a specific locale and its importance to the people.

In *The Way to Rainy Mountain*, for instance, Momaday refers to a crucial mythic moment in the history of the Kiowa. He writes: "There are things in nature that engender an awful quiet in the heart of man: Devil's Tower is one of them. Two centuries ago, because they could not do otherwise, the Kiowas made a legend at the base of the rock" (8).[40] Tsoai, the Kiowa name for Devil's Tower, is, thus, a crucial landmark in the Kiowa imagination, its story an active creation that tells people who they are and where they come from. Such a story, as Vizenor would put it, is the transmotion of Native memories and the sense of presence.

Native stories, totemic creations, and other forms of mental mapping are, for Vizenor, the virtual cartography of Native survivance and sovereignty. Unlike those of Warrior, Cook-Lynn, and other fervent representatives of nationalistic discourse, Vizenor's notion of sovereignty, to which the ideology of nationalism strictly appeals, "does not embrace inheritance or tenure of territory" (*Fugitive Poses* 178). "There is no such word [as *sovereignty*] in the *anishinaabe* language" (178), Vizenor writes. The Native sense of motion and use of the land goes beyond mere reservation territory. According to Vizenor, "The sovereignty of motion is mythic, material, and visionary not mere territoriality, in the sense of colonialism and nationalism. Native transmotion is an original natural union in the stories of emergence and migration that relate humans to an environment and to the spiritual and political significance of animals and other creations. Monotheism is dominance over nature; transmotion is natural reason, and native creation with other creatures" (183).

Vizenor's idea of sovereignty, which he reinvents as *sovenance*, obviously does not operate within the same epistemological framework as the European concept does; more significantly, it becomes a critical lens through which the categories of nationalism and invented blood taxonomies can be deconstructed. In line with some of the most prominent contemporary theorists of sovereignty, such as F. H. Hinsley and Alan James, Vizenor argues that sovereignty is an idea – a "kitschy" European political fiction – that has no connection to the ways of life of indigenous peoples. Similarly, the ideology of nationalism, which strongly relies on the notion of sovereignty, is a further example of "*indian*" simulations. More important the European idea of sovereignty embraced by nationalism in invoking a lineage of racialism as a source of Indian authenticity ends up, Vizenor argues, legitimating the objectivism of social science with its overtly dangerous impulse to categorize, dissect, and analyze. Tracing the history of the term *sovereignty* as well as its significance in the context of the innumerable treaty agreements reached between the United States and Native communities, Vizenor argues that "treaties, then, are not an absolute assurance of native sovereignty" since sovereignty as transmotion is visionary and "motion is a natural human right that is not bound by borders" (*Fugitive Poses* 189, 188–89). Again and again, to the means and declarations of territorial separatism and nationalism Vizenor opposes the ability to move in the imagination, the ability that establishes a sense of presence for Native people.

At the conclusion of his essay on *Fugitive Poses*, Colin Samson argues, "There is clearly a positive, affirmative message of native survivance which comes through [in Vizenor's writing]. The affirmation is always to the autonomous ways of thinking and being of native people" (292). In order to convey this message, Vizenor adopts both trickster strategies and contemporary deconstructivist theories and produces a form of criticism that, in its uniquely "postindian" styling, sets him apart from the other authors discussed in this study. Vizenor's tribal-cum-postmodern and -poststructuralist turn represents a defiant, thought-provoking response to the construction in Euramerican discourse of Indianness. Against the innumerable inventions and reinventions of Natives as "*indians*," simulations of dominance the ultimate goal of which is to fix Natives, to confine them within museum walls, Vizenor deinvents such inventions by offering portraits, not of victims, but of survivors. Survival, for Vizenor, is primarily achieved through the vehicle of stories and humor. Trickster stories, in particular, provide the sense of liberation and comic survivance necessary to oust the invention. Like Wenebojo, the trickster earthdiver who creates a new turtle island by keeping on "throwing earth around," Vizenor's survivors create a new, dynamic identity in stories, overthrowing the simulations and fugitive poses of manifest manners and colonialism.

In the context of a Native American critical theory as I have delineated it in this study, Vizenor's position appears extremely radical. His ongoing attempt to write in the oral tradition produces a critical discourse that disrupts our expectations and forces us to think in new ways. More forcefully and more provocatively than the other theorists that I have discussed, Vizenor combines revolutionary content and revolutionary style, presenting a significant alternative to Western hermeneutics. Rejecting any form of separatism and essentialism as far as Indian identity is concerned, he celebrates a discourse that is communal and comic. Like Sarris and Owens, Vizenor embraces a crosscultural approach, one merging Native epistemology with Western literary forms. His approach, however, is more revolutionary than theirs, attempting as it does to fuse, at every level of discourse, the tribal with the nontribal, the old with the new, the oral with the written. Such a crosscultural, dialogic approach takes an even more radical turn as Vizenor attempts to break free of the confining rules of language and restore the liberative, imaginative freedom inspired by tribal storytelling. As the epigraph to this chapter demonstrates, Vizenor firmly believes that "tribal people were brilliant in understanding that a figure, a familiar figure in an imaginative story, could keep their minds free" (Vizenor qtd. in Blaeser, *Gerald Vizenor* 162). It is this liberation that Vizenor's works constantly seek to convey, through dialogue, through humor, through stories, stories that become, once again, "the canons of survivance" (*Fugitive Poses* 23).

Conclusion

In Louis Owens's *The Sharpest Sight*, Uncle Luther warns the protagonist about the risks, for an individual, of forgetting his stories: "You see, a man's got to know the stories of his people, and then he's got to make his own story too" (91). At the same time, he continues, "We got to be aware of the stories they're making about us, and the way they change the stories we already know" (91). This study began with the question of whether there is such a thing as Native American critical theory and what fundamental assumptions characterize it. As Uncle Luther (or Owens) suggests, Western representations and constructions of Native American people and cultures have become part of the mainstream discourse; those are "the stories" that Europeans make about Natives and Native cultures. Yet it is also crucial for Native people to make their own stories since, as Luther/Owens posits, stories have the power to change the world: "They're always making up stories, and that's how they make the world the way they want it" (91).

Kimberley Blaeser uses Uncle Luther's warning to argue for the necessity of a tribal-centered criticism. Although not completely dismissing Western interpretations of Native literature, Blaeser does hope for a (Native) criticism arising from an indigenous cultural context or, as she puts it, "a critical voice and method which moves from the culturally-centered text outward toward the frontier of 'border' studies" ("Native Literature" 53). I would like to think that the strategies and discursive modes articulated by the authors under analysis in my study have begun to provide the critical center that Blaeser has been looking for.

Despite a general assumption that a "resistance to theory" characterizes the field of Native American studies – the result of a mentality that aligns theory with the privileged terrain of Western discourse – Allen, Warrior, Womack, Sarris, Owens, and Vizenor clearly demonstrate otherwise. As my discussion has indicated, these authors have produced and keep producing discursive strategies and theoretical interpretations of Native American literature and culture that could, indeed, represent the beginning of a Native American critical theory. Unlike critics who approach Native literature from a Western standpoint, imposing external critical voices and methods on Native texts, Allen, Warrior, Womack, Sarris, Owens, and Vizenor have developed hybridized interpretative tools originating largely, if not exclusively, from indigenous rhetoric(s) and worldviews and incorporated into the strategies of Western critical discourse. The diversity of positions taken by each clearly shows that there is no such thing as a monolithic, unified form of discourse for Native theory, only a variety of approaches that, within their differences, still find some common ground.

A first, primary assumption is the idea of inscribing the functions and nature of the oral tradition onto the written page, revitalizing and reimagining a tradition too often reduced, in the Euramerican imagination, to merely cultural artifact and too often theorized as a symbol of the predicted vanishing race. From Allen's gynocentrism to Womack's "Red Stick theory," from Warrior's notion of tradition (closely modeled on Deloria's views) to Sarris's account of Mabel McKay's stories, from Owens's dialogic approach to Vizenor's trickster hermeneutics, these authors suggest meaningful ways in which Native American rhetoric and epistemology can enter the discourse of First World ideology while inevitably remapping the boundaries of the contemporary critical debate. A second assumption, clearly related to the first, is the idea of conveying in writing the dynamic quality of the oral exchange so that, despite the confinement of the printed text, the vitality and power of language are still maintained. The most significant result of this crosscultural "translation," which might constitute a further point of encounter among all the writers discussed, is the multigeneric, heteroglot, and border quality of their texts, texts in which the traditionally objective, authoritative stance of the Western critic is significantly dismantled and the text itself becomes, much like a story, an open form, one involving the direct participation of the reader (listener). Shifting between third and first person, scholarly argument and personal narrative, weaving together bits and pieces of various discourses, Allen, Warrior, Womack, Sarris, Owens, and Vizenor devise new, creative ways of doing theory and, ultimately, challenge the West to reconsider the meanings and values of its own cultural traditions.

Given the cultural and ideological diversity of the authors selected, my study has called attention to the different approaches and methodologies envisioned from within the above-mentioned commonalities. One of the main goals of this discussion has been to point out the heterogeneity of discourses that has resulted; it has also pointed out the "conversation" that these authors' texts carry on with and against the larger discourse of Western, Eurocentric theory. As I argued in the introduction, one of the primary tenets of my study is that there is no such thing as a "pure," authentic Native American theory, as opposed, for example, to a Western critical discourse, since Native American literature itself is the product of Western and Native cultural traditions. Despite critical positions that claim otherwise, Native American writers and critics are inevitably implicated in the discourse of the dominant center, and, from such an unstable, strategic location, they articulate their critical voice. Even though it might be tempting to argue for a kind of separatist discourse – one that, as Allen, Warrior, and Womack point out, relies exclusively on the discursive modes of Native traditions rather than embracing the instruments of Western literary analysis – such Nativist approaches are simply not viable owing to the fact that the Native traditions themselves are inaccessible except in their always-already mediated or hybridized state. More important, such separatist stances risk becoming counterproductive if we want a Native American theory to challenge the binary opposition of Western conceptual frameworks. Any kind of Nativist approach, as I define it in my study, ultimately ends up perpetuating the categories of an us/them universe, merely reversing the terms of the opposition and granting the Indian a privileged position.

As I consider the work of Allen, Warrior, and Womack now, it strikes me as somehow ironic that, from within their separatist positions, these authors, self-consciously or not, to a certain degree conduct a dialogue with the discourse of Eurocentric theory even when such Western theoretical references are intended as a forceful critique of the discourse of the dominant center. Although Allen refuses any association with Western feminist theory, my discussion has suggested ways in which her critical stance, especially in *Off the Reservation*, parallels some of the ideological concerns of ecofeminist discourse. *Off the Reservation* as a whole, then, deeply modeled on Anzaldúa's *mestizaje* theory, is meant as an exploration of the concepts of border crossing and boundary busting, a strategy that makes any kind of separatist discourse logically untenable. Even though Womack's "Red Stick theory" opts for a rigorous Native separatism, his reference to queer theory as a way in which to legitimate a separatist Native discourse makes his overall position ambiguous since, as critics have pointed out, queer theory itself originates out of a poststructuralist, deconstructivist mode. Similarly ambivalent in Warrior's critical position is the question of how effective it is to argue for an authentic tradition of Indian intellectualism based on Mathews's and Deloria's ideas when these Native intellectual figures themselves are highly cosmopolitan and reveal in their work a substantial degree of hybridization with the Eurocentric Western cultural tradition.

Within such a mediative frontier zone of discourse, Native American theory appears to be facing ambiguities similar to those pointed out by Henry Louis Gates Jr. in his discussion of the relation between black literature and literary theory. Rather than inventing valid black critical instruments and methodologies to explicate the "signifying" black differences, Gates suggests ways in which the fused forms of African oral traditions and Western critical theory can produce original ways of reading (interpreting) black literary texts (*Black Literature* 9–10). Such a syncretic maneuver characterizes, I argue, the nature and content of Native American critical theory as well. Despite the critiques leveled against hybrid, crosscultural approaches to Native American literature and theory, critiques advanced primarily by nationalist or indigenist practitioners, I argue that strategies of hybridization and cultural syncretism are already going on in the literature produced by Native American authors; they are the result of the "conjunction of cultural practices" that, as Krupat reminds us, has shaped Native-European relations for more than five hundred years. To envision a Native American theory as a form of authentic indigenous discourse, one uncontaminated by the practices of European analysis, is, thus, simply not possible.

As my discussion has indicated, within the contemporary scenario of the various theoretical "post" isms, a unique kind of relation binds Native American authors to the discursive modes of postcolonial theory. Despite the fact that it is not quite correct to conceptualize the situation of Native American writers as *postcolonial*, and despite the cultural, historical, and geopolitical differences between Native American cultures and so-called postcolonial societies around the world, the writers under analysis in my study do, from the diversity of their own positions, self-consciously or not, carry on a "conversation" with postcolonial theory. Reflecting Spivak's notion of "catachresis," these writers often apply the categories of postcolonial discourse to the Native American experience and, more important, turn the instruments of postcolonial theory against itself. As I hope my discussion of Owens and Vizenor has demonstrated, Native American writers and theorists do also accomplish acts of "mimicry" and "anti-imperial translation" aimed at exposing the ambivalence of the discourse of the metropolitan center. At the same time, however, as in the case of Owens, their critique is also directed toward postcolonial theory itself: toward its blatant ignorance in not recognizing the literature of Native American writers as being among the minority literatures in America and toward the fact that, despite its premises, postcolonial theory often remains another form of Eurocentric discourse, one in which the "acts of crosscultural translation," as intended by Bhabha, remain ironically and inevitably always within the confines of the West. Unlike the postcolonial phenomenon, Native American theory, with its merging of indigenous oral traditions and Western discursive modes, does bring to our attention the ideological and epistemological predicaments of cultures "other" than the West, challenging us to expand our conceptual horizons and significantly embrace those crosscultural encounters so often theorized within postcolonial discourse.

As a non-Native critic presenting this material from the outside, but implicating and exposing my own readerly position as well, it appears quite natural for me to embrace the crosscultural dialogic approach of Sarris, Owens, and Vizenor, rather than the separatist stances of Allen, Warrior, and Womack. On the border of different cultures, a mediator and interpreter of cultures myself, I produce a discourse on Native American theory, not meaning to appropriate or colonize, but hoping to foster genuine crosscultural understanding. However, even though my ideological position might lead me to favor one critical position over another, I do acknowledge the importance of them all in attempting to generate a criticism whose discursive modes originate from the cultural traditions of the texts themselves.

As I argued in my introduction, a study of such complexity cannot and should not hope to be exhaustive. My purpose here was to suggest the parameters that might define Native American critical theory today while dismantling the curious assumption that theory does not belong to the realm of Native American studies. Not only do Native American writers produce critical methodologies concerning the nature and context of Native American experiences, but, more forcefully than their Euramerican counterparts, they are challenging all of us to open up to ways of being in the world that are very different from the models consigned to us by the Eurocentric tradition. If we do envision Native American literature as participating in the discourse of American and world literature, it seems all the more necessary to envision Native American theory in the context of a global theory in order for us to understand our value and meaning in a global community. On the border of various discourses, inside and outside the West, always in the shifting and shimmering fluid zone of trickster, Native American theory calls for multidirectional boundaries that will continue to be crossed as we as a community keep pursuing a crosscultural dialogue. Like the protagonist in Silko's *Ceremony*, we might finally "[see] the pattern, the way all the stories fit together." We might "see" and "hear" the world "as it always was: no boundaries only transitions through all distances and time" (246).

Notes

INTRODUCTION

1. The contemporary debate over tribal identity, integrity, and authenticity also accounts for my semantic choices. In this study, I most often use the term *Native American* as opposed to, e.g., *aboriginal* or *indigenous* mainly because it is accepted and commonly used by the writers whose work is the subject of this study. For the sake of convenience, however, I occasionally retain the familiar *Indian*, even though I am perfectly well aware of the heavily colonial overtones invested in it. As Gerald Vizenor forcefully points out, the term *Indian* has been used since Columbus to create manifold representations of Natives. Yet the *Indian* never existed in reality: "The word Indian . . . is a colonial enactment . . . [a] simulation that has superseded the real tribal names" (*Manifest Manners* 11).

2. Within this context, Native writers and critics such as Jace Weaver have also been excluded from my discussion. *That the People May Live*, Weaver's critical analysis of Native American literature in the last two hundred years, an analysis substantiated by his interesting concept of "communitism," adds very little to a discourse on Native American critical theory that is attempting to generate rhetorical strategies of its own. Similarly, a work such as Owens's *Other Destinies* clearly responds, in its Bakhtinian approach to Native American fiction, to a purpose other than that which my study intends to pursue.

3. While contributing to a discourse on Native American theory and criticism in many important ways, showing how attention to Native intellectual figures such as John Joseph Mathews and Vine Deloria Jr. might benefit a Native American critical discourse, Warrior's critical strategy follows a more traditional Western rhetorical pattern.

4. While Parry and Young's critiques are mainly directed against Said's idea of the *human* – which he opposes to the Western representation of the Orient, but which, ironically, Parry and Young argue, is itself derived from the Western humanist tradition – those critiques acquire conceptual force in the context of a conception of hybridization intended as a synthesizing, dialectical, and progressivist teleology. See Parry 30; and Young 131–32. On the notion of *the hybrid*, see also Bhabha, *The Location of Culture*, 102–22.

5. The concept *transculturation* was, as Lionnet points outs, first advanced by Fernando Ortiz, for whom the term meant the assimilation of Afro-Cuban culture into Hispanic culture. Unlike Ortiz's, Morejon's view of transculturation is, according to Lionnet, a "more dialectic phenomenon" and better responds to Lionnet's notion of *métissage*. See "'Logiques Métisses'" 341.

6. Drawing from Edouard Glissant (one of the most influential theorists of the Creolization process), Bongie posits that all essentialist glorifications of unitary origins – what Glissant refers to as "the univocal pretension of the identitary" – run contrary to the hybridized arguments that have gained such prominence of late in postcolonial theory (Bongie 63). Yet, Bongie argues, in order to avoid the sort of hierarchical thinking often underlying the notion of Creolization, it is necessary to acknowledge the paradoxical coexistence of two different logics. He writes: "What this statement suggests is that the connection between fixed and relational identities is not (simply) a matter of either/or but (also) of both/and" (66).

7. Elaborating on Glissant's formulations, Bongie reads the critic's phrase *identité-relation* in an equivocating manner, suggesting that the hyphen does not so much separate as join both elements interstitially, "the old world of a necessarily circumscribed local identity, and the new world of an increasingly chaotic and globalized cross-cultural relations" (70).

8. Other critics have addressed the homogenizing tendency of postcolonial theory. For a more detailed discussion, see chapter 3.

9. As Owens points out, Said's reference to Native American writing as "that sad panorama produced by genocide and cultural amnesia which is beginning to be known as Native American literature" makes a statement about the kind of imperialist terminology often adopted by postcolonial theorists ("As If an Indian" 210).

10. Spivak uses the notion of catachresis, which I discuss in my chapter on Vizenor's works, primarily in the context of Derrida's theory. According to Spivak, deconstruction must be "catachresized" by testing Derrida's ideological predicaments against non-Western cultural contexts. See Moore-Gilbert 83–91.

1. BACK TO A WOMAN-CENTERED UNIVERSE

1. The category *women of color* is a complex, multiple, and problematic site of representation that resists definition. Chandra Talpade Mohanty claims that the term

(often used interchangeably with *Third World women*) "designates a political constituency, not a biological or even sociological one. It is a sociopolitical designation for people of African, Caribbean, Asian, and Latin American descent, and native peoples of the U.S." "It also refers," she continues, "to 'new immigrants' to the U.S. in the last decade – Arab, Korean, Thai, Laotian, etc.," all of which, she argues, are bound by a *"common context of struggle* rather than color or racial identifications" (Mohanty, "Cartographies of Struggle" 7). On the other hand, bell hooks and Gayatri Spivak warn against the danger of homogenizing differences under the monolithic designation *women of color*, a designation working "to erase class and other differences" (hooks and Childers 78) and to ignore the persuasive significance of "color" within the postcolonial world (Spivak, "Can the Subaltern Speak?" 294). Nevertheless, many critics point out that the term *women of color* was first produced and then legislated by discriminatory racialist practice and that the very name validates racial/ ethnic/color categories. Sandra Kumamoto Stanley argues that, as a "product shaped by the civil rights and women's movement, women of color . . . participated in, as well as critiqued, the 'second wave' of feminism in the late sixties and early seventies" (5), significantly challenging race and class blindness in the white movement. In accordance with white feminists' earlier attempt to decenter a hegemonic male subject, feminists of color seek to dismantle any "mythos of a homogeneous female subject identified with white middle-class norms" (5).

2. The only piece by Allen included in *Making Face, Making Soul* is her poem "Some Like Indians Endure." A few other poems by Joy Harjo, Janice Gould, and Anna Waters are also collected there.

3. Published in 1996, Keating's was the first and remains to date the only book to devote full attention to Allen's critical apparatus while illustrating the possibility of writing the "feminine" in open-ended, nonexclusionary ways. See esp. *Women Reading Women Writing*, chap. 4.

4. I am thinking here of, among others, Donna Haraway's, Judith Butler's, and Theresa de Lauretis's critiques, of which more later.

5. Both Chicano and non-Chicano readers have pointed out how, by privileging in *Borderlands/La Frontera* the pre-Columbian deity Coatlicue, Anzaldúa obscures the plight of present-day Native women in the Americas while inevitably romanticizing an indigenous past for Chicano people. See, e.g., Sánchez; Fregoso and Chabram. Similarly, Lorde has been accused of constructing a monolithic paradigm of black female experience that does not engage black women's differences. See, e.g., bell hooks's critique in *Black Looks*.

On the other hand, Allen's significant exclusion from the contemporary theoretical discourse among women of color goes, I would contend, beyond failed alliances. As a Native American author, one among many marginalized voices in the United States, Allen is positioned even more in the shadows. If, as Owens has posited (see

"As If an Indian" 209–10), Native American writers are, unlike other minority writers in the United States, consistently ignored within contemporary debates on postcolonial theories, a similar lack of attention within the decolonizing project of the women-of-color movement is indicative of the situation of Native American studies within minority discourse.

6. Sandoval applies Louis Althusser's account of ideology and social formation to Third World women, arguing that, when women of color can identify the ideological implications of the categories into which they have been marginalized, they can then begin to create a space for an "oppositional consciousness." Sandoval argues that, since the 1960s, U.S. Third World feminists have practiced what she calls a "differential consciousness," the expression of the new subject position called for by Althusser, one that functions within yet beyond the demands of dominant ideology (3). Compared to Sandoval's critical stance, Allen's position seems more radical since her "new subject position" is meant as a rigid oppositional stance to the demands of dominant ideology. See also Althusser's "Ideology and Ideological State Apparatuses."

7. While in adopting the term *ethnographic discourse* I might at first have been influenced by Renae Moore Bredin's concept of "guerrilla ethnography," intended as an overturning of prototypical "white" ethnographic discourse by women of color, my position departs radically from Bredin's, especially in the context of Allen's critical practice. I will return to Bredin's work later.

8. According to Keating, because myths embody cultures' often unquestioned beliefs about human nature, revisionist mythmaking allows women writers to subvert negative depictions of female identity by telling "their" side of the story and rearranging the narrative events. On women writers' revisionist myths, see DuPlessis; Ostriker.

9. According to Owens, courses in American Indian literature too often constitute little more than excursions into "Indian Territory," one- or two-semester trips that allow students briefly to experience a "touch of the exotic," to come into contact with colorful Natives and authentic Indian spiritualism. Quoting Vizenor's famous line that "some upsetting is necessary," Owens argues that the territory of Native American literature is in no way a "safe space" and that all those entering it will need to reconsider their assumptions. "Literary terrorism," he argues, "is preferable to literary tourism" (*Mixedblood Messages* 46).

10. As critics have pointed out, Irigaray's search for a "female imaginary" epitomizes a general trend in French feminist theory advocating a retreat into aesthetics at the expense of feminist struggle. For a detailed discussion of Irigaray and her critics, see Fuss 55–72.

11. Chicano and non-Chicano critics alike have made similar charges against An-

zaldúa's privileging of Coatlicue, or Lady of the Serpent Skirt, the pre-Columbian deity symbolizing the nondualistic fusion of opposites – destruction/creation, male/ female, light/dark. See Anzaldúa, *Borderlands/La Frontera*. For a critique of Anzaldúa's position, see Fregoso and Chabram.

12. Allen refers to herself as "confluence" in "The Autobiography of a Confluence."

13. Allen notes that, among the Lagunas and Acomas, there are no rulers in the Anglo-European sense of monarchs, lords, and such and that social status is determined by one's mother's clan and position. The term *rulers* clearly represents an alteration to the story on Gunn's part, a result of his Westernized or masculine interpretation of it.

14. The scholarship on such a topic is too extensive to be satisfactorily documented here. For representative pieces, see Swan and Krupat, *Recovering the Word*; Tedlock; Hymes, *"In Vain I Tried to Tell You"*; and Murray.

15. Sarris is quoting Allen, *The Sacred Hoop* 234, 239.

16. I borrow the phrase *real Indian* from Owens, who ironically comments that, since most of what is referred to as postcolonial theory today is produced by "real" Indians from India, when writing and speaking about indigenous Native American literature, we need change neither "noun" nor "modifier" – "as if an Indian were really an Indian" ("As If an Indian" 207).

17. In *The Postcolonial Critic*, Spivak makes it clear that it is not her intention to marginalize the author's position on the story or to dismiss it. Rather, by "revising" Mahasweta's reading, she hopes to prove that her own reading has a different focus (157–58).

18. According to Spivak, Kristeva's arguments regarding the role of the Virgin within cultural subject representation and constitution are "so close to isomorphic generalizations" that they might be effectively contrasted with Mahasweta's critique of the nationwide patriarchal rendering of the Hindu Divine Mother and Holy Child. The story as a whole, she posits, is a satiric indexing of the ideological use of goddesses and mythic god women (*In Other Worlds* 264).

19. That Mother Earth is *the* major American goddess has, in the past few years, been questioned – and not only within a feminist poststructuralist context. Sam Gill, e.g., argues that to conceive of the religious traditions of the hundreds of North American tribes as a single, homogeneous tradition, with the ubiquity and antiquity of Mother Earth as the unifying element, is wrong. Careful examination of the evidence from history and from the tribal cultures on which the discussion of Mother Earth has centered will reveal, he suggests, little evidence corroborating such a position. The story of Mother Earth, Gill claims, "has come into existence in America largely during the last one hundred years and . . . her existence stems primarily from two creative groups: scholars and Indians" (7).

20. Keating's singular interpretation of Anzaldúa's *mestizaje écriture* primarily responds to many U.S. and British feminists' objections to the valorization of the body in writing. By using body writing to deconstruct male/female binary systems, these critics argue that Cixous's notion of *écriture féminine* ultimately reverses the values assigned to each side of the polarity, leaving man as the determining referent. In other words, rather than departing from male/female opposition, Cixous participates in it. See Jones; and Davis.

21. While warning her female colleagues in charge of creating the discipline of women's studies that essentialism is a trap – since women "do not relate to the privileging of essence" (especially through literature) in the same way – in the context of the Subaltern Studies Group Spivak has talked about a "strategic use of a positivist essentialism in a scrupulously visible political interest" (*In Other Worlds* 89, 205).

2. INTELLECTUAL SOVEREIGNTY AND RED STICK THEORY

1. Womack's approach is named after the Red Stick movement, an anticolonial movement strongly inspired by religion and myth. As Womack relates, in 1813–14, a group of traditional Creeks, seeing their land invaded from all sides, came up with a radically different plan for dealing with the colonizer. They turned to tradition, not as a reactionary mode, but as an innovatory mode, initiating new ways of life within the world created by contact (11–12). On the Red Stick movement, see Martin.

2. Since his first critical work, *The Voice in the Margin* (1989), Krupat has been campaigning for a "cosmopolitan literary canon" to which Native American literature belongs. He resumes the same idea in *Ethnocriticism* (1992) and *The Turn to the Native* (1996).

3. In Krupat's view, the nationalists' critical position is based on the legal and political significance of the term *sovereignty*, extending its political implications to literature. As a result, "nationalists tend to see the inclusion of Native American texts in anthologies of *American* literature as appropriation" and would rather see them appear in anthologies of Native literature only, most likely taught in Native American studies or American Indian studies programs. On the other hand, the indigenists' critical position is based on a "geocentric- or place-specific philosophy," but, unlike the nationalists, the indigenists would probably disperse Native literary expression among anthologies (of, e.g., Fourth and Fifth World literature) and departmental locations ("Nationalism" 617–21). Krupat's concept of *oxymoron* is, in *Ethnocriticism*, developed to illustrate how an apparently oppositional and paradoxical discourse (such as an ethnocritical one, located both "on and of the frontier, traversing middles ground while aspiring to a certain centrality") allows, nonetheless, for "polysemous and complex meanings" (28–29).

4. Appiah notes that his father, a cosmopolitan patriot, believed that "there was

no point in roots if you couldn't take them with you" ("Cosmopolitan Patriots" 618). Against the narrow nationalist position, according to which the cosmopolitan is a rootless, diasporic individual, Appiah argues that cosmopolitan patriots can be "attached to a home of [their] own, with its own cultural particularities, but taking pleasure from the presence of other, different places that are home to other different people" (618).

5. Among the essentialists, Warrior includes Ward Churchill and M. Annette Jaimes (at least their earlier work) and Paula Gunn Allen (because of her gynocentric orientation). Critics such as Jack Forbes, Jimmy Durham, and Kimberley Blaeser are cited as contesting the dominating influence of essentialist discourse. Vizenor is cited as "the most controversial critic of essentialism" (*Tribal Secrets* xvii–xviii, 127–28). I would disagree with Warrior as far as Forbes's position is concerned. His essay "Colonialism and Native American Literature" – which Warrior cites as an example of this "contesting strategy" – appears to me a restrictive view of what Native American literature should be. In it, Forbes writes: "Native American literature must consist in works produced by persons of Native identity and/or culture for primary dissemination to other persons of Native identity and/or culture" (19).

6. In the early 1930s, Mathews moved from the town of Pawhuska to a small sandstone house on his allotment land. He named the house "the Blackjacks" after the running scrub oak that dominates that part of Osage country. Out of these years of living alone on the Osage prairie, Mathews wrote *Talking to the Moon*.

7. The complexity of Mathews's cultural background has been clearly pointed out in the course of the recent critical reassessment and reappraisal of his work. In an extensive study of *Talking to the Moon*, LaVonne Ruoff traces in it elements of Thoreau's *Walden* and Muir's *My First Summer in the Sierra*, adding that Mathews's autobiography belongs, in its own right, "within a received literary tradition" ("John Joseph Mathews's *Talking to the Moon*" 5–6). Similarly, in a recent essay, Owens discusses the profound influence of John Steinbeck and of Edward F. Ricketts's *Sea of Cortez* on Mathews's "sophisticated 'Indian' autobiography" ("'Disturbed by Something Deeper'" 168).

8. I borrow the term *Uramerican* from the *Paradoxa* version of Owens's "As If an Indian." Owens ironically suggests that *Uramerican* is, perhaps, the best term with which to define the "original" Americans and distinguish them from the heteroglot immigrants of European descent, those to whom he usually refers as *Euramericans*. I will discuss Owens's essay in the next chapter.

9. Yet, as I will argue in chapter 4, Vizenor's notion of sovereignty is much more complex than Warrior suggests. Extending beyond the boundaries of territoriality, Native sovereignty operates, for Vizenor, within the epistemological field of tribal storytelling. Sovereignty, he argues, "as motion and transmotion is heard and

seen in oral presentations, the pleasures of native memories, and stories" (*Fugitive Poses* 182).

10. Womack uses *Creek* and *Muskogee* as a tribal-specific terms and *Native* as a more general term when referring to the experience of the indigenous people in America.

11. A similar anti-poststructuralist stance is expressed by Jace Weaver, who writes: "It is no coincidence that just as the people of the Two-Thirds World (i.e., non–First World) begin to find their own voices and assert their own agency and subjectivity, postmodernism proclaims the end of subjectivity" ("Indigenousness and Indigeneity" 225). By tracing its theoretical roots in European intellectual discourse, postmodernism (and postcolonialism) inevitably continue, for Weaver, the philosophical hegemony of the West.

12. As I argued in the introduction, it is true that most of what is today considered postcolonial writing ignores Native American writing, this despite the fact that both Native American discourse and postcolonial discourse share interesting ideological parallels. Yet, as my next chapter will illustrate, the relation between Native American literature and postcolonial theory is much more subtle and complex than Womack suggests.

13. As I discuss in the next chapter, Owens's position, which emphasizes cross-cultural communication and hybridized discourse, places him between Sarris's dialogic approach and Vizenor's trickster hermeneutics.

14. Vizenor's ideas regarding trickster are the basis of all his work, whether fiction or nonfiction. However, for a lengthy and straightforward statement about trickster, especially in response to Radin, see the prologue to *The People Named the Chippewa*.

15. Krupat applies Appiah's account of the postcolonial African novel to contemporary Native American fiction, envisioning in the work of Momaday, Silko, Welch, Owens, Vizenor, and many others the same kind of "transnational solidarity" described by Appiah. See *The Turn to the Native*, 30–55.

16. Womack's use of the term *assimilationist* here mirrors Charles Larson's in his early (1978) book on American Indian fiction. From a faulty conception of Indian identity, Larson creates four categories with which to distinguish American Indian novelists: *assimilationists*, *reactionaries*, *revisionists*, and *qualified separatists*.

17. Alexander Posey's wide-ranging career encompassed writing as well as Creek national politics. He was elected to the House of Warriors and served as the superintendent of the Creek Orphan Asylum at Okmulgee, the superintendent of public instruction for the Creek nation, and the superintendent of the Creek boarding schools at Eufala and Wetumka. In addition, he also labored as a fieldworker for the Dawes Commission and was involved in real estate dealings. The owner of the *Eufaula Indian Journal*, he created the persona of Fus Fixico in a series of letters pub-

lished therein; initially dealing with local events around Eufaula, the letters later engaged more serious issues, such as the theft of Indian territory from the Indian nations.

18. The letter is included in Braunlich's biographical study (71–72). As compelling as it is, Braunlich's study does not, Womack points out (*Red on Red* 271), discuss either Riggs's Cherokee identity or his homosexuality.

3. CROSSREADING TEXTS, BRIDGING CULTURES

1. For his discussion of this Clackamas Chinook myth, see Hymes, *"In Vain I Tried to Tell You"* 274–99. Hymes's interpretation is based on Jacobs (esp. 238–42).

2. As I explained in my introduction, even though I am aware that the term *hybridity* might raise innumerable objections among those who consider it akin to *assimilation* and *pluralism*, I use it nevertheless when discussing the highly "mediated" nature of Native American texts. Written in English, and employing Western literary forms, Native American texts employ, nonetheless, elements from a tradition "other" than the written; in this sense, these works can be reread transformatively as indications and figurations of values radically opposed to those of the dominant culture.

3. The four sections in which Sarris's book is arranged resemble the structure of, and his storytelling strategy is similar to that of, many contemporary Native American novels. Writing about Momaday's *House Made of Dawn*, Owens notes that, within Native American cultures, the number *4* is powerful and sacred: "[It] is the number of the seasons, the cardinal directions, balance, beauty, and completion. . . . [T]he very structure of the novel is designed to move us inward toward wholeness and well-being, echoing the centripetal forces dominant in the Indian world" (*Other Destinies* 96). Similarly, *Keeping Slug Woman Alive* aims at achieving order and balance among different discourses and theoretical worldviews. As Sarris states in the final section, "This study is my attempt to doctor and to heal" (199).

4. According to Sarris, *Pomo* "is the name given by ethnographers to several tribes of north central California natives, speaking different but related languages and residing in Lake, Mendocino, and Sonoma counties" (8). He goes on to explain that *Coast Miwok* is the term used by ethnographers to designate those tribes whose territory borders southern Pomo territory. Unlike the Pomo, however, none of the Coast Miwok tribes are today federally acknowledged, and no Miwok reservation exists, although the Miwok do continue to live in the region, interacting with the Pomo as they have always done (see generally Sarris 8–11).

5. Even though Sarris's focus is crosscultural communication as a way to open up ideas in language, some readers have responded suspiciously to the overemphasis in *Keeping Slug Woman Alive* on his own personal experience. Kenneth Roemer, e.g.,

writes: "Sarris, no doubt, will be criticized for making too much of personal contexts" ("Indian Lives" 89).

6. Tompkins argues that, in its notion of meaning as the primary object of the critical act, reader-response criticism has not moved that far from the claims of New Criticism. On the contrary, these polemically opposed movements are, ironically, bound by the assumption that meaning is the ultimate goal of criticism. In both discourses, Tompkins states, "The text remains an object rather than an instrument, an occasion for the elaboration of meaning rather than a force exerted upon the world" (225).

7. Krupat himself acknowledges this risk. He writes: "The danger I run as an ethnocritic is the danger of leaving the Indian silent entirely in my discourse" (*Ethnocriticism* 30).

8. Sarris' notion of performance is based largely on the work of the ethnographer and folklorist Richard Bauman. According to Bauman, "Performance sets up, or represents, an interpretive frame within which the messages being communicated are to be understood [so that] this frame contrasts with at least one other frame, the literal" (qtd. in Sarris 18).

9. The Bole Maru (Dream Dance) cult originated in Pomo and Miwok territory in the winter of 1871–72. Similar to the Plains Ghost Dance movement, the Bole Maru is, as Sarris explains, a "revivalistic religion," a religious and political response to European and Euramerican domination and ideology (65; see also 10–11, 65–68). On McKay's "unique" life, see Sarris 32, 51–62.

10. Drawing from Clifford's analysis of "ethnographic authority" in "On Ethnographic Authority," Sarris intends to resist the "pull toward authoritative representation of the other" by holding in view "the specific contingencies of the exchange" (Clifford qtd. in Sarris 27). Describing his exchange with McKay, Sarris writes: "I must present (or represent) Mabel McKay as she presents herself to me" (27).

11. Similarly, discussing McKay's role as a basket weaver, Sarris notices how her purpose is to bring Pomo basketry outside museums, demonstrating that cultural artifacts have a life, are related to the people who produced them, and can generate questions from and open a discussion with viewers. He writes: "Mabel cannot separate a discussion about the material aspects of her basketry from a discussion about Dreams, doctoring, prophecy, and the ancient basket-weaving rules, since for Mabel these things cannot be talked about or understood separately" (51). See generally Sarris 51–62.

12. "Jenny" is a pseudonym that Sarris uses since his friend did not want her identity revealed.

13. Crucial here is Trinh's idea of storytelling as a living tradition, a regenerating force that disrupts notions of truth and falsity highly valued within Western, scien-

tific (anthropological) discourse. Trinh's notion of the oral tradition relies heavily on Silko's *Ceremony* and *Storyteller*.

14. Bateson argues that culture contact should be considered to have occurred, "not only [in] those cases in which the contact occurs between two communities with different cultures and results in profound disturbance of the culture of one or both groups," "but also in cases of contact within a single community": "In these [latter] cases, the contact is between differentiated groups of individuals, e.g. between the sexes, between the young and old. . . . I would even extend the idea of 'contact' so widely as to include those processes whereby a child is molded and trained to fit the culture into which he was born" (qtd. in Sarris 43). Bateson's ideas also provide further support for Sarris's argument that even an insider might have problems understanding the oral experience.

15. According to Allen, there is an ethical dilemma involved in in working with the oral tradition, i.e., in incorporating elements of the oral tradition unmodified in one's own work. She writes: "The ethical issue is both political and metaphysical, and to violate the traditional ethos is to run risks that no university professor signed up for in any case" ("Special Problems" 379). Interestingly enough, Owens notices (*Other Destinies* 257), Allen herself incorporates elements of Laguna mythology in her novel *The Woman Who Owed the Shadows*, ironically compromising her critique of Silko.

16. It is worth noting that Trinh's strategies as a filmmaker aim at dismantling the monologic unity of Western discourse, a discourse in which the self-other relationship is still conceived as an opposition. In her view, "Otherness becomes empowering critical difference when it is not given, but recreated," for "there can hardly be such a thing as an essential inside that can be homogeneously represented by all insiders" (*When the Moon Waxes Red* 71, 75). Cutting across the boundaries of specific art forms and specific cultures, Trinh's films seem to raise the same kinds of questions as Sarris does in his discussion of the Bole Maru documentary.

17. Sarris distinguishes "narrated autobiographies," in which a recorder-editor "records and transcribes" the oral material provided by the Indian subjects, from "written autobiographies," in which the Indian subjects themselves write up the material, "with or without the assistance of editors" (83–84). Krupat envisions the same distinction as "Indian autobiographies" vs. "autobiographies written by Indians" (*For Those Who Come After* 30–31).

18. Sarris distinguishes between *written* and *oral* American Indian literature. The former is the literary production of contemporary authors, the subject of study by literary critics. The latter is the product of a collaborative act (between the Indians who tell the tales and the [for the most part] non-Indian translators and recorders), often the subject of study by folklorists and anthropologists. According to Sarris, whereas scholars who deal with oral Indian literature are always conscious of the

highly mediated nature of the material in question, those who deal with written Indian literature are not always so conscious (122-23).

19. Sarris borrows the notion of circumscribing and totalizing the Other's culture from Murray (see Murray 98-126).

20. Sarris points out that, even though he refers to the Slug Woman story as one story or one text, it actually consists of two narratives, "A Description of Slug Woman" and "Story about the Slug Woman," and that both have been collected in a pamphlet published by YA-KA-AMA, a Sonoma County Indian education and resource center (see Sarris 172). To the Pomo, Slug Woman is a fearful personage who can poison victims with sickness, something that, as Sarris tells us, one of his family members experienced firsthand (see Sarris 169-72).

21. In *House Made of Dawn*, Abel's loss of voice is indicative of his alienation from a Native worldview, one in which language has creative power. Crucial to his reintegration in that worldview is the recovery of voice through sacred songs and ceremonies.

22. As noticed by the literary historian Amy Kaplan, the frontier as a displacing site is also a paradigm of resistance in the discourse of the borderlands. Drawing from Kaplan, Jose Saldivar argues: "The invocation of the U.S.-Mexico border as a paradigm of crossing, resistance, and circulation in Chicano/a studies has contributed to the 'worlding' of American studies and further helped to instill a new transnational literacy in the U.S. academy" (xiii).

23. Various critics have pointed out the tendency to treat *postcolonial* as a universalizing category that neutralizes significant geopolitical differences between countries. See, among others, Gandhi; Dirlik; Ahmad; and Johnston and Lawson. In her critique of postcolonialism as a discourse that erases the United States as a militaristic power, Shohat argues that it "leaves no space . . . for the struggles of aboriginals in Australia and indigenous peoples throughout the Americas, in other words, of Fourth World peoples dominated by both the First World multi-national corporations and by Third World nation-states" (327).

24. Not only is postcolonialism a universalizing theory, but, by relying on the language of First World poststructuralism, it also ends up mimicking methodologically the colonialist epistemology that it sets out to repudiate. Within this context, the term *hybridity* runs the risk, according to Shohat, of perpetuating the reality of colonial violence if it is not articulated along with questions of hegemony and neocolonial power relations (see Shohat 330). On the other hand, both Dirlik and Ahmad note a refusal in postcolonial discourse to address its relation to a global capitalism.

25. Chakrabarty argues that the disciplinary formation of academic history is inseparable from the story of modernity and its narratives of citizenship, progress, and the nation-state, that the models of the historian's enterprise are always at least cul-

turally "European" and that non-Western scholars cannot afford to remain "ignorant" of such models without appearing "old-fashioned" or "outdated" (224). However, he goes on to assert, there is no cultural relativism in the arena of historiography, as First World historians continue to "produce their work in relative ignorance of non-Western histories" (224).

26. Bart Moore-Gilbert points out how Ahmad's criticism of postcolonial theory is guilty of the same essentialism and determinism for which he takes Said to task. For Ahmad, all Third World writers who take posts – no matter how temporarily – in the Western academy automatically become part of the system of domination. Yet, as Moore-Gilbert points out, Ahmad is also speaking from an elite, privileged position – that of a postcolonial Third World intellectual who has migrated to the First World. Moreover, he is addressing the West, not only in one of its principle languages, but within the parameters of one of its own critical discourses (Marxism). Ultimately, Moore-Gilbert reminds us, "Attacks on postcolonial theory build careers as surely as the production of postcolonial theory itself" (156).

27. The difficulty inherent in understanding Gramsci's thought is compounded for the English-speaking world by the fact that, currently, only partial translations of the *Prison Notebooks* are available.

28. Clarke's appeal has been a primary concern of the ecocritical debate in the past few years. Cheryll Glotfelty, e.g., voices the opinion that ecocriticism, "a predominantly white movement," will become a multiethnic movement only when it opens up to a diversity of voices (xxv). *The Ecocriticism Reader*, the collection in which Glotfelty makes this remark, takes a significant step toward this dialogic endeavor (see Glotfelty and Fromm).

29. Owens argues that the holistic understanding of indigenous inhabitants did not divide the land into areas that could be exploited and areas that should remain "wilderness," remain untouched. *Wilderness* is romantic European notion, a concept that ironically buys into the vanishing mentality.

4. LIBERATIVE STORIES AND STRATEGIES OF SURVIVANCE

1. In an interview with Laura Coltelli, Vizenor points out that the sacred versions of the story are the ones narrating the families of creation, their winds, and animals and birds, all of which are somehow related to the creation of humans. See Coltelli 163–64.

Both *Anishinaabe* (also Chippewa) and *Wenebojo* (also *Naanabozho*) are spelled variably and pronounced differently from region to region. In this chapter, I follow the spelling that Vizenor himself uses.

2. As noted by Elaine Jahner, Vizenor's notion of the sacred stands in stark contrast to ordinary Christian notions. For Vizenor the sacred involves the traditional

(Anishinaabe, in his case) tribal way of designating "the fundamental principle of relationship linking all phenomena" ("Heading 'Em Off at the Impasse" 6). Crucial in this process is the role of language in and through which the sacred manifests itself (see Jahner, "Heading 'Em Off at the Impasse" 6–10).

3. Vizenor's eclectic production includes novels, short stories, poetry, drama, a screenplay, an autobiography, various collection of critical essays, and journalistic pieces. The most prolific of contemporary Native American writers, he is also the most innovative in his tribal-cum-postmodern and -poststructuralist approach to Native American literature.

4. Vizenor's neologisms – including *survivance* – are discussed at various points later in this chapter. Few, it should be noted, are ever clearly defined.

5. Vizenor's notions *wordmaker* and *wordarrow* are clearly indebted to Momaday's essay "The Arrowmaker" and to the story of the arrowmaker (or "the man made of words") that Momaday used to hear as a child. The latter – a story about, Momaday argues, "the efficacy of language" and "the power of words" – tells us something of the risks and responsibilities involved in language and of the necessity of balancing our life with words. See *The Man Made of Words* 9–12.

6. Belladonna's fate as terminal believer has received a sustained amount of critical attention. See, e.g., Velie; Owens, *Other Destinies*; and Blaeser, *Gerald Vizenor*.

7. The radical leader of the American Indian Movement (AIM), Means "posed," according to Vizenor, in photographs with other AIM leaders during the occupation of Wounded Knee; later he "landed" in motion pictures by playing the role of Chingachgook in *The Last of the Mohicans*. According to Vizenor, Means is "one of the most esteemed postindian warriors of simulations in tribal stories and histories" (*Manifest Manners* 19).

8. Jahner also suggests that Vizenor's interest in poststructuralism testifies to his idea that the Indian and the French sides of his Metis heritage could complement each other within the domain of world philosophy ("Heading 'Em Off at the Impasse" 3). In other words, for Vizenor, it becomes a way in which to cross boundaries and cut across ethnic allegiances.

9. As does Owens (see *Mixedblood Messages* 113–31), Vizenor sees *Dances with Wolves* as a reenactment of the popular structural theme of relation between savagery and civilization. At the end, he points out, "Dunbar, the cavalry officer rides out of a warrior tradition with a white woman and leaves the tragic natives to their fate" (Lee, *Postindian Conversations* 85–86).

10. As one of the few critics to have written extensively and insightfully about the connections between Vizenor and Derrida, Jahner provides the solid ground on which to base an analysis of Vizenor's Derridean strategies. Her "Heading 'Em Off at the Impasse" represents, to my knowledge, the most significant attempt to date to

explicate Vizenor's points of convergence with and divergence from poststructuralist theorists.

11. Vizenor's subversion of the written literary tradition and satire of the educational system continue as Almost and his partner, Drain, establish a business selling "blank books" near the local university. One of the professors who supports the business tells them that "blank books made more sense to him than anything he had ever read" ("Almost Browne" 113). (The books are not, it should be noted, completely blank: they contain tribal pictomyths, or, as Almost puts it, "stories that are imagined about a picture, about memories" [113].) When the university bans Almost and Drain from doing business on or near campus, they convert to a mail-order system.

12. Blaeser points out that, since, for Vizenor, both the notion of language and that of performance involve "the active participation of the speaker/writer and listener/reader, . . . therefore, the metaphor of shadow becomes another way of explaining the notion of discourse if we recognize that discourse involves more than an exchange of words" (*Gerald Vizenor* 214).

13. Vizenor explains that the "dead voices" are the languages of the social sciences, the properties of cultural studies, and the absence of Natives in history (Lee, *Postindian Conversations* 137). All these methodologies have, he argues, misreckoned the great teases of Native stories as absence, and, in that sense, they are *dead voices*.

14. On Ku'oosh's observing that "this word is fragile," the narrator comments: "The word he chose to express 'fragile' was filled with the intricacies of a continuing process, and with a strength inherent in spider webs woven across paths through sand hills where early in the morning the sun becomes entangled in each filament of web. It took a long time to explain the fragility and intricacy because no word exists alone, and the reason for choosing each word had to be explained with a story about why it must be said this certain way" (Silko, *Ceremony* 35).

Karl Kroeber has also written about the relation between poststructuralist and deconstructivist theory and Native American oral traditions, relating the transformative process of language, a central tenet of deconstructivist criticism, to the metamorphic quality of coyote stories.

15. Anderson focuses on the work of four contemporary literary journalists in order to show how, in their works, style itself conveys or implies meaning. He writes: "Each [of these writers] define their subjects as somehow beyond words – antiverbal or nonverbal, threatening or sublime, overpowering and intense or private and intuitive – and then repeatedly call our attention to the issue of inexplicability throughout their description and expositions. A self-consciousness about the limits of language is the structuring principles of their work" (5). See also Blaeser, *Gerald Vizenor* 166–80.

16. Kroeber makes a similar argument: "Coyote/coyote . . . is too tricky to be ab-

stractly identified. He transforms, or deconstructs, any definition of him even as he provokes one into making a definition" (78).

17. I use the term *surveillance* here in the Foucauldian sense. Vizenor himself adopts Foucault's ideas to discuss how, with its overtly objective methods, social-scientific discourse has reduced Natives to "double others of surveillance" (*Manifest Manners* 168).

18. The last surviving representative of the Yahi, Ishi was discovered in August 1911 in the corral of a slaughterhouse in Oroville, California, weak and starving. Not knowing what else to do with this "wild man" who understood no English, the county sheriff decided to put him in jail. The story of the discovery of a "primitive man" became headline news and captured the interest of the anthropologists Kroeber and Waterman, professors at the University of California. Ishi was transferred to the Museum of Anthropology on the Berkeley campus, where Professor Kroeber himself became responsible for him. Ishi lived in the museum for five years, working at his old craft of shaping arrows and spears and telling stories. He died of tuberculosis on 25 March 1916. (The interested reader should note that Vizenor's *Ishi and the Wood Ducks* contains a "historical introduction." A more extensive biographical account can be found in Kroeber, *Ishi in Two Worlds*.)

19. Vizenor's fascination with Ishi goes beyond the theoretical. In 1995 it resulted in *Ishi and the Wood Ducks*, a play in four acts, in which his ideas on language significantly approach and overlap Beckett's. More recently it has taken a philosophical turn, in "Mister Ishi: Analogies of Exile, Deliverance, and Liberty," finding parallels between the "wild man" and Albert Camus.

20. Blaeser's ideas on the political nature of style are mainly indebted to Vološinov, esp. his *Marxism and the Philosophy of Language*.

21. In his autobiography Vizenor often adopts the third-person pronoun in order to convey the idea of autobiography as the re-creation of a story rather than the mere recounting of it (see Vizenor, *Interior Landscapes*).

22. I use *authoritative* here to signal the important that Columbus's journal came to assume in the European colonial enterprise in the Americas. It should be noted that the original copy of the journal was lost and that we have only a transcription (substantially altered) made by Fray Bartolomé de las Casas, a Dominican friar and close personal friend of the admiral's.

23. Further excavating the ironies of the Columbus myth, Vizenor reimagines the admiral as a Marrano, a descendant of Jews, whose ancestors had converted to Christianity during the anti-Semitic riots of 1391 (see *Manifest Manners* 113-14) and as a Mayan, thus making of his journey to the Americas a return to his homeland (see *The Heirs of Columbus*).

24. The influence of Eastern thought and literature on his work is revealed else-

where than in *Fugitive Poses*. For example, his 1987 novel *Griever: An American Monkey King in China* weaves the Mind-Monkey tricksterism of Chinese opera, in the person of Sun Wu-k'ung, into its Anishinaabe counterpart. Vizenor's hero in the novel, Griever de Hocus, ends up parodying both communism and capitalism. On the genesis of the novel, see Coltelli 180–82; and also Lee, *Postindian Conversations* 115–26.

25. Other instances of "censorship" include students' often shocked response to the sex and violence in *Bearheart* and the response of the Comparative Ethnic Studies Department to an androgynous nude trickster on the cover of *Shadow Distance: A Gerald Vizenor Reader* (see Vizenor, *Fugitive Poses* 6–10).

26. The title "Penenative Rumours" plays on the term *visionary rumour* used by Jung in *Flying Saucers* to describe the alien abduction story. Elaborating on Jung's theories, Vizenor argues that "the *indian* has been both the absence and the presence of reason in the visionary rumors of modernity" (*Fugitive Poses* 49), suggesting that, as a simulation, the "*indian*" has fulfilled and continues to fulfill the role of the Other, the alien, in the discourse of dominance. About the term *penenative*, Vizenor declares that the word relates to "chance, the playful originary sense of native identity," a humorous play on the feeling of "nostalgia for lost origins," and a further attack on the discourse of the social sciences (Pulitano, interview).

27. This brief summary is, of necessity, reductive. I take Derrida at his word, however, and, approaching his work not as a method but as a process, provide an expanded discussion of his ideas as we encounter them, in appropriated form, in Vizenor's work.

28. Correspondingly, the essay shifts from an academic, objective discursive mode to a first-person narrative mode. Unlike *Manifest Manners*, *Fugitive Poses* introduces autobiographical elements, a further example of Vizenor's attempt to blur established genres.

29. The author of *The Primal Mind* and other books about tribal cultures, Jamake Highwater claimed Blackfoot heritage on his mother's side and Eastern Cherokee on his father's, drawing a significant amount of public attention and becoming one of the most famous Indians of the twentieth century. In 1984, in a column (entitled "A Fabricated Indian?") released by the Universal Press Syndicate, Jack Anderson exposed the fabrication of Highwater's Indian identity by writing that Highwater "lied about many details of his life" (Anderson qtd. in Vizenor, *Manifest Manners* 61; see also 13, 62).

30. The eight "native theaters" are "native by concession" (the inheritance of a Native presence), "native by creation" (the creation of Native characters whose presence has been secured in the history of the nation), "native by countenance" (the possession Indian-looking features), "native by genealogies" (the attribution of iden-

tity on the basis of ancestors and consanguinity), "native by documentation" (the attribution of identity on the basis of the evidence of birth certificates and reservation enrollments), "native by situation" (the attribution of identity on the basis of marriage, service, etc.), "native by trickster stories" (the assumption of shamanic powers, e.g., politicians who have been "touched"), and "native by victimry" (the casting of individuals as representations) (see Vizenor, *Fugitive Poses* 88–91). This last category represents those individuals who are, for Vizenor, "the absolute victims of modernity" (91).

31. Gandhi, e.g., argues that postcolonialism of the sort theorized by Ashcroft et al. unifies disparate societies under "the somewhat dubious premise that their subjectivity has been constituted in part by the subordinating power of European colonialism" (169). For Owen's and Krupat's critique of Ashcroft et al., see chapter 3 above.

32. That is, despite the novel's employment of the diction of literary modernism (a strategy that, according to Owens, helped it on its way to a Pulitzer), it is, in fact, deeply grounded in the complex world of Pueblo and Navajo cultural traditions, a world that, more often than not, remains alien to the metropolitan reader. Momaday's act of mimicry thus perfectly succeeds in writing back to the empire.

33. As critics have pointed out, Bhabha's formulations remain exclusively within the confines of Eurocentric discourse, indebted as they are to an extraordinary number of Western thinkers. Even more significant is the fact that Bhabha tends to take some of these Eurocentric theories at face value. For example, he never questions the applicability of psychoanalysis to non-Western psychic or cultural problematics, accepting, thus, what Spivak describes as its "overtly imperialistic politics" (*In Other Worlds* 262). See also Moore-Gilbert, 140–51.

34. On the other hand, critics have pointed out how, by presenting the nonhybrid alternatives to the postcolonial and insisting that all cultures are mixed and hybrid, Bhabha runs the danger of essentializing the very category of the hybrid. See, among others, Moore-Gilbert; and Young.

35. This "third space" is, according to Bhabha, not so much an identity as a new area of "negotiation of meaning and representation" (Bhabha in Rutherford 211). An example is Rushdie's *Satanic Verses*, in which a process of hybridity, structured around the metaphor of migrancy (of various discourses), ultimately questions the authorship and authority of the Koran.

36. Vizenor defines *natural reason* as a "union of nature and language, not separation." In a sort of existential view, he suggests, it means learning to understand the world, which has no meaning, by what one learns from nature (Pulitano, interview).

37. One of Vizenor's "almost" words, *interimage* suggests the idea of an image

that is almost, but not quite, what it is supposed to be, an "almost" representation that ultimately has no connection to the real.

38. As a reporter for the *Minneapolis Tribune* in 1968, Vizenor had followed the dispute closely. He explains that, a century after the area had been ceded in treaties, the government had established the refuge and, therefore, claimed legal rights over the wild rice harvest. See Vizenor, "Ojibways Seek Right."

39. According to the act, it is unlawful falsely to suggest that any work for sale has been Indian produced. Under the act, an Indian is considered to be someone who "is a member of a federally-recognized or state-recognized tribe, or a person who is certified as an Indian artisan by such a tribe." For a discussion of the irony of such an act, see Vizenor, *Ishi and the Wood Ducks*; and Owens, "Staging *indians*" 239–43.

40. The legend tells of the origins of the Big Dipper. Momaday writes: "From that moment, and so long as the legend lives, the Kiowas have kinsmen in the night sky. Whatever they were in the mountains, they could be no more. However tenuous their well-being, however much they had suffered and would suffer again, they had found a way out of the wilderness" (*The Way to Rainy Mountain* 8).

Bibliography

Achebe, Chinua. "Colonialist Criticism." *Hopes and Impediments: Selected Essays, 1965–1987*. London: Heinemann, 1988. 68–90.

Adorno, Theodor W. "The Essay as Form." *Notes to Literature*. New York: Columbia UP, 1991. 3–23.

Ahmad, Aijaz. *In Theory: Classes, Nations, Literatures*. London: Verso, 1992.

Allen, Paula Gunn. "The Autobiography of a Confluence." *I Tell You Now: Autobiographical Essays by Native American Writers*. Ed. Brian Swann and Arnold Krupat. Lincoln: U of Nebraska P, 1987. 143–54.

——. *Grandmothers of Light: A Medicine Woman Sourcebook*. Boston: Beacon, 1991.

——. *Off the Reservation: Reflections on Boundary-Busting, Border Crossing, Loose Canons*. Boston: Beacon, 1998.

——. Rev. of *This Bridge Called My Back*, ed. Cherríe Moraga and Gloria Anzaldúa. *Conditions* 5 (1982): 121–27.

——. *The Sacred Hoop: Recovering the Feminine in American Indian Traditions*. Boston: Beacon, 1986.

——. "Special Problems in Teaching Leslie Marmon Silko's *Ceremony*." *American Indian Quarterly* 15 (1990): 379–86.

——, ed. *Spider Woman's Granddaughters: Traditional Tales and Contemporary Writing by Native American Women*. Boston: Beacon, 1989.

——, ed. *Studies in American Indian Literature: Critical Essays and Course Designs*. New York: MLA, 1983.

Althusser, Louis. "Ideology and Ideological State Apparatuses (Notes towards an

Investigation)." *Lenin and Philosophy and Other Essays*. London: New Left, 1970. 123–73.

Anderson, Chris. *Style as Argument: Contemporary American Nonfiction*. Carbondale: Southern Illinois UP, 1987.

Anzaldúa, Gloria. *Borderlands/La Frontera: The New Mestiza*. San Francisco: Spinsters/Aunt Lute, 1987.

——, ed. *Making Face, Making Soul/Haciendo Caras: Creative and Critical Perspectives by Feminists of Color*. San Francisco: Aunt Lute, 1990.

Anzaldúa, Gloria, and Cherrie Moraga, eds. *This Bridge Called My Back: Writings by Radical Women of Color*. 2nd ed. New York: Kitchen Table, 1981.

Appiah, Kwame Anthony. "Cosmopolitan Patriots." *Critical Inquiry* 23 (1997): 617–39.

——. *In My Father's House: Africa in the Philosophy of Culture*. Methuen: London, 1992.

Ashcroft, Bill, Gareth Griffiths, and Helen Tiffin. *The Empire Writes Back: Theory and Practice on Post-Colonial Literatures*. New York: Routledge, 1989.

——. *Key Concepts in Post-Colonial Studies*. New York: Routledge, 1998.

Awiakta, Marilou. *Abiding Appalachia: Where Mountain and Atom Meet*. Memphis: St. Luke's, 1990.

——. *Selu: Seeking the Corn-Mother's Wisdom*. Golden, Colo.: Fulcrum, 1993.

Bakhtin, Mikhail M. *The Dialogic Imagination: Four Essays by M. Bakhtin*. Ed. Michael Holquist. Trans. Caryl Emerson and Michael Holquist. Austin: U of Texas P, 1981.

Barthes, Roland. *Camera Lucida*. Trans. R. Howard. New York: Hill & Wang, 1981.

——. *Empire of Signs*. 1970. Trans. Richard Howard. London: Cape, 1983.

Bataille, Gretchen, and Kathleen Mullen Sands. *American Indian Women: Telling Their Lives*. Lincoln: U of Nebraska P, 1984.

Baudrillard, Jean. *Simulations*. Trans. Paul Foss et al. New York: Semiotext(e), 1983.

Berner, Robert. "Other European and American Languages: Native American." Rev. of *Manifest Manners: Postindian Warrior of Survivance*, by Gerald Vizenor. *World Literature Today* 68.3 (1994): 616.

Bhabha, Homi K. "Cultural Diversity and Cultural Differences." *The Post-Colonial Studies Reader*. Ed. Bill Ashcroft, Gareth Griffith, and Helen Tiffin. London: Routledge, 1995. 206–09.

——. *The Location of Culture*. London: Routledge, 1994.

——. *Nation and Narration*. London: Routledge, 1990.

——. "The Other Question: Difference, Discrimination, and the Discourse of

Colonialism." *Literature, Politics, and Theory.* Ed. Francis Baker, Peter Hulme, and Margaret Iversen. London: Methuen, 1986. 148–73.

——. "Postcolonial Criticism." *Redrawing the Boundaries.* Ed. Stephen Greenblatt and Giles Gunn. New York: MLA, 1992. 437–65.

Blaeser, Kimberley. *Gerald Vizenor: Writing in the Oral Tradition.* Norman: U of Oklahoma P, 1996.

——. "Like 'Reeds through the Ribs of a Basket': Native Women Weaving Stories." *Other Sisterhoods: Literary Theory and U.S. Women of Color.* Ed. Sandra Kumamoto Stanley. Chicago: U of Illinois P, 1998. 265–76.

——. "Native Literature: Seeking a Critical Center." *Looking at the Words of Our People: First Nations Analysis of Literature.* Ed. Jeannette Armstrong. Penticton, B.C.: Theytus, 1993. 52–61.

Bongie, Chris. *Islands and Exiles: The Creole Identities of Post/Colonial Literature.* Stanford, Calif.: Stanford UP, 1998.

Bowers, Neal, and Charles L. P. Silet. "An Interview with Gerald Vizenor." *MELUS* 8.1 (1981): 41–49.

Boynton, Victoria. "Desire's Revision: Feminist Appropriation of Native American Traditional Sources." *Modern Language Studies* 26.2–3 (1996): 53–71.

Braunlich, Phyllis. *Haunted by Home: The Life and Letters of Lynn Riggs.* Norman: U of Oklahoma P, 1988.

Bredin, Renae Moore. "Theory in the Mirror." *Other Sisterhoods: Literary Theory and U.S. Women of Color.* Chicago: U of Illinois P, 1998. 228–43.

Bruchac, Joseph. *Survival This Way: Interviews with American Indian Poets.* Tucson: U of Arizona P, 1987.

Brumble, David H. *American Indian Autobiography.* Berkeley: U of California P, 1988.

Butler, Judith. *Gender Trouble: Feminism and the Subversion of Identity.* New York: Routledge, 1990.

Calderon, Hector, and Jose Saldivar, eds. *Criticism in the Borderlands: Studies in Chicano Literature, Culture, and Ideology.* Durham, N.C.: Duke UP, 1991.

Callahan, S. Alice. *Wynema: A Child of the Forest.* Ed. A. LaVonne Ruoff Brown. Lincoln: U of Nebraska P, 1997.

Chakrabarty, Dipesh. "Postcoloniality and the Artifice of History: Who Speaks for 'Indian' Pasts?" *Contemporary Postcolonial Theory: A Reader.* Ed. Padmini Mongia. London: Oxford UP, 1996. 223–47.

Chambers, Ian. *Migrancy, Culture, Identity.* London: Routledge, 1994.

Chambers, Ian, and Lidia Curti, eds. *The Post-Colonial Question: Common Skies, Divided Horizons.* London: Routledge, 1996.

Chinweizu, Onwuchekwa Jemie, and Ihechukwu Madubuike. *Toward the Decolonization of African Literature*. Washington, D.C.: Howard UP, 1983.

Chow, Rey. *Writing Diaspora: Tactics of Intervention in Contemporary Cultural Studies*. Bloomington: Indiana UP, 1993.

Christian, Barbara. "The Race for Theory." *Cultural Critique* 5 (1987): 69–83.

Churchill, Ward. Rev. of *Manifest Manners: Postindian Warriors of Survivance*, by Gerald Vizenor. *American Indian Culture and Research Journal* 18.3 (1994): 313–18.

Cixous, Hélène. "The Laugh of the Medusa." *New French Feminisms*. Ed. Elaine Marks and Isabelle de Courtivron. New York: Schocken, 1981. 245–64.

Clarke, Joni Adamson. "Toward an Ecology of Justice: Transformative Ecological Theory and Practice." *Reading the Earth: New Directions in the Study of Literature and the Environment*. Ed. Michael P. Branch et al. Moscow: U of Idaho P, 1998. 9–17.

Clifford, James. "Diasporas." *Cultural Anthropology* 9.3 (1994): 302–38.

——. "On Ethnographic Authority." *Representations* 1.2 (1983): 118–46.

——. *The Predicament of Culture: Twentieth-Century Ethnography, Literature, and Art*. Cambridge, Mass.: Harvard UP, 1988.

——. "Travelling Cultures." *Cultural Studies*. Ed. Lawrence Grossberg, Cary Nelson, and Paula A. Treichler. Routledge: New York, 1992. 96–112.

Colson, Elizabeth, ed. *Autobiographies of Three Pomo Women*. 1956. Berkeley: U of California P, for the Archeological Research Facility, Department of Anthropology, 1974.

Coltelli, Laura. *Winged Words: American Indian Writers Speak*. Lincoln: U of Nebraska P, 1990.

Cook-Lynn, Elizabeth. "The American Indian Fiction Writers: Cosmopolitanism, Nationalism, the Third World, and First Nation Sovereignty." *Nothing but the Truth: An Anthology on Native American Literature*. Ed. John Purdy and James Ruppert. Upper Saddle River, N.J.: Prentice-Hall, 2001. 23–38.

——. "American Indian Intellectualism and the New Indian Story." *American Indian Quarterly* 20.1 (1996): 57–76.

——. "Cosmopolitanism, Nationalism, the Third World, and Tribal Sovereignty." *Wicazo Ša Review* 9.2 (1993): 26–36. Rpt. as "The American Indian Fiction Writers: Cosmopolitanism, Nationalism, the Third World, and First Nation Sovereignty" in *Why I Can't Read Wallace Stegner*. Ed. Elizabeth Cook-Lynn. Madison: U of Wisconsin P, 1996. 78–96. Also in *Nothing but the Truth: An Anthology on Native American Literature*. Ed. John Purdy and James Ruppert. Upper Saddle River, N.J.: Prentice-Hall, 2001. 23–38.

——. "Who Stole Native American Studies?" *Wicazo Ša Review* 12.1 (1997): 9–28.

Davis, Robert Con. "Woman as Oppositional Reader: Cixous on Discourse." *Gender in the Classroom: Power and Pedagogy*. Ed. Susan Gabriel and Isahia Smithson. Urbana: U of Illinois P, 1990. 96–111.

D'Eaubonne, Françoise. *Le feminisme ou la mort*. Paris: Horay, 1974.

de Lauretis, Teresa de. *Technologies of Gender: Essays on Theory, Film, and Fiction*. Bloomington: Indiana UP, 1987.

Deloria, Vine, Jr. *Behind the Trail of Broken Treaties: An Indian Declaration of Independence*. New York: Delacorte, 1974.

——. *Custer Died for Your Sins: An Indian Manifesto*. New York: Macmillan, 1969. Rpt., with a new preface. Norman: U of Oklahoma P, 1988.

——. *God Is Red*. New York: Grosset, 1973.

——. "Intellectual Self-Determination and Sovereignty: Looking at the Windmills in Our Minds." *Wicazo Ša Review* 13 (1998): 25–31.

——. *Spirit and Reason: The Vine Deloria Jr. Reader*. Ed. Barbara Deloria et al. Golden, Colo.: Fulcrum, 1999.

——. *We Talk, You Listen: New Tribes, New Turf*. New York: Macmillan, 1970.

Deloria, Vine, Jr., and Clifford Lytle. *The Nations Within: The Past and Future of American Indian Sovereignty*. New York: Pantheon, 1984.

Derrida, Jacques. *The Margins of Philosophy*. Trans. Alan Bass. Chicago: U of Chicago P, 1982.

——. *Of Grammatology*. Trans. Gayatri Chakravorty Spivak. Baltimore: Johns Hopkins UP, 1976.

——. *Positions*. Trans. Alan Bass. Chicago: U of Chicago P, 1981.

——. *Writing and Difference*. Trans. Alan Bass. Chicago: U of Chicago P, 1978.

Dilley, Patrick. "Queer Theory: Under Construction." *International Journal of Qualitative Studies in Education* 12.5 (1999): 457–72. 3 Nov. 2002 <http://www.tandf.co.uk/journals/tf/09518398/html>

Dirlik, Arif. "The Postcolonial Aura: Third World Criticism in the Age of Global Capitalism." *Critical Inquiry* 20 (1994): 328–56.

Donovan, Kathleen M. *Feminist Readings of Native American Literature: Coming to Voice*. Tucson: U of Arizona P, 1998.

DuPlessis, Rachel Blau. *Writing beyond the Ending: Narrative Strategies of Twentieth-Century Women Writers*. Bloomington: Indiana UP, 1985.

Eagleton, Terry. *Literary Theory: An Introduction*. Minneapolis: U of Minnesota P, 1983.

Eco, Umberto. *Travels in Hyperreality*. Trans. William Weaver. New York: Harcourt, 1986.

Emerson, Ralph Waldo. *Nature. The Heath Anthology of American Literature* 1. Ed. Paul Lauter et al. 3rd ed. Boston: Houghton, 1998. 1582–1609.

Erdrich, Louise. *Love Medicine*. New York: Bantam, 1984.

Eysturoy, Annie O. "Paula Gunn Allen." *This Is about Vision: Interviews with Southwestern Writers*. Ed. William Balassi, John Crawford, and Annie O. Eysturoy. Albuquerque: U of New Mexico P, 1990. 97–107.

Fanon, Frantz. *Black Skins, White Masks*. New York: Grove, 1967.

——. *The Wretched of the Earth*. New York: Grove, 1963.

Fiori, Giuseppe. *Antonio Gramsci: Life of a Revolutionary*. New York: Schocken, 1973.

Forbes, Jack. "Colonialism and Native American Literature: Analysis." *Wicazo Ša Review* 3 (1987): 17–23.

——. "Intellectual Self-Determination and Sovereignty: Implications for Native Studies and for Native Intellectuals." *Wicazo Ša Review* 13 (1990): 11–23.

Foucault, Michel. *The Archaeology of Knowledge*. Trans. A. M. Sheridan. New York: Pantheon, 1972.

——. *Power/Knowledge: Selected Interviews and Other Writings, 1972–1977*. Ed. Colin Gordon. Hertfordshire: Harvest, 1980.

——. *This Is Not a Pipe*. Trans. James Harkness. Berkeley: U of California P, 1983.

Fregoso, Rosa Linda, and Angie Chabram. "Chicana/o Cultural Representations: Reframing Alternative Critical Discourses." *Cultural Studies* 4.3 (1990): 203–12.

Fuss, Diana. *Essentially Speaking: Feminism, Nature, and Difference*. New York: Routledge, 1989.

Gandhi, Leela. *Postcolonial Theory: A Critical Introduction*. New York: Columbia UP, 1998.

Gates, Henry Louis, Jr. "Beyond the Culture Wars: Identity in Dialogue." *Profession* 9 (1993): 6–11.

——. *Black Literature and Literary Theory*. London: Methuen, 1984.

——, ed. *"Race," Writing, and Difference*. Chicago: U of Chicago P, 1986.

——. *The Signifying Monkey: A Theory of Afro-American Literary Criticism*. New York: Oxford UP, 1988.

Gill, Sam D. *Mother Earth: An American Story*. Chicago: U of Chicago P, 1987.

Glissant, Edouard. *Caribbean Discourse*. Trans. Michael Dash. Charlottesville: UP of Virginia, 1989.

Glotfelty, Cheryll. Introduction. *The Ecocriticism Reader: Landmark in Literary Ecology*. Ed. Cheryll Glotfelty and Harold Fromm. Athens: U of Georgia P, 1996. xv–xxxvii.

Glotfelty, Cheryll, and Harold Fromm, eds. *The Ecocriticism Reader: Landmark in Literary Ecology*. Athens: U of Georgia P, 1996.

Gramsci, Antonio. *Quaderni del carcere*. Ed. Valentino Gerratana. 1975. Torino: Einaudi, 2001.

Greenblatt, Stephen. *The Power of Forms in the English Renaissance*. Norman: U of Oklahoma P, 1982.

Gunn, John M. *Scat-Chen: History, Traditions, and Narratives of the Queres Indians of Laguna and Acoma*. Albuquerque: Albright, 1917. Rpt. New York: AMS, 1977.

Hall, Stuart. "Cultural Identity and Diaspora." *Identity, Community, Culture, Difference*. Ed. Jonathan Rutherford. London: Lawrence, 1990. 222–37.

——. "When Was the 'Postcolonial'? Thinking at the Limits." *The Postcolonial Question: Common Skies, Divided Horizons*. Ed. Ian Chambers and Lidia Curti. London: Routledge, 1996. 242–60.

Hanson, Elizabeth, ed. *Paula Gunn Allen*. Boise, Idaho: Boise State UP, 1990.

Haraway, Donna J. *Simians, Cyborgs, and Women: The Reinvention of Nature*. New York: Routledge, 1991.

Harjo, Joy. "Transformations." *In Mad Love and War*. Middletown, Conn.: Wesleyan UP, 1990. 59.

Harlow, Barbara. *Resistance Literature*. New York: Methuen, 1987.

Harris, David. *From Class Struggle to the Politics of Pleasure: The Effects of Gramscianism on Cultural Studies*. London: Routledge, 1992.

Hartsock, Nancy. "Rethinking Modernism: Minority vs. Majority Theories." *Cultural Critique* 7 (1987): 187–206.

Highwater, Jamake. *The Primal Mind*. New York: Harper, 1981.

Hills, Gordon H. Rev. of *Manifest Manners: Postindian Warriors of Survivance*, by Gerald Vizenor. *Multicultural Review* 3–4 (1994–95): 8.

Hinsey, F. H. *Sovereignty*. New York: Cambridge UP, 1986.

Hodge, Bob, and Vijaay Mishra. "Aboriginal Place." *The Dark Side of the Dream*. North Sydney, N.S.W.: Allen, 1991.

——. "What Is Post-Colonialism?" *Textual Practice* 5 (1991): 399–414.

hooks, bell. *Black Looks: Race and Representation*. Boston: South End, 1992.

——. *Teaching to Transgress: Education as the Practice of Freedom*. New York: Routledge, 1994.

hooks, bell, and Mary Childers. "A Conversation about Race and Class." *Conflicts in Feminism*. Ed. Marianne Hirsh and Evelyn Fox Keller. New York: Routledge, 1990. 60–81.

Hymes, Dell. "Anthologies and Narrators." *Recovering the Word: Essays on Native American Literature*. Ed. Brian Swann and Arnold Krupat. Berkeley: U of California Press, 1987. 41–84.

——. *"In Vain I Tried to Tell You": Essays in Native American Ethnopoetics*. Philadelphia: U of Pennsylvania P, 1981.

Jacobs, Melville. *The People Are Coming Soon: Analyses of Clackamas Chinook Myths and Tales*. Seattle: U of Washington P, 1960.

Jagose, Annamarie. *Queer Theory: An Introduction*. New York: New York UP, 1996.

Jahner, Elaine. "Allies in the Word-Wars: Vizenor's Use of Contemporary Critical Theory." *Studies in American Indian Literatures* 9 (1985): 64–69.

——. "A Critical Approach to American Indian Literature." *Studies in American Indian Literature*. Ed. Paula Gunn Allen. New York: MLA, 1983.

——. "Heading 'Em Off at the Impasse: Native American Authors Meet the Poststructuralists." Unpublished essay, Dartmouth College, n.d.

——. "Indian Literature and Critical Responsibility." *Studies in American Indian Literatures* 5 (1993): 7–12.

——. "Metalanguages." *Narrative Chance: Postmodern Discourse on Native American Indian Literatures*. Ed. Gerald Vizenor. Albuquerque: U of New Mexico P, 1989. 155–85.

Jameson, Frederick. "Third World Literature in the Era of Multinational Capital." *Social Text* 15 (Fall 1986): 65–88.

JanMohamed, Abdul R. "The Economy of Manichaean Allegory: The Function of Racial Difference in Colonial Literature." *Critical Inquiry* 12.1 (1985): 59–87.

JanMohamed, Abdul R., and David Lloyd. "Introduction: Toward a Theory of Minority Discourse." *Cultural Critique* 6 (1987): 5–12.

——, eds. *The Nature and Context of Minority Discourse*. Oxford: Oxford UP, 1990.

Johnston, Anna, and Alan Lawson. "Settler Cultures." *A Companion to Postcolonial Studies*. Ed. Henry Schwarz and Sangeeta Ray. Malden, Mass.: Blackwell, 2000. 361–66.

Jones, Ann Rosalind. "Writing the Body: Toward an Understanding of *L'écriture féminine*." *The New Feminist Criticism: Essays on Women, Literature, and Theory*. Ed. Elaine Showalter. New York: Pantheon, 1985. 361–77.

Jung, C. G. *Flying Saucers: A Modern Myth of Things Seen in the Sky*. London: Routledge, 1959.

Kaplan, Amy. "'Left Alone with America': The Absence of Empire in the Study of American Culture." *Cultures of United States Imperialism*. Ed. Amy Kaplan and Donald E. Pease. Durham, N.C.: Duke UP, 1993.

Kaplan, Amy, and Donald E. Pease, eds. *Cultures of United States Imperialism*. Durham, N.C.: Duke UP, 1993.

Keating, AnaLouise. *Women Reading Women Writing: Self-Invention in Paula Gunn Allen, Gloria Anzaldúa, and Audre Lorde*. Philadelphia: Temple UP, 1996.

King, Thomas, ed. *All My Relations: An Anthology of Contemporary Canadian Native Fiction*. Norman: U of Oklahoma P, 1992.

Kolodny, Annette. *The Lay of the Land: Metaphor as Experience and History in American Life and Letters*. Chapel Hill: U of North Carolina P, 1975.

Kroeber, Karl. "Deconstructionist Criticism and American Indian Literature." *Boundary 2* 7 (1979): 72–87.

Krupat, Arnold. "An Approach to Native American Texts." *Critical Inquiry* 9 (1982): 323–38.

——. *Ethnocriticism: Ethnography, History, Literature.* Berkeley: U of California P, 1992.

——. *For Those Who Come After: A Study of Native American Autobiography.* Berkeley: U of California P, 1985.

——. "Identity and Difference in the Criticism of Native American Literature." *Diacritics* 13 (1983): 2–13.

——. "Nationalism, Indigenism, Cosmopolitanism: Critical Perspectives on Native American Literatures." *Centennial Review* 42.3 (1998): 617–26.

——. "Post-Structuralism and Oral Literature." *Recovering the Word: Essays on Native American Literature.* Ed. Brian Swann and Arnold Krupat. Berkeley: U of California P, 1987. 113–28.

——. *The Turn to the Native: Studies in Criticism and Culture.* Lincoln: U of Nebraska P, 1996.

——. *The Voice in the Margin: Native American Literature and the Canon.* Berkeley: U of California P, 1989.

Lacan, Jacques. "Guiding Remarks for a Congress on Feminine Sexuality." *Feminine Sexuality: Jacques Lacan and the École Freudienne.* Ed. Juliet Mitchell and Jacqueline Rose. Trans. Jacqueline Rose. London: Macmillan, 1982. 86–98.

Larson, Charles R. *American Indian Fiction.* Albuquerque: U of New Mexico P, 1978.

Lee, A. Robert. "The Only Good Indian Is a Postindian? Controversialist Vizenor and *Manifest Manners*." *Loosening the Seams: Interpretations of Gerald Vizenor.* Ed. A. Robert Lee. Bowling Green, Ohio: Bowling Green State UP, 2000. 263–78.

——. *Postindian Conversations: Gerald Vizenor and A. Robert Lee.* Lincoln: U of Nebraska P, 1999.

——, ed. *Loosening the Seams: Interpretations of Gerald Vizenor.* Bowling Green, Ohio: Bowling Green State UP, 2000.

Lee, Dennis. "Writing in Colonial Space." *Boundary 2* 3.1 (1974): 151–68.

Lionnet, Françoise. "'Logiques Métisses': Cultural Appropriation and Postcolonial Representations." *Postcolonial Subjects: Francophone Women Writers.* Ed. Mary Jean Green et al. Minneapolis: U of Minnesota P, 1996. 321–43.

——. *Postcolonial Representations.* Ithaca, N.Y.: Cornell UP, 1995.

Martin, Joel W. *Sacred Revolt: The Muskogees' Struggle for a New World.* Boston: Beacon, 1991.

Mathews, John Joseph. *Talking to the Moon: Wildlife Adventures on the Plains and Prairies of Osage Country.* Norman: U of Oklahoma P, 1945.

McNickle, D'Arcy. *Wind from an Enemy Sky.* New York: Harper, 1979.

Merchant, Carolyn. *The Death of Nature: Women, Ecology, and the Scientific Revolution*. New York: Harper, 1980.

Mitchell, Carol. "*Ceremony* as Ritual." *American Indian Quarterly* 5 (1979): 27–35.

Mitchell, W. J. T. *Picture Theory: Essays on Verbal and Visual Representation*. Chicago: U of Chicago P, 1994.

Mohanty, Chandra Talpade. "Cartographies of Struggle: Third World Women and the Politics of Feminism." *Third World Women and the Politics of Feminism*. Ed. Chandra Talpade Mohanty with Ann Russo and Lourdes Torres. Bloomington: Indiana UP, 1991. 1–47.

——. "Under Western Eyes: Feminist Scholarship and Colonial Discourse." *Boundary 2* 12.3/13.1 (1984): 333–58.

Mohanty, Chandra Talpade, with Ann Russo and Lourdes Torres, eds. *Third World Women and the Politics of Feminism*. Bloomington: Indiana UP, 1991.

Mohanty, Satya. "Epilogue: Colonial Legacies, Multicultural Futures: Relativism, Objectivity, and the Challenge of Otherness." *PMLA* 110.1 (1995): 108–18.

——. *Literary Theory and the Claims of History: Postmodernism, Objectivity, Multicultural Politics*. Ithaca, N.Y.: Cornell UP, 1997.

Momaday, N. Scott. *House Made of Dawn*. New York: Harper, 1968.

——. "The Man Made of Words." *The Remembered Earth*. Ed. Geary Hobson. Albuquerque: U of New Mexico P, 1981. 162–76.

——. *The Man Made of Words: Essays, Stories, Passages*. New York: St. Martin's, 1997.

——. *The Way to Rainy Mountain*. Albuquerque: U of New Mexico P, 1969.

Mooney, James. *The Ghost Dance Religion and the Sioux Outbreak of 1890*. Lincoln: U of Nebraska P, 1991.

Moore-Gilbert, Bart. *Postcolonial Theory: Contexts, Practices, Politics*. London: Verso, 1997.

Mukherjee, Arun P. "Whose Post-Colonialism and Whose Post- Modernism?" *World Literature Written in English* 30.2 (1990): 1–9.

Murphy, Patrick D. *Literature, Nature, Other: Ecofeminist Critiques*. Albany: State U of New York P, 1995.

Murray, David. *Forked Tongues: Speech, Writing, and Representation in North American Indian Texts*. Bloomington: Indiana UP, 1991.

Ngugi, Wa Thiong'o. *Decolonizing the Mind: The Politics of Languages in African Literature*. London: Heinemann, 1986.

Norris, Christopher. *Deconstruction: Theory and Practice*. London: Methuen, 1982.

——. *Derrida*. Cambridge, Mass.: Harvard UP, 1987.

Ong, Walter. *Orality and Literacy: The Technologizing of the Word*. London: Methuen, 1982.

Ostriker, Alicia. *Stealing the Language: The Emergence of Women's Poetry in America*. Boston: Beacon, 1986.

Owens, Louis. "As If an Indian Were Really an Indian: Uramericans, Euramericans, and Postcolonial Theory." *Paradoxa* 15 (2001): 170–83. Rpt. in *I Hear the Train: Reflections, Inventions, Refractions.* Norman: U of Oklahoma P, 2001. 207–26.

——. "'Disturbed by Something Deeper': The Native Art of John Joseph Mathews." *Western American Literature* 35.2 (2000): 163–73.

——. *Mixedblood Messages: Literature, Film, Family, Place.* Norman: U of Oklahoma P, 1998.

——. *Other Destinies: Understanding the American Indian Novel.* Norman: U of Oklahoma P, 1992.

——. "Re: Re: *Mixedblood Messages*." E-mail to Elvira Pulitano. 13 March 2001.

——. *The Sharpest Sight.* Norman: U of Oklahoma P, 1992.

——. "Staging *indians*: Native Sovenance and Survivance in Gerald Vizenor's 'Ishi and the Wood Ducks.'" *I Hear the Train: Reflections, Inventions, Refractions.* Norman: U of Oklahoma P, 2001. 227–43.

——. "Their Shadows Before Them: Photographing Indians." *Trading Gazes: Euro-American Women Photographers among Native North Americans.* Ed. Susan Bernardin, Melody Graulich, Lisa MacFarlane, and Nicole Tonkovich. New Brunswick, N.J.: Rutgers UP, in press.

Parry, Benita. "Overlapping Territories and Intertwined Histories." *Edward Said: A Critical Reader.* Ed. M. Sprinker. Oxford: Blackwell, 1992. 19–47.

Prakash, Gyan. "Postcolonial Criticism and Indian Historiography." *Social Text* 31/32 (1992): 8–19.

Pratt, Mary Louise. *Imperial Eyes: Travel Writing and Transculturation.* London: Routledge, 1992.

Pulitano, Elvira. Interview with Gerald Vizenor. Albuquerque, N.M., 25 March 2001.

——. "Re: *Mixedblood Messages*." E-mail to Louis Owens. 13 March 2001.

Purdy, John. "'And Then Twenty Years Later . . .': A Conversation with Paula Gunn Allen." *Studies in American Indian Literatures* 9.3 (1997): 5–16.

Radin, Paul. *The Trickster: A Study in American Indian Mythology.* New York: Schocken, 1973.

Ramsey, Jarold. *Reading the Fire: Essays in Traditional Indian Literatures of the Far West.* Lincoln: U of Nebraska P, 1983.

Rebolledo, Tey Diana. "The Politics of Poetics." *Making Face, Making Soul / Haciendo Caras: Creative and Critical Perspectives by Feminists of Color.* Ed. Gloria Anzaldúa. San Francisco: Aunt Lute, 1990. 346–55.

Reitenbach, Gail. Rev. of *Keeping Slug Woman Alive*, by Greg Sarris. *American Literature* 66 (1994): 408–09.

Roemer, Kenneth. "Contemporary American Indian Literature: The Centrality of Canon and the Margins." *American Literary History* 6 (1994): 583–99.

——. "Indian Lives: The Defining, the Telling." Rev. of *Sending My Heart Back across the Years*, by Hertha Dawn Wong, and *Keeping Slug Woman Alive*, by Greg Sarris. *American Quarterly* 46.1 (1994): 81–91.

——. Rev. of *Manifest Manners: Postindian Warriors of Survivance*, by Gerald Vizenor. *American Literature* 66 (1994): 871–72.

Roppolo, Kimberley. "Towards a Tribal-Centered Reading of Native Literature: Using Indigenous Rhetoric(s) Instead of Literary Analysis." *Paradoxa* 15 (2001): 263–74.

Rosaldo, Renato. *Culture and Truth*. Boston: Beacon, 1989.

Ruoff, A. LaVonne Brown. "Gerald Vizenor: Compassionate Trickster." *American Indian Quarterly* 9.1 (1985): 67–73.

——. "John Joseph Mathews's *Talking to the Moon*: Literary and Osage Contexts." *Multicultural Autobiography: American Lives*. Ed. James Robert Payne. Knoxville: U of Tennessee P, 1992. 1–31.

Ruppert, James. *Mediation in Contemporary Native American Fiction*. Norman: U of Oklahoma P, 1995.

Rutherford, Jonathan. "The Third Space: Interview with Homi Bhabha." *Identity, Community, Culture, Difference*. Ed. Jonathan Rutherford. London: Lawrence, 1990. 207–21.

Said, Edward W. *Culture and Imperialism*. New York: Knopf, 1993.

——. *Orientalism*. New York: Vintage, 1979.

Saldivar, Jose David. *Border Matters: Remapping American Cultural Studies*. Berkeley: U of California P, 1997.

Samson, Colin. "Overturning the Burdens of the *Real*: Nationalism and the Social Sciences in Gerald Vizenor's Recent Works." *Loosening the Seams: Interpretations of Gerald Vizenor*. Ed. Robert A. Lee. Bowling Green, Ohio: Bowling Green State UP, 2000. 279–93.

Sánchez, Rosaura. "Deconstructions and Denarrativizations: Trends in Chicana Literature." *Bilingual Review* 21.1 (1996): 52–58.

Sandoval, Chela. "U.S. Third World Feminism: The Theory and Method of Oppositional Consciousness in the Postmodern World." *Genders* 10 (1991): 1–24.

Sarris, Greg. *Keeping Slug Woman Alive: A Holistic Approach to American Indian Texts*. Berkeley: U of California P, 1993.

Schweninger, Lee. "A Skin of Lakeweed: An Ecofeminist Approach to Erdrich and Silko." *Multicultural Literature through Feminist/Poststructuralist Lenses*. Ed. Barbara Frey Waxman. Knoxville: U of Tennessee P, 1993. 37–56.

Scwab, Gabriel. "Reader Response and the Aesthetic Experience of Otherness." *Stanford Literature Review* 3 (1986): 107–36.

Seidman, S. "Deconstructing Queer Theory or the Under- Theorization of the Social and the Ethical." *Social Postmodernism: Beyond Identity Politics.* Ed. L. Nicholson and S. Seidman. New York: Cambridge UP, 1995. 116–41.

Serres, Michel. "Panoptic Theory." *The Limits of Theory.* Ed. Thomas M. Kavanagh. Stanford, Calif.: Stanford UP, 1989. 25–47.

Shohat, Ella. "Notes on the Post-Colonial." *Contemporary Postcolonial Theory: A Reader.* Ed. Padmini Mongia. London: Oxford UP, 1996. 322–34.

Silko, Leslie Marmon. *Ceremony.* New York: Viking, 1977.

——. "Language and Literature from a Pueblo Indian Perspective." *Yellow Woman and a Beauty of the Spirit: Essays on Native American Life Today.* New York: Touchstone, 1997. 48–59.

——. *Storyteller.* New York: Seaver, 1981.

Sledge, Linda Ching. "Oral Tradition in Kingston's China Men." *Redefining American Literary History.* Ed. LaVonne Ruoff and Jerry W. Ward. New York: MLA, 1990. 142–54.

Slicer, Deborah. "The Body as Bioregion." *Reading the Earth: New Directions in the Study of Literature and Environment.* Ed. Michael P. Branch et al. Moscow: U of Idaho P, 1998. 107–16.

Smith, Carlton. *Coyote Kills John Wayne: Postmodernism and Contemporary Fictions of the Transcultural Frontier.* Hanover, N.H.: UP of New England, 2000.

Smith, Patricia Clark, and Paula Gunn Allen. "Earthy Relations, Carnal Knowledge: Southwestern American Indian Women Writers and Landscape." *The Desert Is No Lady: Southwestern Landscapes in Women's Writing and Art.* Ed. Vera Norwood and Janice Monk. New Haven, Conn.: Yale UP, 1987. 174–96.

Sollors, Werner. *Beyond Ethnicity: Consent and Descent in American Culture.* New York: Oxford UP, 1986.

Sontag, Susan. *On Photography.* New York: Farrar, 1973.

Spivak, Gayatri Chakravorty. "Can the Subaltern Speak?" *Marxism and the Interpretation of Culture.* Ed. Cary Nelson and Lawrence Grossberg. Basingstoke: Macmillan, 1988. 271–313.

——. "Imperialism and Sexual Difference." *Oxford Literary Review* 8 (1986): 225–48.

——. *In Other Worlds: Essays in Cultural Politics.* New York: Routledge, 1988.

——. *Outside in the Teaching Machine.* New York: Routledge, 1993.

——. *The Postcolonial Critic: Interviews, Strategies, Dialogues.* Ed. Sarah Harasym. New York: Routledge, 1990.

——. "Theory in the Margin." *Consequences of Theory.* Ed. Jonathan Arac and Barbara Johnson. Baltimore: Johns Hopkins UP, 1991. 154–80.

——. "Three Women's Texts and a Critique of Imperialism." *Critical Inquiry* 12 (1985): 243–61.

Standiford, Lester. "Worlds Made of Dawn: Characteristic Image and Incident in Native American Imaginative Literature." *Three American Literatures: Essays in Chicano, Native American, and Asian American Literature for Teachers of American Literature.* Ed. Houston Baker Jr. New York: MLA, 1982. 168–96.

Stanley, Sandra Kumamoto. Introduction. *Other Sisterhoods: Literary Theory and U.S. Women of Color.* Ed. Sandra Kumamoto Stanley. Chicago: U of Illinois P, 1998. 1–19.

St. Clair, Janet. "Uneasy Ethnocentrism: Recent Works of Allen, Silko, and Hogan." *Studies in American Indian Literatures* 6 (1994): 83–98.

Suleri, Sara. *Meatless Days.* Chicago: University of Chicago Press, 1989.

——. "Woman Skin Deep: Feminism and the Postcolonial Condition." *Critical Inquiry* 18 (1992): 756–69.

Swann, Brian, and Arnold Krupat, eds. *I Tell You Now: Autobiographical Essays by Native American Writers.* Lincoln: U of Nebraska P, 1987.

——, eds. *Recovering the Word: Essays on Native American Literature.* Berkeley: U of California P, 1987.

Swanton, John. *Myths and Tales of the Southeastern Indians.* Bureau of American Ethnology Bulletin 88. 1929. Rpt. Norman: U of Oklahoma P, 1995.

Szasz, Margaret Connell, ed. *Between Indian and White Worlds: The Culture Broker.* Norman: U of Oklahoma P, 1994.

Tedlock, Dennis. *The Spoken Word and the Work of Interpretation.* Philadelphia: U of Pennsylvania P, 1983.

Tiffin, Chris, and Alan Lawson, eds. *De-Scribing Empire: Postcolonialism and Textuality.* London: Routledge, 1994.

Tiffin, Helen. "Postcolonial Literatures and Counter- Discourse." *Kunapipi* 9 (1987): 17–34.

Todorov, Tzvetan. *The Conquest of America: The Question of the Other.* Trans. Richard Howard. Ithaca, N.Y.: Cornell UP, 1982.

Tompkins, Jane. "The Reader in History: The Changing Shape of Literary Response." *Reader-Response Criticism: From Formalism to Post-Structuralism.* Ed. Jane Tompkins. Baltimore: Johns Hopkins UP, 1980. 201–33.

Trinh T. Minh-ha. "Not You/Like You: Post-Colonial Women and the Interlocking Questions of Identity and Difference." *Making Face, Making Soul/Haciendo Caras: Creative and Critical Perspectives by Feminists of Color.* Ed. Gloria Anzaldúa. San Francisco: Aunt Lute, 1990. 371–75.

——. "The Undone Interval: Trinh T. Minh-ha in Conversation with Annamaria Morelli." *The Postcolonial Question: Common Skies, Divided Horizon.* Ed. Ian Chambers and Lidia Curti. New York: Routledge, 1996. 3–16.

——. *When The Moon Waxes Red: Representation, Gender, and Cultural Politics.* New York: Routledge, 1991.

——. *Woman, Native, Other.* Bloomington: Indiana UP, 1989.

Veeser, H. Aram, ed. *The New Historicism.* New York: Routledge, 1989.

Velie, Alan. *Four American Indian Literary Masters: N. Scott Momaday, James Welch, Leslie M. Silko, and Gerald Vizenor.* Norman: U of Oklahoma P, 1982.

Verdicchio, Pasquale. "Reclaiming Gramsci: A Brief Survey of Current and Potential Uses of the Work of Antonio Gramsci." *Symposium: A Quarterly Journal in Modern Literatures* 49.2 (1995): 169–76.

Vizenor, Gerald. "Almost Browne." *Shadow Distance: A Gerald Vizenor Reader.* Hanover, N.H.: Wesleyan UP, 1994. 107–14.

——. *Bearheart: The Heirship Chronicles.* Minneapolis: U of Minnesota P, 1990. Rpt. of *Darkness in Saint Louis Bearheart.* Saint Paul, Minn.: Truck, 1978.

——. *Crossbloods: Bone Courts, Bingo, and Other Reports.* Minneapolis: U of Minnesota P, 1976.

——. *Earthdivers: Tribal Narratives on Mixed Descent.* Minneapolis: U of Minnesota P, 1981.

——. *Fugitive Poses: Native American Indian Scenes of Absence and Presence.* Lincoln: U of Nebraska P, 1998.

——. *The Heirs of Columbus.* Hanover, N.H.: Wesleyan UP, 1991.

——. *Interior Landscapes: Autobiographical Myths and Metaphors.* Minneapolis: U of Minnesota P, 1990.

——. *Ishi and the Wood Ducks. Native American Literature: A Brief Introduction and Anthology.* Ed. Gerald Vizenor. New York: Harper, 1995. 299–336.

——. *Manifest Manners: Narratives on Postindian Survivance.* Lincoln: U of Nebraska P, 1999. Rpt. of *Manifest Manners: Postindian Warriors of Survivance.* Hanover, N.H.: Wesleyan UP, 1994.

——. "Mister Ishi: Analogies of Exile, Deliverance, and Liberty." *Ishi in Three Centuries.* Ed. Karl and Clifton Kroeber. Lincoln: U of Nebraska Press, in press.

——, ed. *Narrative Chance: Postmodern Discourse on Native American Indian Literatures.* Albuquerque: U of New Mexico P, 1989.

——. "Ojibways Seek Rights to 'Regulate' Rice on Wildlife Refuge." *Minneapolis Tribune,* 13 Sept. 1968.

——. *The People Named the Chippewa: Narrative Histories.* Minneapolis: U of Minnesota P, 1984.

——. "Postindian Autoinscriptions: The Origins of Essentialism and Pluralism in Descriptive Tribal Names." *Pluralism and the Limits of Authenticity in North American Literatures.* Ed. Winfried Siemerling and Katrin Schwenk. Iowa City: U of Iowa P, 1996. 29–39.

——. "The Ruins of Representations: Shadow Survivance and the Literature of Dominance." *Another Tongue: Nation and Ethnicity in the Linguistic Borderlands.* Ed. Alfred Arteaga. Durham, N.C.: Duke UP, 1994. 139–67.

——. *Shadow Distance: A Gerald Vizenor Reader.* Hanover, N.H.: Wesleyan UP, 1994.

——. "Trickster Discourse: Comic Holotropes and Language Games." *Narrative Chance: Postmodern Discourse on Native American Indian Literatures.* Ed. Gerald Vizenor. Norman: U of Oklahoma P, 1989. 187–211.

——. *The Trickster of Liberty: Tribal Heirs to a Wild Baronage at Petronia.* Minneapolis: U of Minnesota P, 1988.

——. *Wordarrows: Indians and Whites in the New Fur Trade.* Minneapolis: U of Minnesota P, 1978.

Vološinov, V. N. *Marxism and the Philosophy of Language.* Cambridge, Mass.: Harvard UP, 1993.

Warren, Karen J. "The Power and the Promise of Ecological Feminism." *Environmental Ethics* 12.2 (1990): 125–46.

Warrior, Robert A. "Intellectual Sovereignty and the Struggle for an American Indian Future." *Wicazo Ša Review* 8 (1992): 1–20.

——. *Tribal Secrets: Recovering American Indian Intellectual Traditions.* Minneapolis: U of Minnesota P, 1995.

Weaver, Jace. "Indigenous and Indigeneity." *A Companion to Postcolonial Studies.* Ed. Henry Schwarz and Sangeeta Ray. Malden, Mass: Blackwell, 2000. 221–35.

——. "Native American Authors and Their Communities." *Wicazo Ša Review* 12.1 (1997): 47–87.

——. *That the People May Live: Native American Literatures and Native American Community.* New York: Oxford UP, 1997.

Wiget, Andrew, ed. *Critical Essays on Native American Literature.* Boston: Hall, 1985.

——. Rev. of *Narrative Chance: Postmodern Discourse on Native American Indian Literatures,* ed. Gerald Vizenor. *Modern Philology* 89 (May 1991): 476–79.

Womack, Craig S. *Red on Red: Native American Literary Separatism.* Minneapolis: U of Minnesota P, 1999.

Young, Robert. *White Mythologies: Writing History and the West.* London: Routledge, 1990.

Ziff, Larzer. *Writing in the New Nation: Prose, Print, and Politics in the Early United States.* New Haven, Conn.: Yale UP, 1991.

Index